Universal Design for Transition

Universal Design for Transition

The Educators' Guide for Equity-Focused Transition Planning

Second Edition

by

LaRon A. Scott, Ed.D.
University of Virginia
Charlottesville

and

Colleen A. Thoma, Ph.D.
Virginia Commonwealth University
Richmond

with invited contributors

·P·A·U·L·H·
BROOKES
PUBLISHING Co ®

Baltimore • London • Sydney

Paul H. Brookes Publishing Co.
Post Office Box 10624
Baltimore, Maryland 21285-0624
USA

www.brookespublishing.com

Typeset by Absolute Service Inc., Towson, Maryland.
Manufactured in the United States of America by

The individuals described in this book are composites or real people whose situations are masked and are based on the authors' experiences. In all instances, names and identifying details have been changed to protect confidentiality.

Library of Congress Cataloging-in-Publication Data

Names: Scott, LaRon A., author. | Thoma, Colleen A., author.
Title: Universal design for transition : the educators' guide for
    equity-focused transition planning / by LaRon A. Scott, Ed.D.,
    University of Virginia, Charlottesville and Colleen A. Thoma, Ph.D.,
    Virginia Commonwealth University, Richmond, with invited contributors.
Description: Second edition. | Baltimore, Maryland : Paul H. Brookes
    Publishing Co., [2024] | Previous editon: 2009. | Includes
    bibliographical references and index.
Identifiers: LCCN 2023028396 (print) | LCCN 2023028397 (ebook) | ISBN
    9781681256023 (paperback) | ISBN 9781681256030 (epub) | ISBN
    9781681256047 (pdf)
Subjects: LCSH: Instructional systems--Design. | Students with
    disabilities—United States. | Inclusive education—United States. |
    BISAC: EDUCATION / Inclusive Education | EDUCATION / Special Education /
    General
Classification: LCC LB1028.38 .T55 2023 (print) | LCC LB1028.38 (ebook) |
    DDC 371.9/0473—dc23/eng/20230714
LC record available at https://lccn.loc.gov/2023028396
LC ebook record available at https://lccn.loc.gov/2023028397

British Library Cataloguing in Publication data are available from the British Library.

2027   2026   2025   2024   2023

10   9   8   7   6   5   4   3   2   1

Contents

About the Downloads

Purchasers of this book may download, print, and/or photocopy selected resources in the text for educational use.

To access the materials that come with this book:

1. Go to the Brookes Download Hub: http://downloads.brookespublishing.com

2. Register to create an account (or log in with an existing account)

3. Filter or search for the book title *Universal Design for Transition: The Educators' Guide for Equity-Focused Transition Planning, Second Edition*

About the Authors

LaRon Scott, Ed.D., Associate Professor, Department of Curriculum, Instruction & Special Education, University of Virginia, Ridley Hall, 278, 417 Emmet Street South, P.O. Box 400260, Charlottesville VA 22904

LaRon A. Scott, Ed.D., is a faculty member at the University of Virginia. He studies recruitment, preparation, and retention of historically marginalized teacher educators, notably special education teachers, and postsecondary transition programming and postschool outcomes for Black youth with intellectual and developmental disabilities. He also focuses on the critical implications of implicit bias in shaping the conditions for historically marginalized educators, and how historical and contemporary local, state, and federal policy shapes the treatment of minoritized special educators. Dr. Scott has a stellar publication record including numerous peer-reviewed articles, books, and nearly 100 presentations. He has served as reviewer for several top journals in special education. He worked as a mental health case manager and special education classroom teacher and transition coordinator before completing his master's and doctoral degrees. He has experience with teaching and research related to personnel preparation, teacher program development, program accreditation, and program administration. Dr. Scott has received numerous awards for his work, including the Patricia L. Sitlington Research Award from the Division on Career Development and Transition, the Education Award from the American Association on Intellectual and Developmental Disabilities, and numerous other research, teaching, and service awards.

Colleen A. Thoma, Ph.D., Professor, Virginia Commonwealth University, School of Education, 1015 W. Main Street, Box 842020, Richmond VA 23284-2020

Colleen A. Thoma, Ph.D., is a respected faculty member and researcher specializing in special education and supporting youth with disabilities as they prepare to transition to adult life. She has more than 25 years of experience in the field as an educator, consultant, and researcher. Dr. Thoma is known for her dedication and commitment to improving the lives of individuals with intellectual and developmental disabilities through her work in research, personnel preparation, and professional development.

She has published numerous articles, books, and book chapters on the topic of transition education, and she is a sought-after speaker at national and international conferences. Dr. Thoma currently is a professor at Virginia Commonwealth University, where she teaches courses in special education, mentors doctoral students, and conducts research on evidence-based practices for individuals with disabilities. In her free time, she enjoys traveling and spending time with her family (especially her granddaughter) and dogs.

About the Contributors

Kathryn M. Abrams, M.A., Ph.D., is currently a program coordinator with the UI REACH program at the University of Iowa in Iowa City, Iowa. Prior to beginning at Iowa, she worked as the director of the Washington State University Responsibility Opportunity Advocacy and Respect (ROAR) program for 3 years. She recently completed her dissertation, which explored using virtual reality to teach science vocabulary to individuals with intellectual and developmental disabilities. Dr. Abrams helped bring together programs from the Northwest Region by forming a regional alliance and has been active in a variety of Think College Affinity Groups. Her research interests include supporting students in inclusive postsecondary education settings through the use of emerging technologies in special education. Dr. Abrams previously taught special education in kindergarten through Grade 12 settings in both Arizona and Colorado.

Edwin Obilo Achola, Ph.D., is currently an associate professor of special education at California State University Long Beach. Dr. Achola earned his Ph.D. degree in Special Education and Disability Policy from Virginia Commonwealth University. In the last 15 years, Dr. Achola has worked as a classroom teacher, teacher educator, and researcher—concentrating primarily on issues of equity for students with disabilities in the United States and Kenya. His research and teaching activities have focused on culturally responsive and sustaining pedagogy in transition planning, personnel development, and higher education for students with disabilities. Dr. Achola has coauthored a number of book chapters and published research articles on various topics in the field of transition planning and diversity. His research themes include meaningful involvement of culturally diverse families in transition planning, transition assessments, development of culturally responsive transition plans as well as postsecondary education success for traditionally marginalized youths.

Abdulaziz Alsaeed, M.Ed., is a graduate research assistant at the Kansas University Center on Developmental Disabilities and a doctoral student in the Department of Special Education. Mr. Alsaeed's research focuses on two research lines of inquiry around: 1) assessing student self-determination to inform research-based practice to promote self-determination to improve school and postschool outcomes and 2) supporting educators to implement instructional designs that target enhancing self-determination in effective ways (e.g., enhancing implementation fidelity). He is a former teacher of elementary school students with and without disabilities.

Rachel W. Bowman, M.A., is a doctoral student in special education at Virginia Commonwealth University in Richmond, Virginia. She is currently studying the role of mentorship in retaining a diverse teaching force. She has been a research assistant with the Minority Educator Recruitment, Retention, and Equity Center (MERREC) for 2 years. Her research interests include mentorship, teacher retention, teacher diversity, and the universal design for transition. Ms. Bowman previously worked as a teacher of the Deaf and Deaf-Blind in New York City, Washington, D.C., and Arlington, Virginia.

Katherine R. Brendli Brown, Ph.D., is an extension associate for the Yang Tan Institute on Employment and Disability in the School of Industrial and Labor Relations at Cornell University. At Cornell, she supports multiple projects, including the Autism Transition to Adulthood Initiative (ATTAIN) to explore factors that predict successful transitions to adulthood for young people with autism. Dr. Brendli Brown also develops materials, conducts trainings, and provides technical assistance supporting content specialists on the Office of Special Education (OSE) Educational Partnership regional teams, as a member of the New York State Education Department's Special Education Technical Assistance Partnership for Data. She is passionate about conducting, translating, and applying scholarly research focused on self-determination/self-advocacy, inclusive higher education, and promoting positive transition experiences and outcomes for people with intellectual and developmental disabilities.

Lauren P. Bruno, Ph.D., is an assistant research professor at Kansas University Center on Developmental Disabilities (KUCDD) at the University of Kansas in Lawrence. Her research is broadly focused on improving transition outcomes for youth with disabilities. Through her research, she seeks to improve the preparation of preservice and in-service educators' ability to implement evidence-based transition and use the universal design for learning and universal design for transition frameworks (including the use of assistive technology) to improve postschool outcomes of youth with disabilities. In addition, Dr. Bruno seeks to enhance access to postsecondary educational opportunities for youth with intellectual and developmental disability. Prior to entering academia, she worked as a high school special educator for students with significant disabilities in Virginia. Prior to beginning at KUCDD, Dr. Bruno was an assistant professor of special education at Washington State University where she continues to support the WSU Responsibility Opportunity Advocacy and Respect (ROAR) program. She also worked as a postdoctoral research scholar with the University of Iowa REACH program. Dr. Bruno remains actively involved in supporting the transition of young adults with disabilities through participation in Think College Affinity Groups and serves as an active member in the Division on Career Development and Transition.

Melissa J. Cuba, Ph.D., is a visiting assistant professor of special education at the University of Maine College of Education and Human Development's School of Learning and Teaching. Her line of research focuses on developing and enhancing evidence-based practices and policies to mitigate the disproportionality of multilingual learners (who are classified as English learners) in special education and improve student outcomes. Dr. Cuba has published research on factors that impact opportunities and outcomes for multilingual learners and articles on instructional practices that support these students. She draws from 15 years of prekindergarten through Grade 12 practitioner experience working with multilingual learners with and without disabilities and the teachers who support them.

Meagan Dayton, M.S., is a doctoral student in the Special Education and Disability Leadership program at Virginia Commonwealth University in Richmond, Virginia. She is currently finishing her second year in the program and plans to base her dissertation on the use of affinity groups to support special education teachers of color. Ms. Dayton's research interests include recruiting, retaining, and supporting special education teachers of color. She has previously taught special education in the prekindergarten through Grade 12 setting in Virginia.

Stacie L. Dojonovic Schutzman, Ph.D., is the coordinator for the Online Transition Certificate and Master's Program at The University of Kansas. In addition, she serves as the associate executive director of the Division on Career Development and Transition. Dr. Dojonovic Schutzman has experience as a transition coordinator in both urban and suburban school districts. Through service, scholarship, and practice, she has been recognized for engaging diverse audiences in order to implement research to practice to improve the postschool outcomes of all youth. She has more than 20 years' experience serving in public schools as a transition coordinator. During this time, she developed, implemented, and disseminated a U.S. Department of Education grant, Project M.O.V.E. (Mentoring Opportunities for Vocational Exploration), which has expanded and evolved into a 4-year model transition program. Through partnerships with universities, pursuit of evidence-based practices, connections and involvement with the Division of Career Development, Vocational Evaluation and Career Assessment professionals, and the Council for Exceptional Children, Dr. Dojonovic Schutzman has developed a commitment to improving the postsecondary outcomes of ALL youth by supporting the implementation of evidence-based practices in classrooms and schools.

Imani Evans, M.A., CCC-SLP, is a doctoral student in Special Education and Disability Leadership at Virginia Commonwealth University. She is currently completing her second year in her Ph.D. program. Her research interests include collaborative practices to support inclusion in urban and high-need schools, diversifying the special education workforce, and disproportionality in special education. Ms. Evans has a background in pediatric speech-language pathology. She has worked in private practice, early intervention, and kindergarten through Grade 5 public schools in both Washington, D.C., and Richmond, Virginia.

Kim W. Fisher, Ph.D., is an assistant professor in the Department of Special Education at Illinois State University. She earned her Ph.D. in special education from the University of Illinois at Urbana-Champaign. Dr. Fisher is also a Fellow of the American Association on Intellectual and Developmental Disabilities.

Regina H. Frazier, M.S., is a doctoral student in Special Education and Disability Leadership at Virginia Commonwealth University, VA. She is currently completing her second year in her Ph.D. program. Ms. Frazier has served as a public school assistant principal. Her research interest is in special educators' preparation in reading instruction and issues in the field regarding the preparation and retention of special educators. Ms. Frazier is an active member of the Council for Exceptional Children (CEC), serving in various roles and mediums of engagement, including work with the division for Culturally & Linguistically Diverse Exceptional Learners, Council of Administrators of Special Education (CASE), Division on Career Development, and Transition, and the Teacher Education Division of CEC.

Mayumi Hagiwara, Ph.D., is an assistant professor in the Department of Special Education at San Francisco State University (SF State). Dr. Hagiwara's research focuses on inclusive education for students with intellectual and developmental disabilities, developing family–school partnerships, using culturally sustaining transition practices, and promoting self-determination for people with intellectual and developmental disabilities across contexts (e.g., school, home, community). She serves as a project coordinator for an inclusive postsecondary education project for young adults with intellectual and developmental disabilities at SF State. Dr. Hagiwara teaches undergraduate and graduate courses to prepare future teachers for students with extensive support needs. Her scholarly goal is to examine culturally sustaining transition practices from diverse perspectives and lived experiences (e.g., student, family, school, community) and educate future teachers to facilitate student-directed transition planning by honoring their cultural contexts, strengths, and assets. Dr. Hagiwara is a former special education teacher for students with extensive support needs across grade levels.

Michelle A. C. Hicks, M.S., is currently a doctoral student in the special education and disability policy program at the Virginia Commonwealth University School of Education. She received her master's degree in education from Old Dominion University and her bachelor's degree at Hampton University. Her research interest is improving the postsecondary outcome for students with blindness and visual impairment. Ms. Hicks has previously taught students with specific learning disabilities, specific emotional disabilities, and visual impairment. She is also an American Association of Colleges for Teacher Education (AACTE) Holmes Scholar.

Jarrod Hobson, M.S., is a current doctoral student in special education and PRISE (Preparing Research Intensive Special Educators) Scholar at Virginia Commonwealth University. Previously, Mr. Hobson was a special education teacher in the greater Richmond, Virginia, area. His research interests include education policy (special education workforce) and technology skill development/decision making. He currently works as an inclusive education coordinator for the Virginia Department of Education's Technical Training and Assistance Center at James Madison University. In addition, Mr. Hobson works on the I'm Determined Project, which focuses on providing individuals with disabilities and their families opportunities to develop skills associated with self-determination.

Sarah K. Howorth, Ph.D., BCBA-D, is an assistant professor of special education and program coordinator for the special education graduate programs in the School of Learning and Teaching, part of the University of Maine College of Education and Human Development. Her research interests include social skills and social coaching of individuals with autism, and the use of emerging technology such as virtual reality and augmented reality to support behavioral, academic, and transition skills instruction for individuals with disabilities. Dr. Howorth is a board-certified behavior analyst and has more than 20 years of experience in special education. She also has expertise in the following areas: assistive technology, reading comprehension, positive behavior interventions and supports, and improving employment and transition outcomes for individuals with autism and intellectual disabilities.

Roger Ideishi, JD, OT/L, FAOTA, is the program director of occupational therapy and a professor of Health, Human Function, and Rehabilitation Sciences at The George Washington University School of Medicine and Health Sciences. His research area is the development and evaluation of community programs with a focus on arts and disability for the neurodiverse community. He is a cofounder of Philadelphia's

Chinatown Disability Advocacy Project. Dr. Ideishi is a recognized advisor and educator on arts inclusion partnering with more than 100 arts organizations across the United States and internationally, including in Ireland, Russia, Romania, China, and Japan. He received the 2017 Art-Reach Philadelphia Cultural Access Impact Award, the 2019 Kennedy Center Achievement in Accessibility Leadership Award, and in 2021 Dr. Ideishi was named as one of the 50 national cultural leaders creating a more inspired, inclusive, and compassionate world by The Kennedy Center.

Rebekka J. Jez, Ed.D., is currently an assistant professor at the University of San Diego. She earned her Ed.D. degree from the University of San Francisco in 2011. She taught in special education for more than 14 years, and in 2013 she was a Fulbright Scholar in South Africa. Dr. Jez's research focuses on supporting educators from around the world in culturally responsive/sustaining inclusive practices, trauma-informed/healing practices, holistic academic assessment, postsecondary transition for kindergarten through Grade 12 learners, and critical collaboration practices to bring learners, families, educators, and communities together. She has served on the Division of Special Education and Services board of directors since 2019. Dr. Jez has published multiple articles, chapters, and briefs on collaborative projects in the work she has done in the United States, South Africa, Jamaica, and Tanzania. She is the co-editor of *Teacher Education Quarterly* and serves on the editorial board of the *African Journal of Teacher Education and Development*.

Genna Kieper, M.A., is currently a doctoral student and serves the Washington State University (WSU) Responsibility Opportunity Advocacy and Respect (ROAR) program as their employment services coordinator. They earned their master's degree in educational psychology from WSU in 2021. Genna's research focuses on self-determination theory, gender theory, and the self-regulation and coregulation of learning in workplace environments for people with intellectual and developmental disabilities (I/DD).

Scott Kupferman, Ph.D., is an associate professor at the University of Colorado Colorado Springs and director of the National Collaborative for Disability and Technology, a federally funded network of more than 300 people with disabilities, researchers, and technology companies who codevelop and coresearch accessible technology. He received his Ph.D. degree in special education and rehabilitation from Utah State University. Dr. Kupferman's honors include selection as a Fulbright Scholar in Japan and an invitation to serve as a delegate at the United Nations in Geneva; he is also a recipient of the U.S. Department of Education Commissioner's Award for Excellence.

Leena Jo Landmark, Ph.D., is currently a professor of special education at Sam Houston State University. She is also the director of research and grants for the Garrett Center on Transition and Disability Studies. Dr. Landmark researches topics related to individuals with disabilities, such as self-determination, transition planning, classroom management, family involvement, leadership experiences, and postsecondary educational practices.

Donald D. McMahon, Ph.D., is an associate professor of special education at Washington State University (WSU) in Pullman, Washington. His research interests include augmented reality, virtual reality, inclusive postsecondary education (PSE), wearable devices, universal design for learning, assistive technology, and instructional technology. At WSU, Dr. McMahon coordinates the VR2GO Lab. He is one of the faculty mentors for the WSU Responsibility Opportunity Advocacy and Respect (ROAR) PSE program for students with intellectual and developmental disabilities.

He is also the co-coordinator of special education programs at WSU. Dr. McMahon is an active member of the PSE community as a member of several Think College Affinity Groups and as a presenter at national conferences. He presents professional development to school districts and states, and he has articles in more than 17 publications involving inclusive PSE programing and students.

Ashley J. Miller, Ed.D., is an assistant professor for the Department of Special Education at West Chester University in Pennsylvania. She received an educational doctorate in innovation and leadership with a focus on special education from Wilmington University. Before teaching at the postsecondary level, Dr. Miller served as a high school learning support in Chester County, Pennsylvania, for nearly 10 years and had the rare privilege of serving as interim assistant principal and interim principal at a unique middle school in northern Philadelphia. Dr. Miller's research interests include transition services, culturally and linguistically diverse teaching, and teacher wellness. When Dr. Miller is not inspiring future educators in the classroom, she is renovating her home or spending quality time with her best friend and spouse of more than 18 years and their dog Caico.

Yetta Myrick is the mother of a young adult son diagnosed with an autism spectrum disorder and intellectual disability. She is the founder and president of DC Autism Parents (DCAP), a 501(c)(3) nonprofit organization in the District of Columbia. Ms. Myrick has served as the Centers for Disease Control and Prevention's Act Early ambassador to the District of Columbia since 2016 and is currently leading the D.C. Act Early COVID-19 Response Team Project. She holds a bachelor of arts degree in communication studies from The Catholic University of America. In 2021, she was appointed to the Interagency Autism Coordinating Committee. In addition, Ms. Myrick is a member of DC Developmental Disabilities Council and the Got Transition National Family Health Care Transition Advisory Group. She believes deeply that parental involvement is key to obtaining quality services for all children and that an informed parent is an engaged parent.

Marcus Poppen, Ph.D., is an associate professor of special education at Washington State University, where he works to advance career development and employment outcomes for youth and young adults with disabilities. His work is focused on supporting positive postsecondary outcomes for young adults with disabilities, including those involved in the juvenile justice system, foster care system, and/or living with mental health concerns through the implementation of evidence-based transition services and supports.

Sheida K. Raley, Ph.D., is an assistant research professor at the University of Kansas (KU) Center on Developmental Disabilities and an assistant professor in the Department of Special Education. Dr. Raley's research focuses on assessment and intervention related to self-determination for all students, including students with extensive support needs learning in inclusive contexts. The goal of her research is to understand how to enable all students, including students with and without disabilities, to build abilities and skills associated with self-determination. Dr. Raley has a particular interest in identifying instructional strategies and supports for general and special educators to use in inclusive classrooms. She is currently the co–principal investigator or co-investigator on multiple federally funded projects related to understanding, assessing, and evaluating evidence-based practices. Dr. Raley teaches courses in the KU Department of Special Education program focused on self-determination and strengths-based approaches. She is a former teacher for elementary and middle school students with extensive support needs.

Deborah L. Rooks-Ellis, Ph.D., is an associate professor of early childhood education at Coastal Carolina University. She earned her doctorate degree from the University of Arizona. Her research interests include teacher education, family–school partnerships, and how instructional strategies are implemented within the complexities of classrooms.

Amber Brown Ruiz, Ph.D., CR, is a postdoctoral researcher at Washington State University (WSU) for the WSU Responsibility Opportunity Advocacy and Respect (ROAR) program. She received her Ph.D. degree in special education and disability policy at Virginia Commonwealth University. She has a growing scholarship agenda aimed at improving postsecondary transition outcomes for students of color with disabilities through collaborative and culturally responsive transition service delivery models. Dr. Ruiz's research is derived from her practitioner experience as a former vocational rehabilitation counselor.

Karrie A. Shogren, Ph.D., is director of the University of Kansas Center on Developmental Disabilities, senior scientist at the Life Span Institute (aka Schiefelbusch Institute for Life Span Studies), and professor in the Department of Special Education, all at the University of Kansas. Her research focuses on assessment and intervention in self-determination and supported decision making for people with disabilities. She has led multiple grant-funded projects, including assessment validation and efficacy trials of self-determination interventions in school, secondary transition, and community contexts. She teaches courses in the special education doctoral program, including on self-determination and strengths-based approaches to disability. Dr. Shogren has published more than 180 articles in peer-reviewed journals, is the author or coauthor of 10 books, and is the lead author of the Self-Determination Inventory, a recently validated assessment of self-determination, and the Supported Decision-Making Inventory System, the first assessment of the supports needed to involve people with intellectual and developmental disabilities in decisions about their lives.

Joshua Taylor, Ph.D., is an assistant professor of special education in the College of Education at Washington State University. His research focuses on promoting lifelong success for individuals with autism and developmental disabilities through implementation of evidence-based practices in inclusive school, work, and community settings. He earned a Ph.D. degree in special education from Virginia Commonwealth University (VCU) with a focus on research-to-policy implementation. Dr. Taylor's background is in public school settings, where he has more than 10 years of experience as a special education teacher and autism specialist in Arlington Public Schools (Virginia) and most recently as a research, training, and technical assistance associate with the VCU's Rehabilitation Research and Training Center.

Holly N. Whittenburg, Ph.D., is currently an assistant professor of special education at Washington State University and codirector of the Washington Transition Program. She earned her Ph.D. degree in education with a concentration in special education and disability leadership from Virginia Commonwealth University. Dr. Whittenburg's research focuses on employment-related skills interventions for transition-age youth with disabilities, approaches to creating more opportunities for inclusive work experiences, and the effects of special education and vocational rehabilitation law and policies on the transition experiences of students with disabilities. She has published more than 20 articles and book chapters related to transition and employment and is a co–principal investigator on a federally funded model demonstration program project for transition and postsecondary programs for students with intellectual disabilities. Dr. Whittenburg also works extensively with schools and vocational rehabilitation agencies. In her free time, she enjoys running, reading, and spending time with her family.

Kendra Williams-Diehm, Ph.D., is a professor and director with Zarrow Center for Learning Enrichment, located within the special education program in the Jeannine Rainbolt College of Education at the University of Oklahoma. She holds both the Zarrow Family Endowed Chair and the Brian E. and Sandra L. O'Brien Presidential Professorship. Her primary research interests include comprehensive transition services with a focus on appropriate transition assessment and self-determination for students with intellectual and developmental disabilities. A secondary research interest focuses on the intersection of cultural and successful transition outcomes. Dr. Williams-Diehm taught special education at both the elementary and secondary level and still considers herself to be an educator first.

Heather J. Williamson, Ph.D., is an associate professor at Northern Arizona University in the Center for Health Equity Research and the Department of Occupational Therapy. She is a Fellow of the American Association on Intellectual and Developmental Disabilities.

Preface

Universal Design for Transition: The Educators' Guide for Equity-Focused Transition Planning, Second Edition, reintroduces readers to universal design for transition (UDT) with a bit of a twist. In the first edition, *Universal Design for Transition: A Roadmap for Planning and Instruction* (Thoma et al., 2009), we introduced our readers to a new concept called universal design for transition to support the planning for the transition from school to adult life for students with disabilities. Since that time, the UDT framework has grown in popularity. We cite an increase of the UDT framework used in research (e.g., see Alzahrani, 2018, 2021; Scott et al., 2022), and requests we have received from numerous school districts about providing professional development to educators. Finally, we have heard from hundreds of teacher educators about their use of UDT in classrooms. Although we consider the growing popularity and use of UDT a positive matter for the field, we are also motivated to reintroduce educators to the UDT framework using culturally responsive and sustaining approaches. By "culturally responsive and sustaining," we mean approaches that reduce opportunity gaps related to student academic achievement and transition planning success (e.g., health, education, school, community living, self-determination). In this text, *culturally responsive and sustaining teaching* is meant to describe how educators appreciate and affirm students' sociocultural identities, values, heritages, communities, and backgrounds, as well as recognizing and constructing ways to leverage and sustain students' cultural differences in teaching and learning while remaining reflexive and reflective during practice. Throughout this book, on most occasions we default to the term *culturally sustaining* when describing UDT and culturally responsive approaches, as we acknowledge that the term has varied and picked up different meanings over time (e.g., culturally responsive teaching, culturally relevant pedagogy, culturally sustaining pedagogy).

We anticipate that this book will advance what we know, and what we thought we knew, about approaches for meeting the academic and functional/transition needs of students with disabilities, particularly those from historically marginalized groups. In the first iteration, we got to know LaRon Scott, a high school special education teacher and coauthor who overcame challenges to teaching both functional and academic content to prepare postsecondary education students with disabilities for lives after high school. As a novice high school special education teacher, he struggled to meet the needs of his diverse group of students. LaRon frequently grappled with choosing between *what* to teach, *when* to teach, and *how* to teach his diverse group of students content to advance their academic knowledge while also meeting their unique functional and transition needs (see Thoma et al., 2009).

Transition planning is an extremely important focus of the Individuals with Disabilities Improvement Act (2004) and, most recently, the Workforce Innovation and Opportunity Act (2014). With that said, students with disabilities from historically marginalized backgrounds continue to experience disparities in education, support services, and adult outcomes. And, more than a decade after meeting LaRon, we posit that classroom teachers continue to struggle with opportunities to bridge academic, functional, and transition skills. For this reason, we have renewed our efforts to prepare and support teachers through using unique approaches to bridging academic, functional, and transition skills. This renewal could not come at a more critical time in the field of education/special education. For example, despite some researchers' and practitioners' efforts to focus on improving the academic achievement, social/ emotional learning, and transition education outcomes, students with disabilities, especially those from marginalized genders and racial and linguistic backgrounds (to name just a few) continue to experience inequities that adversely impact their school, employment, independent living, postsecondary, and self-determination outcomes (to name a few). For instance, researchers indicated that Black/African American and Latine students with disabilities are likely to experience more adverse academic and postschool outcomes than White students with disabilities (Booth et al., 2016). When discussing these disparate outcomes, several researchers described one of the barriers to success for students of color, which has been that the overwhelmingly White teacher workforce lacks cultural competence (Bonilla-Silva, 2017; Ladson-Billings, 2017; Milner, 2020) despite research indicating that cultural competency improves the instructional quality for teachers and leads to increased academic achievement for students of color (Khalifa et al., 2016). Thus, a major goal of this current edition of *Universal Design for Transition* is to place greater emphasis on acknowledging the rich cultural heritages of historically marginalized children and youth when planning their academic and transition curriculum.

Some would argue that policy has taken a race-evasive approach and therefore has not gone far enough to eliminate barriers for these young people. Others might argue the need for school reform at the state and/or local levels. Whatever the argument, efforts to narrow the achievement gap for students from historically marginalized backgrounds must take center stage. With that said, building educators' (e.g., teachers') cultural competency as a commitment to closing achievement gaps and shaping equitable learning experiences underlies arguably one of the most valuable fixes to inequitable education and transition outcomes for students from historically marginalized backgrounds.

Improving postschool outcomes for students from historically marginalized backgrounds was the first priority for our team when we thought about a second iteration of UDT. We realized that we did not go far enough with the first UDT book in providing a foundation for supports and services to specifically address the transition needs of these groups of students. And even though we were concerned with blending academic and transition planning to meet the needs of "diverse" groups of students, we assert that we needed to go deeper into these issues to truly make the type of impact in the field that can change the lives of students who are most vulnerable. Therefore, we introduce you to UDT 2.0—with a specific focus and call for equitable practices that blend academic and transition planning.

We organized the book into three major sections. Section I, Culturally Sustaining UDT: Overview and Components, provides an overview of the basics of UDT while also incorporating tenets of culturally responsive teaching and culturally sustaining pedagogical approaches.

Chapter 1 provides an overview of UDT 2.0 and culturally responsive/sustaining practices. These UDT components and practices include the following:

- Assessment (Chapter 2)

- Self-determination (Chapter 3)

- Multiple resources and perspectives (collaboration; Chapter 4)

Section II, Culturally Sustaining UDT Across Domains, addresses multiple transition domains, which are disaggregated into separate chapters:

- Employment (Chapter 5)

- Postsecondary education (Chapter 6)

- Community living (Chapter 7)

- Social inclusion and engagement (Chapter 8)

Finally, Section III, Culturally Sustaining UDT Planning: Implementation, includes other topics related to UDT that should be considered when delivering academic and transition planning:

- Individualized education planning (Chapter 9)

- Embedding technology (Chapter 10)

- Guidance for putting everything together to implement a UDT framework (Chapter 11)

Each chapter in this book begins with the voice of one or more educators (who are also chapter authors or coauthors) who have dedicated, in some form, their professional career (and often their personal life) to advocating for a diverse body of students with dis/abilities. Many of our educators, like LaRon, faced challenges with balancing teaching academic and functional/transition skills to students in schools. However, each educator was able to facilitate changes using approaches they learned from the first iteration of *Universal Design for Transition* in 2009. Each educator also prioritized designing instruction and plans that valued the sociocultural identity of their students. Also featured throughout chapters are case studies that provide context for real-world examples and experiences of activities in education settings. We also offer additional tips, resources, and documents throughout for practice and use for our readers. All together, we believe that this current iteration of UDT focusing on using culturally responsive and sustaining pedagogical approaches will support the *how* to meet the functional/transition needs of an increasingly diverse prekindergarten through Grade 12 student population. We hope this text will help shape the future of equitable academics and functional/transition planning for all youth but particularly those from historically marginalized communities.

REFERENCES

Alzahrani, M. A. (2018). The importance of teachers' universal design for transition principles knowledge in preparing students who are deaf and hard of hearing for the life after school in Saudi Arabia. *Creative Education, 9*(3), 513.

Alzahrani, H. (2021). *Teachers', paraprofessionals', and administrators' perceptions of the effectiveness of community-based programs on individuals with intellectual disability transitioning to employment* (doctoral dissertation, Saint Louis University).

Bonilla-Silva, E. (2017). *Racism without racists: Color-blind racism and the persistence of racial inequality in America.* Rowman & Littlefield.

Booth, J., Butler, M. K., Richardson, T. V., Washington, A. R., & Henfield, M. S. (2016). School–family–community collaboration for African American males with disabilities. *Journal of African American Males in Education (JAAME), 7*(1), 87–97.

Individuals with Disabilities Education Improvement Act (IDEA) of 2004, Pub. L. No. 108-446, 20 U.S.C. §§ 1400 *et seq* (2004).

Khalifa, M. A., Gooden, M. A., & Davis, J. E. (2016). Culturally responsive school leadership: A synthesis of the literature. *Review of Educational Research, 86*(4), 1272–1311.

Ladson-Billings, G. (2017). The (r)evolution will not be standardized. In D. Paris & H. S. Alim (Eds.), *Culturally sustaining pedagogies: Teaching and learning for justice in a changing world* (pp. 141–156). Teachers College Press.

Milner, H. R., IV. (2020). *Start where you are, but don't stay there: Understanding diversity, opportunity gaps, and teaching in today's classrooms* (2nd ed.). Harvard Education Press.

Scott, L., Bruno, L., Gokita, T., & Thoma, C. A. (2022). Teacher candidates' abilities to develop universal design for learning and universal design for transition lesson plans. *International Journal of Inclusive Education, 26*(4), 333–347.

Thoma, C. A., Bartholomew, C. C., & Scott, L. A. (2009). *Universal design for transition: A roadmap for planning and instruction.* Paul H. Brookes Publishing Co.

Workforce Innovation and Opportunity Act of 2014, Pub. L. No. 113-128, Stat. 129 (2014). https://www.govinfo.gov/content/pkg/PLAW-113publ128/pdf/PLAW-113publ128.pdf

Acknowledgments

We acknowledge the hard work of our contributors who dedicate their professional and personal careers to solving some of the world's most complex challenges. This book would be impossible without the support and dedication from our contributors (see About the Contributors).

We acknowledge the historically marginalized students and families who shared their stories with us to provide guidance about changes they would like to see in the transition planning process. We learned so much from all of you who gave so generously of your time.

We acknowledge and thank our hard-working doctoral students, who were funded by a grant from the Office of Special Education, Policy and Research Intensive Special Educators (PRISE), for their creative ideas and support with pulling this book together: Jarrod Hobson, Regina Howard, Michelle Hicks, Monica Grillo, Meagan Dayton, Rachel Bowman, and Imani Evans.

Last but not least, we also thank our families who support us no matter what. This book would not be possible without your ongoing love and support.

For Dwight VanRossum and Morgan Scott (Papa loves you)
Mike, Chris, Stephanie, and Violet Thoma

I

Culturally Sustaining UDT:
Overview and Components

1

UDT to Provide Culturally Competent Academic and Transition Instruction

LaRon A. Scott, Rachel W. Bowman, Meagan Dayton, Imani Evans, Amber Brown Ruiz, Colleen A. Thoma, and Lauren Bruno

Essential Questions

▶ How has universal design for transition (UDT) evolved over time?

▶ In what ways does the UDT framework promote blending academic and functional/transition skills and making connections to academic and postschool goals?

▶ What does culturally competent academic instruction entail? How should it infuse transition planning and practices for a growing culturally and linguistically diverse (CLD) kindergarten through Grade 12 (K–12) student body?

▶ What are the core principles of UDT?

What we have learned over numerous decades is that teachers face multiple responsibilities when attempting to meet both the academic and transition goals of students with disabilities. For example, teachers who prepare students with disabilities for life beyond high school, while simultaneously focusing on academic achievements, face seemingly conflicting demands from academic and transition-related education policies. For example, the Individuals with Disabilities Education Improvement Act (IDEA) was reauthorized in 2004, with a renewed emphasis on access to the general education environment, functional achievement, and transition planning (Bassett & Kochhar-Bryant, 2006). Transition was previously defined as an "outcome-oriented process" that encouraged movement from school to post-school activities; however, IDEA officials redefined transition as a "results-oriented process," shifting their focus from simply promoting transition to highlighting the school leaders' obligations to facilitate achievement of positive transition outcomes through purposeful improvement of functional skills for students with disabilities (Bassett & Kochhar-Bryant, 2006, p. 4). In addition to IDEA 2004, the Workforce Innovation and Opportunity Act (WIOA, 2014) was developed to add an additional layer of transition policy implications. The transition requirements under WIOA focus on the collaboration of teachers, vocational rehabilitation counselors, and other stakeholders (including families and youth with disabilities), with emphasis particularly on improving employment and independent living outcomes. WIOA divides the responsibility for organizing transition supports, services, and education among different organizations, each with different missions, responsibilities, and approaches, with special educators playing a major role in coordinating these efforts.

On top of the complex and demanding responsibilities required by these policies, in 2015, legislators passed the Every Student Succeeds Act (ESSA), which emphasized high, standards-based academic achievement for all students, including individuals with disabilities. A major focus of ESSA was to create a more equitable education system in which educators prepare historically underserved students to meet the high demands of the current century. ESSA is used to emphasize access for students to learning opportunities involving higher-order thinking skills, use of multiple measures to assess school performance and progress, resource equity, and evidence-based interventions (Cook-Harvey et al., 2016). The passage of ESSA created additional pressure for special education teachers to balance high academic standards while simultaneously meeting the functional and transition needs of students with disabilities (Scott et al., 2019).

An additional challenge for teachers is providing academic instruction and transition planning that is culturally competent. Investigators who focused on transition education for students of color with disabilities have highlighted the importance of cultural competence in transition planning and education services in K–12 schools (Achola, 2019; Banks, 2014, Brown Ruiz & Scott, 2021; Suk et al., 2020). In particular, researchers noted that the transition provisions of IDEA (2004) are based in White ideology (Halley & Trujillo, 2013). Although reasons for the disparate outcomes for students of color with disabilities are complex, it is critically important for special education teachers to be able to understand and apply culturally relevant and sustaining practices in instructional planning to meet the academic and transition needs of students with multiple sociocultural identities, especially students of color with disabilities (e.g., Brown Ruiz & Scott, 2021; Suk et al., 2019). Despite the increasing body of literature in which researchers focused on developing special educators' cultural competence for delivering instruction and guiding transition planning, studies indicated that teachers *still* struggle to understand ways to teach culturally responsive academics while also meeting the transition needs of students with disabilities (Scott & Bruno, 2018). To date, we have not come across a strategy that shows teachers how to implement culturally responsive instruction while concurrently incorporating research-/evidence-based transition practices for students with disabilities, especially those of color. Thus, a major goal of this current iteration of *Universal Design for Transition* is to place greater emphasis on acknowledging the rich cultural heritages of historically marginalized children and youth when planning their academic and transition curriculum.

To address the challenges that teachers face in meeting both the academic and transition needs of their students, Thoma et al. (2009) created a conceptual framework for combining academic and transitional teaching—universal design for transition, or UDT. This chapter will describe the evolution of UDT, an approach to transition that is grounded in universal design (UD) and in universal design for instruction (UDI) and universal design for learning (UDL). In the UDT approach, the principles of UDI and UDL are applied to, and enhanced by, best practices for transition planning and services.

This chapter introduces you to the concept of UDT to bridge the perceived discrepancies between providing academic instruction and transition planning that is culturally competent. Although UDT is the newer iteration, it is based on the established principles of UD, particularly its educational application in UDI and UDL. Furthermore, we present UDT and culturally sustaining pedagogies as a way of promoting equity to meet the needs of students from historically marginalized backgrounds, particularly students of color with disabilities. However, before we go further with UDT, we must go back to where it all started, and that is with UD. Table 1.1 outlines the evolution of these four different concepts.

UNIVERSAL DESIGN

According to The Center for Universal Design, UD can be defined as "[t]he design of products and environments to be usable by all people, to the greatest extent possible, without the need for adaptation or specialized design" (2008, para. 2). This concept of design emerged in response to legislative and social changes that occurred more than 6 decades ago. "Barrier-free" designs in architecture and community living were implemented after legislation focusing on nondiscriminatory practices began to emerge in the 1950s. This concept continued to be a focus in architecture and urban planning and was supported by legislation such as the Rehabilitation Act (1973), Fair Housing Act (1968), and Americans with Disabilities Act (1990).

Table 1.1. Evolution of universal design

Term	Field	Major features
Universal design	Architecture/product design	Access for all
Universal design for instruction	Education: teaching strategies	Access to what is being taught
Universal design for learning	Education: learning	Access to learning that seeks to ensure that methods, materials, and assessment/engagement are all accessible
Universal design for transition	Special education	Access to preferred adult lifestyles through a process of self-determined planning, instruction, collaboration, and support services

The term *universal* implies that methods or design are not specific to one person or one ability level but rather are beneficial to all individuals (Wehman, 2006). UD in architecture focuses on proactively removing barriers within the community to create access for all individuals, including the removal of structural barriers within community buildings. We see several examples of UD each day in the buildings in which we work and shop. Automatic doors are one example. They are designed to enable individuals using wheelchairs to enter and exit buildings independently; however, these doors also provide easier access to individuals who are carrying packages and pushing carts and/or baby strollers. Other examples of UD in architecture and product design include curb cuts on sidewalks, closed captioning for television shows, and elevators in buildings. Curb cuts and elevators make it possible for a large number of individuals to navigate streets, sidewalks, and buildings independently, including individuals with disabilities who use wheelchairs and walkers, children on bikes, people pushing strollers, or professionals toting rolling briefcases. Closed captioning on televisions not only benefits individuals with hearing impairments but is also useful for patrons of sports bars and spouses who watch television at night while their significant other sleeps. These architectural and product designs extend beyond their original use and support access for all.

Universal Design in the Classroom

The concept of barrier-free design has been applied not only in the physical environment of the classroom but also in the instructional methods and materials that are used to teach students. The terms *UDI* and *UDL* characterize efforts to create universal access to education for all students, including those with cognitive, physical, and emotional disabilities. Both approaches build on the concept of UD and focus on removing both physical and cognitive barriers in the classroom, thus providing an instructional design that removes barriers to learning (Council for Exceptional Children, 2005). Whereas UDI focuses primarily on the way that instruction is provided to students, UDL focuses on the entire educational process, including how information is taught, which materials are used, how students engage in learning activities, and how progress is assessed. UDL is flexible and is based on the premise that there is no one-size-fits-all approach to student learning; teachers must deliver instruction in multiple ways and allow students multiple ways of expressing mastery.

As mentioned previously, UDT was developed and grounded in the UDL framework (Thoma et al., 2009). Thus, to understand and incorporate UDT, it is important to get a good understanding of UDL.

Universal Design for Learning

The goals of UDL are to make learning accessible for all students, support inclusion, and ensure that all students have their academic needs met. UDL has three main principles: multiple means of engagement, multiple means of representation, and multiple means of action and expression (Center for Applied Special Technologies [CAST], 2018). The principle of *multiple means of engagement* is based on the idea that if students are not engaged, they are not learning. Engagement does not stay static from student to student or even in an individual student (CAST, 2018); therefore, the methods teachers use to engage their students must be varied. Teachers can achieve varying methods by using student choice as often as possible, varying activities, giving feedback, and teaching students how to self-regulate (CAST, 2018).

The rationale of *multiple means of representation* is that not all students learn best from the same instructional approach, so teachers must provide different kinds of instructional approaches to address a range of learning needs (CAST, 2018). Teachers can provide different instructional approaches by varying their teaching modalities (i.e., audio and visual), using tools such as guided notes and graphic organizers to present information in different formats, using visuals to support understanding, and explicitly teaching background knowledge, vocabulary, and big ideas (CAST, 2018).

All students learn differently; therefore, they also best convey their understanding of concepts differently, which makes providing *multiple means of action and expression* essential for all students to have an equitable chance of showing what they have learned (CAST, 2018). Teachers can achieve equitable learning by varying response types (e.g., pen and paper, typing, drawing), allowing students to respond in ways that are most effective for them, and directly teaching students skills for goal setting and self-monitoring (CAST, 2018).

It is important to note that UDL is not a set method for instruction but rather a framework for instructional design that is built on the principle that all students can learn; multiple means of content delivery and student assessment should be part of daily lessons and planning to enhance this learning process. Figure 1.1 provides a visual representation of the three characteristics of UDL, highlighting some examples of instructional, assessment, and/or planning practices that fit each of these categories. For additional information, see the UDL Guidelines on the CAST website at https://udlguidelines.cast.org/.

Additional Components in UDT

UDL principles are core components of UDT. However, implementing a UDT framework ensures that instruction also helps with preparing students for life after school (Scott & Bruno, 2018; Thoma et al., 2009). The distinction originates from the inclusion of the transition/functional components that are added to the UDL principles. The additional principles of UDT include the following:

Multiple life domains

Multiple means of assessment

Individual self-determination

Multiple resources and perspectives

For an in-depth look at these principles, see Table 1.2.

When teachers focus on *multiple life domains* for their students, they focus on all areas of transition rather than only on career or education (Thoma et al., 2009). Focusing on all areas of transition involves preparing students for education, careers, independent living, leisure activities, and any other areas that students may need help with to prepare them for life after school (Scott & Bruno, 2018). The term *multiple means of assessment* denotes teachers using different types of assessments that can be sourced to evaluate student needs and create a snapshot of the students' skills, needs, and desires for adult life (Scott & Bruno, 2018). The use of informal assessments is particularly important because teachers can personalize the assessment to the student and assess skills in real-world settings (Thoma et al., 2016). *Individual self-determination* is the third component unique to UDT, and it is a true foundational principle of any transition planning (Thoma et al., 2016). When teachers incorporate

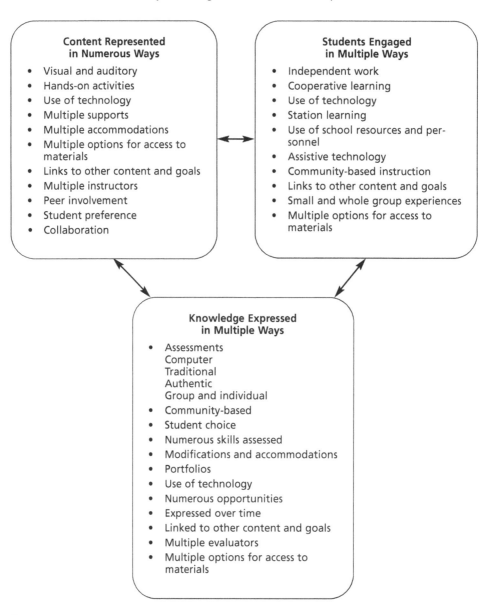

Figure 1.1. Universal design for learning.

self-determination in their approaches, they focus on student wants and needs when setting goals for students' adult lives. Teachers should also explicitly teach students self-determination skills to support themselves in and after school (Scott & Bruno, 2018). Finally, UDT involves the use of *multiple resources and perspectives*. When teachers use multiple resources and perspectives, it means that they are involving individuals from the students' schools, homes, and communities when making decisions. The use of multiple resources and perspectives allows for different points of view from people involved from different domains of a student's life. It also ensures that students are connected to community resources that will help them after they leave school (Scott & Bruno, 2018).

Table 1.2. Universal design for transition characteristics

Multiple life domains	Multiple means of assessment	Individual self-determination	Multiple means of representation	Multiple means of engagement	Multiple means of expression	Multiple resources/perspectives
Focus is on the transition to a complete, integrated plan for life rather than on multiple, divided life segments.	Focus is on collecting an array of information about the student that provides holistic data upon which decisions are made.	Student is the focus of the process, with their preferences and interests serving as the basis for transition services. Student is the causal agent.	Transition planning and services are developed so that they include materials, services, and instruction that include a range of methods.	Transition planning and services are developed to ensure that there are multiple ways that students can be involved in the process.	Transition planning and services are developed to ensure that students can communicate their preferences and interests and demonstrate progress in multiple ways.	Transition planning and services are developed collaboratively, pooling resources (financial, human, and/or material), and using natural supports and/or generic community services as well as disability-specific ones.
Includes a focus on the typical transition/life domains of employment, community living, postsecondary education, transportation, recreation and leisure, and community integration; supports are examined for the range of applicability. For example, instruction in writing (during English class) can include writing for employment (creating a résumé and cover letter), writing for the transition to postsecondary education (writing a college admissions essay, writing for an advanced placement class), writing for community living (writing a letter of complaint to a landlord), and/or writing for recreation/leisure (writing in a journal).	Assessments include a range of methods, and they are chosen based on the students' needs and the disparity between student long-range goals and the current information on student strengths/needs and abilities. For example, for a student who is interested in becoming a nurse, assessment should focus on understanding a wide range of skills (aptitude, computer skills, ability to work with others, interest in and awareness of this career). Information should also be gathered in multiple ways (computers, informal and formal, authentic work tasks, on-site employment assessments).	Students do not need to do it all themselves, but self-determination needs to be a focus for the entire transition planning team, *ensuring* that the student chooses needed supports that achieve their long-range adult life goals. Using a person-centered planning method (discussed in Chapter 2) is one way to engage students and plan with them, not for them.	Methods employ a variety of instructional strategies, including the use of authentic learning objectives (i.e., tasks that adults perform in their lives and on the job). For example, rather than have students complete a paper-and-pencil test to demonstrate their understanding of geometry, they could build a walkway by designing its size and shape, determining the amount of materials necessary, and completing the project.	Instructional design provides opportunities for individuals to be engaged in many different ways to meet multiple objectives. For instance, by involving students in developing a movie, they can engage academic content (in the details of the storyline) as well as functional skills like communication, working with others, and using technology.	Assessment of student progress can occur in multiple ways, ensuring that students with disabilities are able to demonstrate what they know. These options, when incorporated into transition planning and services, support individual self-determination. For example, students should have the opportunity to express their knowledge and interests in multiple ways, including the use of technology, group work, class and individualized education program, participation, paper-and-pencil work, and authentic task completion.	Transition planning and services reflect the range of supports available to individuals with and without disabilities, and the best of collaborative planning where stakeholders work together to break down barriers to provide appropriate supports. Employers, peers, community agency representatives, family members, teachers, and guidance counselors are all examples of people who can be included in the transition process and can offer different perspectives in a collaborative process.

MEETING THE NEEDS OF A DIVERSE PUBLIC SCHOOL POPULATION

As briefly discussed previously, in addition to meeting the complex demands and responsibilities related to educational policies that are enacted, teachers further need to meet the needs of an increasingly CLD student population with learners who vary in characteristics, learning needs, and academic and social skills (Kieran & Anderson, 2019). To ensure that all learners can access the curriculum, teachers must acquire new knowledge and skills to respond to these individual learner needs. The increasing number of students with disabilities in general education classrooms, paired with multiply marginalized learners, makes the mastery of culturally responsive instruction a top priority (Kieran & Anderson, 2019; Santamaria, 2009). In classrooms with a wide range of instructional levels, teachers are tasked with ensuring that learning is rigorous, flexible, and varied in order for all students to maximize individual growth and success (Kieran & Anderson, 2019; Santamaria, 2009)—posing an opportunity to link strengthening practice and pedagogy that support the needs of a more diverse student population.

Culturally Responsive Teaching

Classrooms that are becoming more diverse further highlight teachers' need to develop the skills necessary to provide *culturally responsive teaching* practices. Discussion of culturally responsive teaching often includes several related terms—*culturally responsive pedagogy, culturally relevant pedagogy,* and *culturally sustaining pedagogy* (CSP). The nuances of these terms and practices are explored in this section, but they all serve the same overarching goals.

Culturally responsive teaching requires that educators approach instruction in a way that is proactive and responsive to the sociocultural context and integrates cultural content that empowers and illuminates learners (Gay, 2002, 2018; Kieran & Anderson, 2019; Santamaria, 2009). The goal of using *culturally relevant pedagogy* is to empower students intellectually, socially, emotionally, and politically, grounding cultural references within instruction, so that all students realize that their cultural heritages are also valuable assets when learning (Kieran & Anderson, 2019; Ladson-Billings, 1995; Santamaria, 2009).

Culturally relevant pedagogy was first developed in response to literature in which researchers overwhelmingly viewed African American learners through a deficit lens (Ladson-Billings, 1995, 2014). Based on culturally relevant pedagogy, researchers shifted focus by studying classrooms in which successful teaching of African American learners occurred (Ladson-Billings, 1995). As a result of examining the thinking and practices of model teachers, culturally relevant pedagogy was used to provide practical recommendations to improve teacher education programs, preparing future generations of teachers who value their students' assets and bring appreciation to their work with African American students (Ladson-Billings, 1995, 2014). *Culturally responsive* and *culturally sustaining pedagogy* builds on the tenets of culturally relevant pedagogy, expanding the focus into practices that support the learning of many populations of multiply marginalized learners, including Latine, Asian, Native American, and African American students (Ladson-Billings, 2014, 2017).

Culturally responsive and sustaining pedagogy includes several key components (Alim & Paris, 2017; Gay, 2002, 2018):

1. Developing and sustaining a knowledge base and community regarding cultural diversity

2. Designing culturally relevant curricula by including ethnic and cultural diversity content

3. Creating classroom climates that are conducive to learning for multiply marginalized students

4. Developing effective cross-cultural communications

5. Delivering instruction matching the learning styles of diverse students

Throughout the text, we often use culturally responsive teaching with the hope of movement toward culturally sustaining pedagogy and practice. Alim and Paris (quoted in Ferlazzo, 2017) explain that a goal of CSP is to decenter Whiteness in education because of the harmful impact it has on historically multiply marginalized students:

> Culturally sustaining pedagogy exists wherever education sustains the lifeways of communities who have been and continue to be damaged and erased through schooling. As such, CSP explicitly calls for schooling to be a site for sustaining—rather than eradicating—the cultural ways of being of communities of color.

To accomplish learning for multiply marginalized students effectively, teachers must engage in activities to increase and sustain their cultural competence and sociopolitical consciousness (Alim & Paris, 2017; Kieran & Anderson, 2019; Ladson-Billings, 1995; Santamaria, 2009); therefore, teachers must set aside time to examine their own practices, develop knowledge of their students' communities, strengthen community and familial relationships, and intensify their collaboration with other professionals (Brown Ruiz & Scott, 2021; Kieran & Anderson, 2019; Santamaria, 2009). Although academic rigor, transition planning, differentiated instruction, and culturally responsive teaching are each valuable and necessary, blending of the concepts in daily practice, without a model for unification, poses a mounting challenge for teachers.

UDT and Culturally Responsive Teaching

Although UDT principles focus on providing equal access and learning for all students with disabilities, the initial iteration did not specifically highlight the unique elements that are needed to meet the needs of students with disabilities from marginalized cultural backgrounds. To truly provide for all students equally, we contend that UDT must be used concurrently with culturally responsive (sustaining) teaching. Brown-Jeffy and Cooper (2011) have situated the early conceptual frameworks for culturally responsive and relevant teaching from the foundational work of scholars, such as Drs. Geneva Gay and Gloria Ladson-Billings, developing a framework with five core principles: 1) identity and achievement, 2) equity and excellence, 3) developmental appropriateness, 4) teaching the whole child, and 5) student–teacher relationships.

The first principle, identity and achievement, involves teachers reflecting on their identities and the identities of their students to understand how the identities may affect interactions and to address the idea of *color blindness*, to acknowledge systemic inequities, affirm differences, and validate other cultures and their viewpoints (Brown-Jeffy & Cooper, 2011). The second principle is equity and excellence, which involves teachers having high expectations for all their students, while also understanding that different students have different needs, and incorporating rich multicultural content into the curriculum so that all students understand the value of other cultures (Brown-Jeffy & Cooper, 2011). The third principle is developmental appropriateness, which involves teachers getting to know students with regard to both their academic understanding and their understanding of societal problems and then building on that knowledge by using their students' strengths and being aware of potential vulnerabilities (Brown-Jeffy & Cooper, 2011). The fourth is teaching the whole child, which involves understanding students' cultures and empowering them to believe in the value of those cultures while also acknowledging that they are individuals with their own ideas (Brown-Jeffy & Cooper, 2011).The final principle is student–teacher relationships, which involves creating a warm and open classroom environment where students can be valued as individuals and as a part of a cultural group (Brown-Jeffy & Cooper, 2011). Many of these core principles can easily be incorporated into the UDT framework (see Figure 1.2).

Multiple Means of Engagement	**Multiple Means of Representation**	**Multiple Means of Expression**
Build relationships with students to understand their backgrounds, interests, and what motivates them.	*Present content and information in different ways to reach all students.*	*Allow students to demonstrate their knowledge and skills and feel pride in their knowledge.*
Equal Access *Understand that different students have different needs.* **Caring** *Understand the systematic barriers that students face.*	**Multicultural Content** *Incorporate this in a meaningful way that supports students and allows them to feel proud of and validated in their culture.* **Teaching Styles** *Feature different types of success, not just the traditional.*	**Counter-narratives** *Provide positive examples to combat systematic prejudices.* **Interaction** *Understand different people communicate differently and work to avoid miscommunication.*

Multiple Life Domains	**Multiple Means of Assessment**	**Student Self-Determination**	**Multiple Resources and Perspectives**
Consider culture, family, and individual likes and plan for all future life domains, not just education or career.	*Collect a variety of information about students using unbiased, personalized assessments.*	*Consider students' preferences and value their culture. Teach self-advocacy.*	*Use all the community supports available and have a diverse and knowledgeable team.*
Validate Home and Community Cultures *Consider and incorporate a student's home and community cultures when planning and instructing in all life domains, including education, employment, independent living, and recreation.*	**Assessment** *Use diverse forms of assessment and keep high standards.* **Empower Students' Knowledge** *Allow students to value and demonstrate their personal and community knowledge.*	**Skill Development in Cultural Context** *Culture affects how students perceive and respond to learning and decide what is meaningful to them. Students also have their own independent ideas, so do not stereotype.*	**Bridge Home, School, and Community** *Show interest in students' lives outside school. Consider what they and their families value.*

☐ = Universal Design for Transition Principles   ☐ = Culturally Responsive Pedagogy Principles

Figure 1.2. Incorporating culturally responsive practice into universal design for transition (UDT). (*Sources:* Brown-Jeffy & Cooper, 2011; Scott et al., 2019.)

For example, multiple means of representation involves presenting information in different ways, but it also can include presenting information from different perspectives. When assessing students' knowledge using multiple means of action and expression, teachers can consider the cultures of students in the classroom when creating various assignments. While focusing on multiple resources and perspectives, teachers can also involve the student's family and community to get a more holistic understanding of the student's interests and goals. By combining the UDT and culturally responsive teaching frameworks in such ways, teachers can provide equitable access to academics and transition planning for multiply marginalized students with disabilities. As a model for how to do this, we present a case study of a young woman named Tatianna and the ways her teacher, Ms. Rose, used UDT in instructional planning for Tatianna.

CASE STUDY: Tatianna

Applying the UDT and Culturally Responsive Teaching Framework

Tatianna is a 16-year-old Afro-Latine student with a learning disability who lives in Washington, D.C. She is interested in computer science. Each summer, Tatianna goes to coding camp with her sister and enjoys seeing her final work products. In college, Tatianna wants to major in computer science; however, historically, White males have dominated the computer science field and the field has not been well disposed to individuals with disabilities.

Ms. Rose, Tatianna's high school special education teacher, recently learned about UDL to support her students. However, Ms. Rose realized that some of her methods may need to be adjusted to infuse UDL into transition planning, because she is concerned about having ample time to work on the goals with students individually. Likewise, Ms. Rose wants to explore ways to promote diversity, equity, and inclusion to ensure that students like Tatianna reach their goals, while also being conscious of centering and promoting racial equity in practice in her classroom.

Tatianna's disability largely impacts her executive functioning skills. She has been focusing on transportation skills and getting around the city, because her mom and sister cannot take her to school and to an internship site after school. Tatianna must be at school at 8 a.m., and after school at 4:30 p.m. she must travel five blocks to participate in her computer science internship. The school day ends at 3:30 p.m., and it takes Tatianna 20 minutes to get to the internship site by metro or 35 minutes by walking. The metro stop by her school is a 3-minute walk from her last class and the metro arrives at 3:45 p.m. daily, but Tatianna is late for her internship most days because she gets sidetracked using the metro. After considering Tatianna's academic and transition goals, Ms. Rose implemented a lesson plan using the UDT framework. (A blank reproducible copy of this lesson planning template is provided with the other online resources for this book, which are available at the Brookes Download Hub. For details about how to access the downloads, see the About the Downloads section in the front of the book.)

▶ LESSON PLAN

Universal Design for Transition and Culturally Responsive Teaching

Purpose: Students will use real-world data to graph and interpret data on a scatterplot while gaining experience planning and evaluating transportation options.

Objective: Given previous practice with scatterplots and resources for planning transportation, students will work in heterogeneous cooperative groups to 1) choose an interesting destination in their city, 2) describe three practical methods of transportation (e.g., metro, rideshare [e.g., Uber]), bus, bicycle), 3) calculate the time and cost associated with each route, and 4) plot their findings on a scatterplot and discuss the relationship between travel time and cost with 80% accuracy.

Universal Design for Learning Principles

1. **Multiple means of engagement**
   a. Whole-group discussion: Review terms, introduce the topic, and brainstorm ideas.
   b. Small-group discussion: Respond to the following prompt: "You have a friend visiting you from outside the city. They asked to see your favorite Washington, D.C. location. Where would you take them?" Students in their groups could discuss their favorite places to go, places they went on field trips, or a destination they always wanted to visit.
   c. Activity: Utilize technology to gather data, and then plot a linear relationship based on desired destination.
   d. **Culturally responsive teaching principles:** Use experiences from students' lived experiences.

2. **Multiple means of representation**
   a. Clarify with concrete examples of transportation and places you may want to travel within the city.
   b. Show pictures or videos of the metro, buses, bike share programs, and so forth, for students.
   c. Review and demonstrate how to interpolate data onto a scatterplot.
   d. Provide definitions of vocabulary words with visual examples.
   e. **Culturally responsive teaching principles:** Reduce barriers to print, use explicit instruction, and support multiple literacies.

3. **Multiple means of action and expression**
   a. Physical action: Students could act out the physical motions of different means of transportation, use hand signals for left and right when giving directions, practice swiping or tapping a metro card, or use manual signs to connect the vocabulary to a familiar motion.
   b. Expression and communication: Verbally explain the linear relationship, plot points on a graph and draw the relationship, and conduct whole and small group discussion.

    c. Executive function: Go through the motions of using technology to access different routes, locate your metro card or bike share key.

    d. **Culturally responsive teaching principles:** Honor different methods of communication, and use metacognitive strategies to increase understanding.

Transition Principles

1. **Multiple life domains**

    a. Students will learn how to plan and compare different transportation routes by how much time they will take and how much they will cost. Students will gain practice in reading bus routes, comparing metro routes, estimating the cost of a rideshare service (e.g., Lyft), and exploring other transportation options, such as a bike share program.

    b. Students will also engage in goals related to multiple transition domains (e.g., employment, postsecondary education, health care/independent living, leisure and recreation) by learning about low-cost ways to spend time outside of their home and travel between home and other adult life activities.

    c. **Culturally responsive teaching principles:** Promote active citizenship.

2. **Self-determination**

    a. Students are encouraged to explore their interests outside of school and problem-solve with peers and other students about the best way to access these destinations.

    b. Students will also engage in decision making related to multiple transition domains (i.e., employment, postsecondary education, health care/ independent living and leisure and recreation) by learning about low-cost ways to spend time outside of their home and travel between home and other adult life activities.

    c. In addition, this lesson addresses self-determination by encouraging students to explore their interests outside of school.

    d. **Culturally responsive teaching principles:** Allow for choice in activities to increase relevance.

3. **Multiple resources and perspectives**

    a. Collaborative planning with a group.

    b. Use different resources such as Google Maps, metro map, bus route, and travel-planning apps.

    c. Refer back to and utilize individual transition goals in the individualized education program (IEP) developed by the IEP team that included students' families and community members.

    d. **Culturally responsive teaching principles:** Provide opportunities for collaboration, and view diversity in a group as a strength.

4. **Multiple means of assessment**

    a. Students will be assessed by their ability to express (write, draw, verbalize) how to use transportation and their verbal description or physical ability to interpolate data into a scatterplot.

b. Students can also fill out exit tickets describing linear relationships as strong, weak, positive, or negative; they could also have a prompt to draw a strong positive relationship and quickly do so.

c. Students can also be observed discussing their findings within their groups.

d. **Culturally responsive teaching principles:** Assessments are designed to help students construct meaning from their world.

Resources: Use Google Maps, metro and bus maps, scatterplots, and slides with pictures of transportation options and destinations.

Accommodations and modifications: Provide written, verbal, and visual directions broken out into steps to complete.

Evaluation: Students should be able to interpolate two out of three data points correctly, and correctly identify the type of linear relationship. Students will be evaluated through informal observations and exit tickets.

Ms. Rose wanted to address some of Tatianna's needs in navigating transportation while simultaneously teaching rigorous grade-level content. Ms. Rose knew that utilizing UDT would allow her to address Tatianna's academic and transition needs while providing rich content for the rest of her class. She also wanted to incorporate culturally responsive teaching into her lesson to ensure that she would meet the needs of her CLD class. Ms. Rose planned strategies that used elements from both culturally responsive teaching and UDT.

CREATING A CULTURALLY RESPONSIVE UDT LESSON: STEP BY STEP

The following sections outline how Ms. Rose created the lesson described previously, which met the following Common Core State Standard (National Governors Association Center for Best Practices and Council of Chief State School Officers [NGACBP/ CCSSO], 2010): "CCSS.MATH.CONTENT.HSS.ID.B.6: Represent data on two quantitative variables on a scatterplot and describe how the variables are related."

Step 1: Create the Learning Objective

Based on the standard, Ms. Rose created the following learning objective: Given previous practice with scatterplots and resources for planning transportation, students will work in heterogeneous cooperative groups to 1) choose an interesting destination in their city, 2) describe three practical methods of transportation (e.g., metro, rideshare [e.g., Uber], bus, bike), 3) determine the time and cost associated with each route, and 4) plot their findings on a scatterplot and discuss the relationship between travel time and cost with 80% accuracy.

Step 2: Provide Multiple Means of Engagement

To provide multiple means of engagement, Ms. Rose understood that she needed to increase her students' interest by giving them options for remaining motivated and interested in the lessons (Thoma et al., 2009). Ms. Rose knew that Tatianna needed to practice navigating public transportation so that she could eventually travel to her internship independently. The other students in the class also needed reasons to engage in the lesson.

To help the students be more purposeful in their learning, Ms. Rose asked the students to work in cooperative groups and respond to the following prompt: *You have a friend visiting you from outside the city. They asked to see your favorite Washington, D.C. location. Where would you take them?* In groups, students could discuss their favorite places, places they went on field trips, a destination they always wanted to visit, and places they wanted to show their friends. In the groups, students chose destinations such as the International Spy Museum, the Holocaust Museum, the Pentagon City Mall, and the Museum of African American History and Culture. By engaging in the activity, Ms. Rose demonstrated awareness by allowing students to choose destinations that were personally or culturally relevant to their interests and backgrounds (Ladson-Billings, 1995). Then, Ms. Rose showed the students how to use Google Maps to enter their starting points and destinations to find various available transportation options. Then, within their groups, they chose three options for transportation to their destinations. Tatianna's group decided on the metro, the bus, and walking.

Step 3: Utilize Multiple Means of Representation

Ms. Rose wanted to utilize multiple means of representation so her lesson would be accessible to Tatianna and members of the rest of the class (CAST, 2018; Scott & Bruno, 2018). Ms. Rose began the lesson by explaining the purpose of transportation and clarified with solid examples of places students might want to go in Washington, D.C. Ms. Rose then asked her students to brainstorm different means of transportation to the locations. She displayed pictures of the varying responses to support students who were unfamiliar with the transportation methods. Then, Ms. Rose connected the pictures to the academic content by presenting the objective and then reviewing what the students knew about scatterplots and reviewed vocabulary, such as *quantitative variables* and *linear relationships,* using visuals and explanations. Ms. Rose reduced barriers to print by offering verbal explanations or visual examples to supplement her written material (Kieran & Anderson, 2019).

Step 4: Plan for Multiple Means of Action and Expression

To accommodate different learning approaches (Thoma et al., 2009) and respect students' differing methods for sharing their knowledge (Kieran & Anderson, 2019), Ms. Rose planned for students to express their understanding in multiple ways, using visual and tactile strategies in addition to graphing and writing. Because many students in the class were unfamiliar with various modes of transportation, Ms. Rose asked the students to determine physical motions to represent different means of transportation. Tatianna suggested pretending to swipe a MetroCard to symbolize using the metro. Another student proposed acting out steering a large wheel to represent the bus. Rehearsing the physical motions needed for travel also helped promote executive function skills. Later in the lesson, students expressed their understanding of time and cost associated with each method of transportation by plotting information they found on Google Maps into a scatterplot on graph paper. In addition, students had the option of verbally explaining where to plot different points while a group member helped to interpolate the data.

Step 5: Address Multiple Life Domains

Because one of the components of UDT is preparing students with disabilities for multiple domains of postsecondary life (Thoma et al., 2009), Ms. Rose wanted to ensure that her lessons would do the same. Throughout the lesson, Tatianna and her classmates practiced accessing and evaluating transportation options using Google Maps. By exploring transportation options that varied in cost, Ms. Rose demonstrated mindfulness of her students' diverse socioeconomic backgrounds and ensured that her lesson was inclusive for all (Kieran & Anderson, 2019). Students were instructed to record the time and cost associated with each option on their scatterplots and were asked to compare them. Within the groups, students noticed a negative linear relationship between time and cost involved in travel (i.e., the faster they could travel, the more expensive it was likely to be).

All the skills were used to help prepare the students to plan local travel independently and responsibly. Planning travel is a skill that can be used to help the students prepare for travel to employment sites, postsecondary education classes, and medical appointments, and for recreation and leisure activities, while learning about low-cost ways to spend time outside of their homes and meeting the same high academic standards.

Step 6: Utilize Multiple Means of Assessment

To evaluate students' mastery of academic and transition skills, Ms. Rose wanted to utilize different assessment materials based on her students' needs (Scott & Bruno, 2018) and account for student diversity in assessment styles (Brown-Jeffy & Cooper, 2011). To evaluate their ability to interpolate data into a scatterplot, Ms. Rose chose to use an informal checklist. She allowed students to demonstrate their knowledge using their choice of physical demonstrations or verbal descriptions throughout the lesson. Ms. Rose conducted informal observations by visiting each group. She listened to their discussions to assess whether students understood the assignment and she prompted quieter students to ensure they were understanding. Finally, Ms. Rose asked each student to complete an exit ticket as they left the classroom. They could either draw or describe a positive and negative linear relationship. This component of UDT does not merely focus on assessing students' understanding of the lesson, but it also assesses what was learned from the lesson/unit plan that could inform transition planning. For this lesson, much was learned about students' ability to use a variety of transportation options that could be used to meet their postschool goals in areas such as employment, leisure/travel, independent living, community involvement, and/or postsecondary education.

Step 7: Promote Individual Self-Determination

To promote self-determination, Ms. Rose chose to use student-centered planning and encouraged her students to draw on their preferences when making independent decisions (Scott & Bruno, 2018). In addition, Ms. Rose understood the importance of bridging home, school, and community life (Brown-Jeffy & Cooper, 2011). Throughout the lesson, Tatianna and her classmates used self-determination skills to practice making independent living decisions. The students discussed and decided where to spend their leisure time. They also used real-world information to problem-solve by considering and choosing which transportation methods worked best for their budgets and schedules. By incorporating her students' interests and existing knowledge,

Ms. Rose acknowledged the value of her students' experiences and empowered them in their decision making (Brown-Jeffy & Cooper, 2011).

Step 8: Incorporate Multiple Resources and Perspectives

To align with the UDT framework, Ms. Rose needed to incorporate various resources, supports, and perspectives into her lessons (Scott et al., 2019). Ms. Rose wanted to provide opportunities for collaboration, both within the entire class and within small groups, which helped to build an inclusive community of learners (Kieran & Anderson, 2019). She also incorporated different tools for planning travel, including Google Maps, metro and bus apps, and travel-planning apps. In addition, Ms. Rose referred to Tatianna's individual IEP transition goals, which were developed with Tatianna, her family members, and her IEP teammates.

Reflection

In your own words, what does it mean to provide academic instruction that is culturally competent? What are some ways you currently try to infuse cultural competence into your academic instruction and transition planning? After reading this chapter, do you have any additional ideas for doing so?

WRAP-UP: INTRODUCTION TO CULTURALLY COMPETENT UDT

In sum, Ms. Rose's efforts to effectively blend academics, transition, and culturally responsive teaching to support Tatianna's needs meant that she needed to fully understand how to apply these seemingly different frameworks. Thus, ensuring equitable practices for Tatianna and her classmates required that Ms. Rose fully understand and commit to these activities. Being a teacher can often require one to juggle multiple responsibilities. However, as presented, opportunities to unify academics, transition, and culturally responsive teaching are possible when embracing these ideas and with upfront development. This chapter provides insight into how one teacher combined these efforts. Subsequent chapters will include details regarding each UDT component and added tips for implementing, as well as broader topics (e.g., collaboration, planning an IEP) using culturally responsive/sustaining strategies using a UDT framework. We hope these ideas will empower educators to plan academics and functional/transition supports and services with their diverse group of students in mind.

KEY RESOURCES: UDL AND TRANSITION

Print Resources

Culturally Responsive and Sustaining Readings

The following list includes decades of readings about culturally sustaining pedagogies that can assist with understanding the use in instruction and classroom environments for students from multiply marginalized backgrounds.

Gay, G. (2018). *Culturally responsive teaching: Theory, research, and practice.* Teachers College Press.

Ladson-Billings, G. (1995). Toward a theory of culturally relevant pedagogy. *American Educational Research Journal, 32*(3), 465–491.

Universal Design and Universal Design for Transition

The following list of readings provides information about planning and implementing UDL and UDT in education settings.

Lord Nelson, L. (2021). *Design and deliver: Planning and teaching using universal design for learning* (2nd ed.). Paul H. Brookes Publishing Co.

Scott, L., Bruno, L., Gokita, T., & Thoma, C. A. (2022). Teacher candidates' abilities to develop universal design for learning and universal design for transition lesson plans. *International Journal of Inclusive Education, 26*(4), 333–347.

Thoma, C. A., Bartholomew, C. A., & Scott, L. A. (2009). *Universal design for transition: A roadmap for planning and instruction.* Paul H. Brookes Publishing Co.

Online Resources

Center for Applied Special Technologies (CAST)

http://www.cast.org

This website provides a wealth of information about UDL. The organization provides resources, videos, and other supports for understanding each principle of UDL. Examples and other interactive tools are provided on the website.

REFERENCES

Achola, E. O. (2019). Practicing what we preach: Reclaiming the promise of multicultural transition programming. *Career Development and Transition for Exceptional Individuals, 42*(3), 188–193.

Alim, H. S., & Paris, D. (2017). What is culturally sustaining pedagogy and why does it matter. *Culturally sustaining pedagogies: Teaching and learning for justice in a changing world, 1,* 24.

Americans With Disabilities Act of 1990, Pub. L. No. 101-336, 42 U.S.C. § 12101 *et seq.* (1990). https://www.ada.gov/pubs/adastatute08.htm

Banks, J. (2014). Barriers and supports to postsecondary transition: Case studies of African American students with disabilities. *Remedial and Special Education, 35*(1), 28–39.

Bassett, D. S., & Kochhar-Bryant, C. A. (2017). Strategies for aligning standards-based education and transition. *Focus on Exceptional Children, 39*(2). https://doi.org/10.17161/foec.v39i2.6825

Brown-Jeffy, S., & Cooper, J. E. (2011). Toward a conceptual framework of culturally relevant pedagogy: An overview of the conceptual and theoretical literature. *Teacher Education Quarterly, 38*(1), 65–84. http://www.jstor.org/stable/23479642

Brown Ruiz, A., & Scott, L. A. (2021). Guiding questions for a culturally responsive framework during preemployment transition services. *TEACHING Exceptional Children, 53*(5), 369–375. https://doi.org/10.1177/0040059920982312

CAST. (2018). *Universal design for learning guidelines version 2.2.* http://udlguidelines.cast.org

Center for Universal Design. (2008). About UD: Universal design principles. https://teaching-//resources.delta.ncsu.edu/boost-motivation-with-universal-design-for-learning/

Centers for Disease Control and Prevention. (n.d.). *Signs and symptoms of autism spectrum disorders.* https://www.cdc.gov/ncbddd/autism/signs.html

Cook-Harvey, C. M., Darling-Hammond, L., Lam, L., Mercer, C., & Roc, M. (2016). *Equity and ESSA: Leveraging educational opportunity through the Every Student Succeeds Act.* Learning Policy Institute.

Council for Exceptional Children. (2005). *Universal design for learning: A guide for teachers and education professionals.* Pearson/Merrill Prentice Hall.

Every Student Succeeds Act, 20 U. S. C. § 6301 (2015). https://www.congress.gov/114/plaws/pubi95/PLAW-114publ95.pdf

Ferlazzo, L. (2017, July 6). Author interview: "Culturally Sustaining Pedagogies." *Education Week.* https://www.edweek.org/teaching-learning/opinion-author-interview-culturally-sustaining-pedagogies/2017/07

Gay, G. (2002). Preparing for culturally responsive teaching. *Journal of Teacher Education, 53*(2), 106–116. https://doi.org/10.1177/0022487102053002003

Gay, G. (2018). *Culturally responsive teaching: Theory, research, and practice.* Teachers College Press.

Halley, K. F., & Trujillo, M. T. (2013). Breaking down barriers: Successful transition planning for culturally and linguistically diverse exceptional students. *Journal of Educational Research and Innovation, 2*(1), 1.

Individuals with Disabilities Education Improvement Act (IDEA) of 2004, Pub. L. No. 108-446, 20 U.S.C. §§ 1400 *et seq* (2004).

Kieran, L., & Anderson, C. (2019). Connecting universal design for learning with culturally responsive teaching. *Education and Urban Society, 51*(9), 1202–1216. https://doi.org/10.1177/0013124518785012

Ladson-Billings, G. (1995). Toward a theory of culturally relevant pedagogy. *American Educational Research Journal, 32*(3), 465–491. https://doi.org/10.3102/00028312032003465

Ladson-Billings, G. (2014). Culturally relevant pedagogy 2.0: AKA the remix. *Harvard Educational Review, 84*(1), 74–84. https://doi.org/10.17763/haer.84.1.p2rj131485484751

Ladson-Billings, G. (2017). The (r)evolution will not be standardized. In D. Paris & H. S. Alim (Eds.), *Culturally sustaining pedagogies: Teaching and learning for justice in a changing world* (pp. 141–156). Teachers College Press.

National Governors Association Center for Best Practices and Council of Chief State School Officers. (2010). *Common Core State Standards: Mathematics.* http://www.corestandards.org/Math/

Rehabilitation Act of 1973, Pub. L. No. 93-112, 29 U.S.C. §§ 701 *et seq.* (1973). https://drexel.edu/~/media/Files/autismoutcomes/publications/National%20Autism%20Indicators%20Report%20-%20July%202015.ashx

Santamaria, L. (2009). Culturally responsive differentiated instruction: Narrowing gaps between best pedagogical practices benefiting all learners. *Teachers College Record, 111*(1), 214–247.

Scott, L., & Bruno, L. (2018). Universal design for transition: A conceptual framework for blending academics and transition instruction. *The Journal of Special Education Apprenticeship, 7*(3). https://doi.org/10.3233/JVR-180974

Scott, L., Bruno, L., Gokita, T., & Thoma, C. A. (2019). Teacher candidates' abilities to develop universal design for learning and universal design for transition lesson plans. *International Journal of Inclusive Education*, 1–15. https://doi.org/10.1080/13603116.2019.1651910

Suk, A. L., Sinclair, T. E., Osmani, K. J., & Williams-Diehm, K. (2020). Transition planning: Keeping cultural competence in mind. *Career Development and Transition for Exceptional Individuals, 43*(2), 122–127.

Thoma, C. A., Bartholomew, C. C., & Scott, L. A. (2009). *Universal design for transition: A roadmap for planning and instruction.* Paul H. Brookes Publishing Co.

Thoma, C. A., Agran, M., & Scott, L. A. (2016). Transition for black youth with disabilities: What do we know and what do we need to know? *Journal of Vocational Rehabilitation, 45*(2), 149–158. DOI: 10.3233/JVR-160819.

Wehman, P. (2006). Life beyond the classroom: *Transition strategies for young people with disabilities.* Paul H. Brookes Publishing Co.

Workforce Innovation and Opportunity Act of 2014, Pub. L. No. 113-128, Stat. 129 (2014). https://www.govinfo.gov/content/pkg/PLAW-113publ128/pdf/PLAW-113publ128.pdf

2

Assessment

Colleen A. Thoma, Michelle A. C. Hicks, Jarrod Hobson,
Kendra Williams-Diehm, and Stacie L. Dojonovic Schutzman

DIGGING DEEPER: What Teachers Have to Say

Sometimes, the need for transition assessment is so overwhelming. I am not certain what constitutes transition assessment. I know about transition surveys, but how do I find time to interview students when they are included in the general education classroom? If I email a student a transition survey and ask them to complete the survey, how do I know if it is the student themselves responding? However, how do I find the time in their school day to pull them from their classes? I do not want my students to miss valuable instruction, and often when I pull a student, they think they are in trouble. Often, parents ask me to help their children develop postsecondary goals or complete career exploration activities but do not want their children to miss class. What can I use besides a transition survey? Some of my students cannot complete the survey. How can I make sure that students can access transition assessment? It is hard to find time to prepare my students for college, working, and participating in social and recreational opportunities in their community. Then, you want me to pull kids from their general education classrooms to administer transition assessments. How do I then find tools that are accessible and meaningful for all students? This is why I am overwhelmed because I cannot do this by myself and ensure that it is meaningful to my students. It seems that I will need the support of their classroom teachers, families, and the students themselves. Having myself and all their classroom teachers use a universal design for transition (UDT) approach to our lesson plans allows transition assessment to occur within the classroom and not as an add-on. This is more meaningful, and students do not have transition assessment being done to them but can participate in ongoing assessment while learning. UDT allows for the time within the classroom, accessibility, multiple methods, and the responsibility to be shared with the student. It also eliminates the stress many of my students felt when I would pull them from their classrooms and administer an assessment to them rather than taking an ongoing, student-centered approach to transition assessment. Now, instead of being one more add-on, transition assessment is occurring with the student within the classroom (this reflection was provided by Stacie Dojonovic).

Essential Questions

▶ What are transition assessments and how can they be incorporated into a UDT framework?

▶ What are the major UDT transition assessment domains? Why is each domain important?

▶ What are some ways educators can blend UDT transition assessments and culturally responsive and sustaining practices?

An understanding of transition assessment needs to start with the root of the word *assessment,* which comes from the Latin *assidere,* which translates to mean "to sit with" (Harper, n.d.; Sax & Thoma, 2002). Capturing comprehensive information about a student's individual strengths, preferences, interests, and needs (SPINs) is needed to help the team determine a transition individualized education program (IEP) plan that is based on the student's goals for the future. It's also important that the knowledge others—family members, friends, special educators, and other school personnel—have about an individual student is used to guide the development of transition plans. But that is not always easy to do, especially because many schools and districts have an overreliance on the more formal transition assessment instruments that often fail to capture the student's strengths, needs, interests, and dreams for the future and fail to reflect the knowledge that others have about the student, particularly if those individuals are not invited to the transition planning meeting. Those who do attend can feel uncomfortable sharing what they know about the student, from their day-to-day interactions with them, that is not part of a formal standardized assessment. Throughout this chapter, we emphasize the value of using informal assessments as well as formal ones. *Informal transition assessment* refers to an assessment without validity and reliability; they are often curriculum based and may be teacher made (Pulos & Martin, 2018; Thoma & Tamura, 2013). Typically, *informal assessment* refers to observations, interviews, checklists, portfolios, and other nonstandardized ways to measure student knowledge and skills.

This chapter will encourage you as the educator, as well as family members, friends, and the student, to place greater value on what you know from being part of a student's life. This information needs to be the central focus of the planning process or the risk is that the student's team will put a plan in place based on insufficient information. The transition assessment process should honor what we know and have learned throughout the time spent with the individual student, not merely what is gathered through a more traditional, professional-centered approach to the transition assessment process. It should be a student-centered, ongoing, age-appropriate, and comprehensive process. When this transition process is done annually, transition goals are defined and evolve as the student evolves through the process. In a UDT framework, this includes what is learned about the student's SPINs for adult life as they engage in academic classes, not merely what is learned through an individualized transition assessment process.

We begin this chapter by describing the transition assessment procedures required by the Individuals with Disabilities Education Improvement Act (IDEA) of 2004. Next, we describe the relationship between transition assessment and transition domains—comprehensive goals as well as goals for employment, postsecondary education, independent living, and self-determination skills.

In the latter half of the chapter, we explore how teachers can infuse transition assessment into the general education curriculum using a UDT framework. Here, we give particular attention to how teachers can ensure that transition assessments are culturally sustaining and supportive for underrepresented minority (URM) youth with disabilities.

TRANSITION ASSESSMENT REQUIRED BY IDEA

Transition assessments, when done well, create a picture of the student's SPINs, and together they help create a plan for academic and transition services that help the student achieve their goals for adult life. But what do transition policy and evidence-based practices (EBPs) require as part of this process? At one time, a one-to-one interview with the student prior to the transition IEP meeting was deemed adequate. Over the years, recommendations for transition planning and services changed in line with research and the development of new assessment instruments and tools. IDEA (2004) requires that transition plans should include "appropriate measurable post-secondary goals based on *age-appropriate transition assessments related to training, education, employment, and, where appropriate, independent living skills*" (§300.320(b)). In fact, the entire transition planning process *must* be occurring on an annual basis to better reflect changes in plans, goals, and skills that typically occur during adolescence as teenagers become more aware of the world around them.

A good model for the overall transition assessment and transition planning/services process is included in Figure 2.1. In this model adapted from Deardorff (2020), the first steps of the process use exploration tools and interest inventories that gather basic information from the student and family members to determine beginning thoughts/goals for the future. Next, this information can be used to identify student-selected postsecondary goals, which should guide the next step, the holistic, age-appropriate transition assessment process. The results of the assessment process should then inform the development of transition goals in the IEP, which are implemented with the student throughout the year. This process is implemented each year during the transition years (age 16 or earlier if needed).

The transition assessment process itself should 1) use a variety of assessments, 2) use at least one formal assessment, and 3) include more than one stakeholder

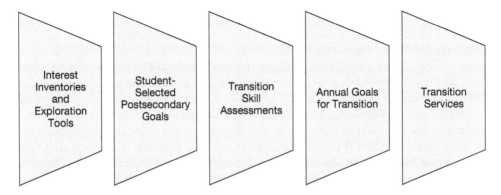

Figure 2.1. Transition model. (From Deardorff, M. E. [2020]. Effects of professional development on transition plan components [Doctoral Dissertation, University of Oklahoma]. SHAREOK. https://shareok.org/handle/11244/324417; adapted by permission.)

(Prince et al., 2014). These assessments, as stated previously, should address skills related to employment, postsecondary education, and independent living (if needed). (The phrase "if needed" implies that some students with disabilities might not need any additional help to transition to adult roles and responsibilities—but who doesn't need help with some of these skills, such as money management and budgeting, home/apartment maintenance, using transportation or driving a car, ensuring safety in the home, and so forth?) In addition to these three areas, effective transition assessment and services should also include student self-determination, which has been demonstrated to be related to improved postschool outcomes in all three of these areas (Wehmeyer & Palmer, 2003) as well as to an increase in perceived quality of life (Lachapelle et al., 2005).

Unfortunately, there can be a perception that formal assessments are more useful than informal ones. This perception is believed to persist for two reasons. First, formal assessments are recommended to ensure best practice in transition planning (Prince et al., 2014). Second, educators are inundated with a heavy educational emphasis on evidence-based practices and standardized assessment. It is true that formal assessments must have evidence of their reliability and validity—that is, evidence that the assessment consistently measures (reliability) a specific knowledge or skill (validity). However, these formal assessments should not be the only type of assessment used during the transition planning process and often cannot provide critical information. Informal assessments can provide the following:

- Information about how well the student can implement a specific skill in real-world settings

- An opportunity to engage in dialogue to gain a better understanding about why a student might want a specific goal

- Rich details about what family members know about the student from their interactions at home and in their communities

- The thought process to capture *why* a student has chosen a specific career area

It is important that at least one formal assessment be included in the process but also that the entire transition assessment process include a variety of assessments to create that holistic view of the student that helps to develop a transition plan that more accurately captures the student and family goals for the future.

We recommend having more than one stakeholder participate in the transition assessment process for a number of different reasons. As stated previously, family and community members see a student in different settings while they are actually navigating their neighborhoods, interacting with others, and participating in community activities that are important to them. These are opportunities to assess the student that most school-based special education teachers and/or transition specialists do not have but that provide critically important pieces of information in determining transition goals as well as services. Other stakeholders to consider involving in transition assessments include the vocational rehabilitation (VR) counselor, who is responsible for providing Pre-Employment Transition Services (Pre-ETS) as required by the Workforce Innovation and Opportunity Act (2014) to youth who are transition age. These required services include the following:

- Job exploration counseling

- Work-based learning experiences, which may include in-school or after-school opportunities, experiences outside of the traditional school setting, and/or internships

- Counseling on opportunities for enrollment in comprehensive transition or postsecondary education programs

- Workplace readiness training to develop social skills and independent living

- Instruction in self-advocacy

The Workforce Innovation Technical Assistance Center website includes a page on Pre-ETS. For more information, use the following link to visit the page, click on the question "What are the *required* pre-employment transition services?" and then use the additional links to navigate to more details about the areas listed previously: http://www.wintac.org/topic-areas/pre-employment-transition-services

Not only are VR counselors additional stakeholders who can conduct some of these transition assessments, but they are also highly knowledgeable about the information and skills needed to be successful in meeting goals related to employment. They have access to a range of employment assessment tools, both formal and informal, eliminating the need for school-based personnel to explore options and possibly struggle with implementing those assessments and/or finding time to do so.

TRANSITION DOMAINS AND ASSESSMENT

Another benefit to involving multiple stakeholders in the transition assessment process is that it provides an opportunity to implement an assets-based approach to transition assessment and planning that honors the student's and family's unique cultural strengths and capital (Achola, 2019). Too often, transition goals and services reflect a bias for postschool outcomes that are based on the preferences for White, middle-class individuals. For example, many communities and cultures believe in multigenerational housing situations where a young adult is not expected to live on their own but does often have responsibilities within the family household. In addition, adult roles can differ based on one's gender, race/ethnicity, religion, and desires for the future. Involving families in transition assessment provides an opportunity for them to share their family's background including culture, religion, language, country of origin (if not a native-born citizen), values, and adult expectations. All of these can contribute to the development of a transition plan that takes into account the cultural expectations of their communities.

The next sections identify a few commonly used assessment tools related to different transition domains. The Chapter 2 appendix provides some additional transition assessment resources that can be used to assess 1) all transition goals, 2) employment goals, 3) postsecondary education goals, 4) independent living goals, and 5) self-determination goals.

Assessing Comprehensive Transition Goals

The desire to develop and use a single transition assessment instrument is appealing for simplicity. Having one assessment to address all three transition areas (employment, postsecondary education, and independent living) as well as self-determination could take all the confusion out of choosing an appropriate transition assessment. However, we know that an effective age-appropriate transition assessment battery requires multiple assessments, both formal and informal. Formal assessments are those that have been evaluated for reliability and validity. This makes the use of formal assessments more comfortable for school personnel and provides greater confidence in reporting the results of the assessments to the other members of the team.

Informal assessments do not have that level of support for their use; however, they typically provide information that is more nuanced, detailed, and contextual. They involve such things as observations, interviews, many curriculum-based assessments, and situational or environmental assessments. They can provide greater details that can be more easily tied to transition planning.

Assessing Goals for Postsecondary Education

Many considerations surround a student's preparation for postsecondary education. These include typical college application preparation through acquiring transcripts, developing essays, gathering letters of recommendation, and completing college enrollment assessments. In addition, one must consider alternatives to college if the student and family believe another route is more appropriate after high school, including immediately entering the workforce or prioritizing other types of postsecondary training. If postsecondary education is on the table, there are many other considerations beyond the typical process for preparing for college. The student's daily classroom participation provides educators with opportunities to observe and evaluate skills associated with college readiness. Many of these skills overlap with the self-determination domain (e.g., goal setting, problem solving, taking initiative, identifying supports). Thus, the student must have opportunities to develop and incorporate self-determination within secondary classrooms. As educators prioritize this, it is important that they are responsive to the individual student's experience and how their cultural norms may impact how self-determination manifests. Educators should also consider other prerequisite skills (e.g., time management, socialization, general foundational academic skills) that are part of the daily secondary classroom that will continue to be present as the student goes off to college. Many times, these skills will not be the main focus of the lesson. However, there are still opportunities to build them into the lesson, collect data, and inform further instruction needed in these skills.

Assessing Goals for Employment

Employment decisions often generate through a student's expressed interest in a career. There are many ways to provide opportunities to expand and explore careers based on student interest. A strong foundational understanding of a student's interests, strengths, and needs, paired with employment connections and a vast understanding of opportunities within the community, can open many doors. A student's lack of knowledge of careers can limit what they share in interest inventories and student interviews. However, making connections to the student's general interests and the things they bring to the classroom can lead to ideas that would not have been generated through generic transition planning. A student may have an occupation in mind but may have limited knowledge of other opportunities in the world because of their limited experience. It is our responsibility to also present a multitude of ideas and opportunities for the student to learn about and weigh into their future career(s). By generally thinking about the types of careers in which a student expresses interest and finding out their "why," we can provide additional considerations to the student to explore.

Some students may not know or feel like this question is difficult to answer. Therefore, we may need to present evidence from our understanding to help guide this process. For example, suppose a student says they are unsure of their career interests. Through an interest inventory and a student interview, you don't have much information to report. You then provide the student with evidence gathered through classroom observations and work samples to conclude that the student 1) is comfortable taking the lead in group projects, 2) is easily engaged by problem solving, 3) does not like to write lengthy passages, and 4) loves being physically active. As a result of this information, you may present some information for exploratory purposes on becoming a personal trainer. This is one of many possible job routes that emerges from the information gathered. The student may find they are not interested in this route, or you might have initiated the beginning steps of their lifelong career.

Assessing Goals for Independent Living Skills

Independent living encompasses a large and diverse set of skills that prepare individual students to assume adult roles and responsibilities. It includes decisions about where a student with a disability wants to live as an adult; it also encompasses goals that provide opportunities to have an "enviable and dignified life" (Turnbull, 2020). What does that mean? Well, it means different things to different people, but it can include such aspects as having friendships, enjoying recreation and leisure activities, participating in faith-based or culturally based groups and organizations, assuming adult roles and responsibilities within one's family, financial literacy, and so much more. When one thinks of the kinds of preferences an individual student might have, it is very difficult to think about how any student might not need transition goals that address these areas. As with postsecondary education, an abundance of skills is associated with living independently. Some examples that could be incorporated into the academic classroom include money management, self-care, gardening, and preparing meals. These skills can be directly assessed through traditional transition planning; however, incorporation of these skills into the academic classroom will provide additional evidence on students' level of independence. Beyond these skills, teachers can provide opportunities to learn about housing markets, different types of housing opportunities, and how to manage relationships with roommates. These skills, which may be more tailored to independent living, can be infused into the academic curriculum by pairing with academic standards and/or carefully choosing elective classes.

Assessing Self-Determination Skills

Self-determination refers to a range of skills that allow individuals to become causal agents in their lives (Wehmeyer, 2015). This means that they set the direction for their own lives, not that they do everything themselves, which is an important distinction. Too often, if students need some assistance to achieve their goals or even to identify their goals for adult life and communicate them to others, they are thought to be unable to learn self-determination skills. Instead, we should think of self-determination as a continuum and honor times when students choose goals that are not individualistic but rather reflect a more family-oriented focus that aligns with their cultural backgrounds. Self-determination skills can be assessed through typical transition means; however, the student's ability to exhibit these skills on a daily basis is likely a stronger indicator of their ability to also display these skills outside of the school building. Providing the student with opportunities to take control of the day-to-day decisions in their secondary school is one method for assessing self-determination goals, empowering the student, and developing a plan that continues to build on these crucial skills. This can range from daily choices surrounding how they access the daily lesson to how they participate in class and how they provide output based on what they have learned. A key area teachers could focus on through this process is the student's active involvement and participation in the IEP meeting. This sets an important standard in the IEP process, emphasizing the student's responsibility and control while also giving them time to practice for situations in their postsecondary life in which they will have to be a self-advocate and drive decision making with various levels of support.

But, as Stacie (the special educator who shaped her reflections to start this chapter) points out, it can be difficult for educators to juggle the transition assessment requirements along with teaching and assessing academic knowledge and skills. Although transition assessment and planning are a requirement for all students with disabilities according to IDEA (2004), it can be difficult to adequately address these procedures when special educators are already struggling with providing access to the general education curriculum and preparing students with disabilities to participate in high-stakes academic assessments as required by their state. It is possible to infuse aspects of transition assessment into academic instruction and assessment, using a UDT framework, so that information about a student's knowledge and skills to meet common goals for adult life is collected and used to inform the development of transition goals. This does not negate the need to conduct individualized transition assessments on an annual basis. Rather, it provides an opportunity to gather some of the information through activities and instruction already occurring during the school day, or through assessment activities conducted by the additional stakeholders (family, VR counselors, community partners).

INFUSING TRANSITION ASSESSMENT INTO THE GENERAL EDUCATION CURRICULUM USING A UDT FRAMEWORK

A comprehensive approach that involves a variety of formal and informal assessments is vital for effective age-appropriate transition planning. Assessment data can be generated using general education curriculum and assessments. We can intentionally develop lessons to include transition components by infusing these or seeking out naturally occurring opportunities that occur within the classroom that provide data on transition-related skills.

Table 2.1 offers three suggestions for building in time to assess skills needed for transition to adult life. As you were reading, ideas may have already occurred to you regarding how you could build in time to work on transition skills. Hopefully, the following suggestions will spark ideas of how transition assessment might be added into assignments you may already have planned. For example, a fairly common assignment for middle school or even upper elementary students is to interview a person. Why not suggest that the student interview one of their elders and add a question about what future roles the elder thinks the student would be able to fill in the community? Or suggest that the student interview an adult mentor or coach to find out what strengths and weaknesses the adult may see in the student? Often, these people would not be available to attend IEP meetings, but the interview would act as a way to hear the important viewpoints from the student's community.

This chapter offers some suggested ways teachers can infuse transition assessments into academic instruction, but they are not the only way that a UDT framework can be applied to the transition assessment process. A number of formal and informal assessments can be infused into academic instruction, providing information about students' SPINs that can be used to guide transition assessment. The Chapter 2 appendix, lists some other examples that can be explored (many of them are free) and used, depending on the academic course.

One suggested way to infuse assessment into everyday lesson planning is to take a step back from the assessment designed to provide evidence of the student's current academic ability level and consider the additional functional skills present that can also be evaluated. For example, a class project to create a presentation can also assess level of competence with programs like Microsoft PowerPoint or Google Slides. Even the soft skills of communication could be assessed. The case study of Jesse that follows illustrates a way to find the hidden skills in everyday class assignments.

CASE STUDY: Jesse

Using Academic Projects to Assess Functional Skills for Transition

Suppose a student of yours, Jesse, is tasked with working in a small group to complete a presentation explaining the scientific method. Although Jesse has expressed to you that they have no relative interest in pursuing a field of study or career in science, that doesn't rule out the opportunity to gather information related to transition with this student. Many skills are involved in working in a group that can be assessed simultaneously while the final (academic) assessment is completed. This variety of skills for group work can translate into many different areas of school and beyond. This includes the dynamic atmosphere of working with others, socialization, time management, self-advocacy, expressive and receptive language, and opportunities to serve in various roles, just to name a few. In addition, the final product of this assignment involves an oral presentation. Although content may be the main focus of this assessment, there are additional functional skills used during oral presentations that can be used to gather information about transition readiness. These can include such things as interviewing for jobs, being ready to take classes in college, and standing up for one's rights. Although the general education purpose is to show the understanding of the scientific method, the teacher can derive a vast

Table 2.1. Suggestions for building in assessments

Assessment	Infusion into curriculum	Possible results
PERC Self-Advocacy Checklist (See https://ganinfo.org/wp-content/uploads/2011/07/Self-Advocacy-Checklist.pdf)	At the beginning of school, ice-breaker type activities are usually incorporated into the class routine. Have the students rate their comfort with the PERC Self-Advocacy Checklist. Introducing themselves to new classmates and new teachers will help gauge their comfort in speaking with possible employers and new co-workers. Then, throughout the year, this can be revisited when discussing interview skills. Often, these soft skills of talking to people and explaining any possible needs may have prevent people from sustaining their employment.	Present-level statement: X feels comfortable in the school setting sharing and requesting help. X completed the PERC Self-Advocacy Checklist and felt that they need practice talking to adults outside of school (e.g., possible and future employers). Transition goal: When in a new situation (e.g., job interview) with an unfamiliar adult, X will articulate their strengths and areas of need __ out of __ observable interactions.
Elective class reflection (See https://instrc.indiana.edu/pdf/transition_matrix/AA%20Elective%20Class%20Reflection.pdf)	This authentic assessment would be a good way to incorporate transition assessment and writing. This can be used as a culminating activity at the end of the year or before choosing new electives for the upcoming school year. Having a journal topic that can help assess the amount of knowledge and skills a student has gained from a particular elective class will help the student make connections between coursework and postsecondary life.	Present-level statement: X completed an *elective class reflection* on (insert date); X described the art skills that were learned in their Introduction to Photography class this school year. X developed their "Photoshop skill" and a "better understanding of how the composition of a photo works." They also expressed that this would help them in their chosen career as a photojournalist (parent's suggestion) or "Instagram influencer" (X's suggestion). In the upcoming school year, it is recommended that X takes Advanced Photography. Current course of study statement: Advanced Photography will continue to build X's skills in Photoshop and other photography software.
Student dream (sheet) board (See https://instrc.indiana.edu/pdf/transition_matrix/Student%20Dream%20Sheet.pdf)	This assessment could be used as a standalone worksheet to be given. However, using multiple means for representation, have students turn this into a dream (vision) board. Students can cut out pictures showing places they would like to live, colleges they might want to attend, cars they might want to drive, or jobs they would like to have. Then, presenting their collage to the class or even to the individualized education program team would be another option to support self-determination.	Present-level statement: X created and shared their *student dream board* on (insert date), at which time (insert chosen college) was their goal college to attend. Goal: Before selecting coursework, X will access (selected college's) website to find acceptance requirements to compare with their transcripts.

amount of information to provide evidence that would support decision making in the IEP process, particularly guiding moments for the team to navigate the transition process.

Another way to infuse assessment within the planning process is to look for opportunities to intentionally infuse transition assessment components while also simultaneously assessing the academic curriculum. This approach may target specific types of information that you are looking to explore. For example, if you are doing a unit math test on elapsed time, several skills for employment could be addressed—such as reading a time card, knowing how to run required breaks as a supervisor, and time management, to name a few. The continuation of Jesse's case study illustrates a way to add this type of assessment piece.

CASE STUDY: Jesse, *continued*

Infusing Transition Components Into Writing Assignments

Now, suppose one of your co-teachers identifies some additional needs for working with Jesse on their writing. Specifically, Jesse is struggling with editing and revising. This academic skill of editing and revising could be analyzed from the same lens that was applied to the previous example of group work. Learning how to edit and revise a written document has many implications for Jesse's future. However, for this lesson, you choose to intentionally infuse transition components into the writing prompts instead of focusing on these generalizable skills. That way, you will keep editing in mind for future focus.

To generate a writing passage to edit or revise, you present Jesse with a variety of topics designed to show their personal interests, goals, desires, and dislikes in the major areas of transition. Jesse develops writing samples to describe their postsecondary goals for themselves, interests in postsecondary education, and where they may want to live when they get older. Although Jesse is still working on the original goal of editing and revising, the artifacts developed are authentic representations of the student's perspective and a valuable form of self-expression.

CULTURALLY SUSTAINING AND SUPPORTIVE TRANSITION ASSESSMENTS FOR UNDERREPRESENTED MINORITY YOUTH WITH DISABILITIES

Youth with disabilities who are members of historically marginalized populations experience some of the worst transition outcomes of any group of students with disabilities. Specifically, research consistently documents that young adults from predominantly nonmainstream ethnic and cultural communities are less likely to have better employment outcomes (Trainor, 2008; Trainor et al., 2014), postsecondary education success (Newman et al., 2009), and satisfaction with the transition experience (Geenen et al., 2003). As a result of these abysmal transition outcomes, experts have recommended that changes to the process should use approaches "that value students' cultural and ethnic resources as capital to build upon rather than as a barrier

to learning" (Achola, 2019, p. 188). These culturally responsive and sustaining practices have been shown to positively impact educational outcomes as a whole as well
as intergroup relations (Carjuzaa, 2012; Zirkel, 2008). Transition assessment provides an opportunity to learn more about individual students' identities (e.g., cultural,
racial, religious, gender, language, disability) and how those influence their goals for
adult life.

Achola (2019) provided guidance about how school-based professionals and other
stakeholders engaged in the transition assessment process can incorporate an assets-
based approach in the process. He recommends that the starting point is to communicate with the student and family members to gain an understanding of their cultural
values and preferred adult roles and responsibilities. It also provides an opportunity
to learn about the communities in which students live. A community resource map
or community assets mapping process provides an opportunity to explore a student's
community in relation to its strengths as they relate to the student's goals for adult
life. This is especially useful when the student's and family's communities are different from the other members of the transition team. In addition, it addresses the community assets in relation to the student's identities and goals for adult life.

CASE STUDY: Mr. David

Exploring Strengths Within a Student's Community

Mr. David did not live in the community surrounding the school, which was home for
most of the students on his caseload. This community was home to a highly diverse
population in terms of culture, race/ethnicity, language, and religion. It was also home
to a large number of students who qualified for free and/or reduced price lunches.
He realized that in the past, he saw the community in terms of its needs and had not
explored its strengths or assets. In speaking with students and their families, he asked
them to identify some of the strengths of living in their community, and he pointed
them to the Creately website's page on community asset mapping to help them
record what they found (see https://creately.com/usage/community-asset-mapping/).
He also used the tool to record what he found when doing his own exploration of the
community. Then, he combined the assets everyone had identified, and he realized
that the community provided a number of resources that could support the goals for
adult life of many of his students, including faith-based groups, gender-focused affinity
groups, cultural centers, financial literacy resources, and recreational opportunities that
together can help a young adult build an adult life.

The transition plans and goals that were identified as a result of his incorporation
of culturally responsive and sustaining practices looked much different from those
developed prior to using this approach.

USING TRANSITION ASSESSMENT
INFORMATION TO DEVELOP GOALS

The purpose of transition assessment is to inform the transition plan and goals for
adult life for a student with a disability. Clark (2007) refined that purpose, bringing it
in line with culturally responsive and sustaining practices as well as the UDT framework, stating that "Transition assessment is a process of obtaining, organizing, and

using information to assist all individuals with disabilities of all ages and their families in making all critical transitions in those individuals' lives, both successful and satisfying" (p. 2).

Sitlington et al. (2010) reminded educators that students are the most important people in the transition assessment process. Students, rather than a psychologist or educator, need to be able to interpret the results of the assessments and use the results to plan. This is in contrast to academic assessments that are selected by the teacher and often administered to a student and interpreted by the teacher. Transition assessments need to actively engage the student beginning with selection of the procedures and ending with interpretation of the results as they relate to that student's individual goal setting and transition planning.

Transition assessment under a UDT framework requires some additional steps in planning for the transition IEP meeting; that is, finding ways to be sure that the information gathered throughout the year during academic coursework and by collaborative partners such as the family, community members, VR counselors, and others is highlighted, shared, and treated with respect.

Some special educators take responsibility for collecting all assessment information prior to the meeting so the information can be shared comprehensively with the student, family, and other transition stakeholders. Others find ways to involve the student in gathering and reporting that information. A third option would be to schedule time for all stakeholders to share the assessment information they collected while in the meeting.

CASE STUDY: Mr. David, *continued*

Using a Student-Led Process for the Transition IEP Meeting

Mr. David considered a range of options for sharing the transition assessment data that was collected throughout the year, but often he found that when he shared information collected by a family member, it was not given the attention that was given to data collected through formal assessments administered by the school psychologist. When it came time for the transition IEP meetings this year, he decided to use a student-led IEP process. He spent time with his students preparing them for their meetings, with a particular focus on the transition assessment data collected in their communities, assessment information from their general education classes, and student's own goals for adult life. He shared a common format for general education teachers to use to summarize transition and academic information from their classes, and he had the students ask those teachers to fill them out. He also found some transition assessments that collaborators could complete with the student online so the results were readily accessible. Then, he prepared each student to share this information during the meeting, Mr. David found that this process helped everyone participate, provided more useful information for transition planning, and provided more focus on the students' goals for their adult lives.

More information about the IEP process can be found in Chapter 9, and tips for setting goals in transition domains (employment, postsecondary education, and independent living) can be found in other chapters of this book. An example of a format that can be used by general education teachers to summarize assessment information (like the one used by Mr. David) can be found in Figure 2.2.

Describe student's academic strengths and weaknesses (based on content, not behavior):	
MATH: ENGLISH: HISTORY: SCIENCE:	MATH: ENGLISH: HISTORY: SCIENCE:
Describe student's behavior in class (ability to work with others, ability to focus on tasks/ goals, ability to ask for help; ability to advocate for self):	
MATH: ENGLISH: HISTORY: SCIENCE:	MATH: ENGLISH: HISTORY: SCIENCE:
Describe student strengths/needs related to adult roles and responsibilities that you learned from class:	
MATH: ENGLISH: HISTORY: SCIENCE:	MATH: ENGLISH: HISTORY: SCIENCE:
Transition goals: Please create a goal for this student pertaining to your class curriculum that can provide information about adult roles and responsibilities.	
MATH: ENGLISH: HISTORY: SCIENCE:	MATH: ENGLISH: HISTORY: SCIENCE:

Figure 2.2. Template for general education teacher input on student strengths and needs. (From Cavendish, W., Connor, D. J., & Rediker, E. [2016]. Engaging students and parents in transition-focused individualized education programs. *Intervention in School and Clinic, 52*[4], 1–8; adapted by permission of SAGE Publications. Permission conveyed through Copyright Clearance Center, Inc.)

Reflection

Think about the actions Mr. David took to learn about his students' community and to ensure that meaningful assessment information was part of students' transition IEP meetings. Consider one of your own students who is preparing to transition into adulthood. What types of informal assessments could you use to evaluate that student's strengths and needed supports in relation to transition? What actions could you take to learn about that student's community?

WRAP-UP: ASSESSMENT IN UDT

The role of assessment in transition planning is more than just checking a box or merely asking a student and their family about their goals for adult life. Assessment is meant to supply useful information that will allow the student and the IEP team to make decisions about ways to help support the student as they take on their role as adults. The results from transition assessment are to be added to the present levels of academic achievement and functional performance (PLAAFP) in the IEP. In addition, the results of both formal and informal assessments will help teams to create targeted and specific goals for the transition plan, identifying the students' vision for adult life as well as additional supports, instruction, and/or resources needed.

Applying the UDT framework to transition assessment provides the opportunity to gather information about student SPINs while they are working on learning academic content. As stated previously in this chapter, this does not mean that the need for more individualized assessments no longer exists. However, it provides an opportunity for more targeted individualized assessments once an understanding of the student's identities, community assets, and family values are understood as well as their strengths related to the school's learning environment. Mr. David found that his interactions with families during transition planning were smoother when he began with this information. He used this information as a beginning point for the transition team's discussion, and they explored more options for individual students than was previously possible. For example, for Rebecca, who wanted to transition to college and who identified both as a student with a learning disability and as lesbian, the team identified a goal of learning about campus safety as well as identifying student groups that support lesbian, gay, bisexual, transgender, intersex, queer/questioning, asexual, and more identities (LGBTQ+), students on various college campuses.

Referring back to the case study of Jesse, the information from Jesse's writing can be used to provide a firsthand narrative of typical transition assessment data while providing the teacher with pathways to explore the content further. For example, the student may use this information to take on a bigger role in the IEP meeting. Another example includes the opportunity to triangulate these data with additional transition data, such as the parent's perspective on similar topics. In addition, a pathway for linking relevant community partners may be generated through the insight gained from the content of Jesse's writing. Although the main academic objective, editing and revising, continued to be the main focus, a targeted planning decision to intentionally focus on prompts that would provide insight on the perspectives of the student provided key information essential for the transition planning process.

Ultimately, incorporating a UDT framework into the transition planning process addresses two challenges faced by school-based transition personnel. First, it identifies opportunities throughout academic instruction to also learn more about the SPINs of students with disabilities and incorporate that information into the transition planning process. Of course, there is some up-front planning that needs to be done to organize this information and bring it to the team. Second, and no less important, is that it offers a way to incorporate strategies that honor the strengths and assets of historically marginalized students with disabilities, their families, and their communities. Transition plans can then be developed that honor students' identities and their desired adult roles and responsibilities.

▶ **Tips for Transition Assessment**

1. **Use a variety of and multiple student-centered assessments that include both informal as well as formal assessments.** We need to individualize, involve the student in the selection process, and use multiple methods to validate the results of the assessments. If you interview a student and they state their career interest, then validate it with another assessment or by interviewing parents to see whether this is a career that their child has ever discussed. It is important to use a strengths-based, person-centered approach.

   Informal assessments include, but are not limited to, portfolios of a student's work, checklists (created by the teacher or by the student), visual or audio recordings of a student's performance, community-based assessments, observations, interviews, class projects, and teacher-created tests designed to measure student knowledge.

2. **Value the student and family as the richest sources of information about the student's SPINs.** The individual student is the best source for identifying their SPINs as they relate to the demands of current and future working, educational, living, and personal and social environments. We need to collect this information from not just the students and families but from people who actually observe them in community settings. Results are used to assist the student in making informed choices related to training, education, employment, and where appropriate, independent living. When we involve the student, they not only develop self-determination skills but they also provide the meaning to the transition assessment plan.

3. **The selection of an assessment tool should be based on what the student needs to know about their future.** Questions to ask when selecting instruments include the following: *Where do I want to learn after leaving high school? What do I need to take in high school? What do I need to learn now to make this happen? Where do I want to work after leaving high school? What type of job do I want that I can obtain in high school? What do I need to learn now to make this happen? Where do I want to live after leaving high school? What social activities can I participate in in high school? What do I need to learn now to make this happen?* Select instruments and methods that are appropriate for your students; consider the nature of their disability, reading level, postschool ambitions, and community opportunities.

4. **Plan authentic assessments for postsecondary education, postsecondary employment, and postsecondary independent living.** When determining how to assess students in their future learning, living, and working settings, most would agree that an ideal assessment tool would be one that evaluates students' knowledge and skills when performing real-world tasks. Traditional assessment practices, such as standardized tests, may not enable educators to accurately identify students' skills, strengths, and support needs that will contribute to success in school, employment, or living settings. Conducting authentic assessment takes planning. Start with the end in mind and align the assessment with student goals, interests, and skills to tasks in that environment. It will take collaboration with families, communities, colleges, and employers to develop and implement the assessment. The outcome of this assessment will provide real-world information regarding student interests, strengths, skills, and conditions for success. A common authentic assessment is a student compiling a portfolio throughout their classes.

KEY RESOURCES: ASSESSMENT

Print Resources

Collier, M. L., Griffin, M. M., & Wei, Y. (2016). Facilitating student involvement in transition assessment: A pilot study of the Student Transition Questionnaire. *Career Development and Transition for Exceptional Individuals, 39*(3), 175–184. https://doi.org/10.1177/2165143414556746

Neubert, D. A., & Leconte, P. J. (2013). Age-appropriate transition assessment: The position of the Division on Career Development and Transition. *Career Development and Transition for Exceptional Individuals, 36*(2), 72–83. https://doi.org/10.1177/2165143413487768

Rowe, D. A., Mazzotti, V. L., Hirano, K., & Alverson, C. Y. (2015). Assessing transition skills in the 21st century. *TEACHING Exceptional Children, 47*(6), 301–309. https://doi.org/10.1177/0040059915587670

Scheef, A. R., & Johnson, C. (2017). The power of the cloud: Google Forms for transition assessment. *Career Development and Transition for Exceptional Individuals, 40*(4), 250–255. https://doi.org/10.1177/2165143417700844

Online Resources

Indiana University Transition Assessment Matrix
https://instrc.indiana.edu/transition-resources/transition-matrix.html

This website provides tools for conducting authentic assessments. These simple transition assessment tools allow you to capture transition-related services and activities happening in the classroom, during community-based instruction, in a career/technical education classroom/program, and throughout a student's school year. Authentic assessments can help inform transition and transition IEP decision making.

Center for Change in Transition Services
https://www.seattleu.edu/ccts/resources/assessment/

This website provides resources to help students with disabilities assess their capacity to transition into an independent life. Areas of assessment include career, independent living, interests, preference/personality, and self-determination.

Zarrow Institute on Transition & Self-Determination
https://www.ou.edu/education/zarrow/resources/assessments

This website provides access to several high-quality transition assessments. Currently, there are both formal transition assessments and informal assessments available, and the majority are free. The Transition Assessment and Goal Generator (https://tagg.ou.edu/tagg/) website has assessments built into an online platform. This includes assessments for career skills, self-determination, nonacademic skills, and independent living.

REFERENCES

Achola, E. (2019). Practicing what we preach: Reclaiming the promise of multicultural transition programming. *Career Development and Transition for Exceptional Individuals, 42*(3), 188–193.

American Association for Intellectual and Developmental Disabilities (2019). *Supports Intensity Scale.* Author.

Brady, R.P. (2020). *Picture Interest Career Survey* (3rd ed.). Paradigm Education Solutions.

Carjuzaa, J. (2012). The positive impact of culturally responsive pedagogy: Montana's Indian education for all. *International Journal of Multicultural Education, 14*(3), 1–17.

Cavendish, W., Connor, D. J., & Rediker, E. (2016). Engaging students and parents in transition-focused individualized education programs. *Intervention in School and Clinic, 4,* 1–8.

Clark, G. (2007). *Assessment for transition planning* (2nd ed.). PRO-ED.

Curriculum Associates (2021). *Brigance Transition Skills Inventory-2.* Author.

Deardorff, M. E. (2020). *Effects of professional development on transition plan components* [Doctoral Dissertation, University of Oklahoma]. SHAREOK. https://shareok.org/handle/11244/324417

ESTR Publications (2021) *Transition Rating Scales 3.0.* Author.

Geenen, S., Powers, L., Lopez-Vasquez, A., & Bersani, H. (2003). Understanding and promoting the transition of minority adolescents. *Career Development for Exceptional Individuals, 26,* 27–46.

Harper, D. (n.d.). Etymology of *assess. Online Etymology Dictionary.* https://www.etymonline.com/word/assess

Harrison, P. & Oakland, T. (2015). *Adaptive Behavior Assessment System* (3rd ed.). Pearson.

Hart, D., Boyle, M., & Jones, M. (2017). *Foundational Skills for College and Career Learning Plan.* Think College.

Individuals with Disabilities Education Improvement Act (IDEA) of 2004, Pub. L. No. 108-446, 20 U.S.C. §§ 1400 *et seq* (2004).

Lachapelle, Y., Wehmeyer, M. L., Haelewyck, M. C., Courbois, Y., Keith, K. D., Schalock, R., Verdugo, M. A., & Walsh, P. N. (2005). The relationship between quality of life and self-determination: An international study. *Journal of Intellectual Disability Research, 49,* 740–744.

Martin, J.E., Huber-Marshall, L.H., Maxson, L.M., & Jerman, P.L. (2007). *Choicemaker self-determiantion curriculum* (2nd ed.). Sopris West.

Martin, J. E., & Marshall, L. H. (1995). ChoiceMaker: A comprehensive self-determination transition program. *Intervention in School and Clinic, (30),* 147–156. doi.org/10.1177/105345129503000304.

McCarney, S.B. & Arthaud, T.J. (2012). *Transition Behavior Scale* (3rd ed.). Hawthorne Educational Services.

Mesibov, G., Thomas, J. B., Chapman, M., Schopler, E. (2007). *TTAP: TEACCCH Transition Assessment Profile* (2nd ed.). PRO-ED.

Newman, L., Wagner, M., Cameto, R., & Knokey, A. M. (2009). The post-high school outcomes of youth with disabilities up to 4 years after high school. A report from the National Longitudinal Transition Study-2 (NLTS2). SRI International. www.nlts2.org/reports/2009_04/nlts2_report_2009_04_complete.pdf

Patton, J.R. & Clark, G.M. (2009). *TPI-3: Transition Planning Inventory* (3rd ed.). PRO-ED.

Prince, A. M. T., Plotner, A. J., & Yell, M. L. (2014). Postsecondary transition and the courts: An update. *Journal of Disability Policy Studies, 25*(1), 41–47. https://doi.org/10.1177/1044207314530469

Pulos, J. M., & Martin, J. E. (2018). *Transition assessment.* In L. L. Stansberry Brusnanhan, R. A. Stodden, & S. H. Zucker, *Transition to adulthood: Work, community, and educational success* (pp. 19–33). Council for Exceptional Children.

Sax, C. L. & Thoma, C. A. (2002). *Transition assessment: Wise practices for quality lives.* Paul H. Brookes Publishing Co. *Children, 71,* 401–414.

Sitlington, P. L., Neubert, D., & Clark, G. (2010). *Assess for success: A practitioner's handbook on Transition Assessment* (2nd ed.). Corwin Press.

Trainor, A. A. (2008). Using cultural and social capital to improve postsecondary outcomes and expand transition models for youth with disabilities. *The Journal of Special Education, 42,* 148–162. https://doi.org/10.1177/0022466907313346

Trainor, A. A., Murray, A., & Kim, H. (2014, August). *Postsecondary transition and English learners with disabilities: Data from the second National Longitudinal Transition Study* (WCER Working Paper No. 2014-04). University of Wisconsin–Madison. https://wcer.wisc.edu/docs/working-papers/Working_Paper_No_2014_04.pdf

Thoma, C. A., & Tamura, R. (2013). Demystifying Transition Assessment. Paul H. Brookes Publishing Co.

Turnbull, A. (2020). *An enviable and dignified life.* Minnesota Developmental Disabilities Council. https://mn.gov/mnddc/ann-turnbull/ann-turnbull-02.html

Wehmeyer, M. L. (2015). Framing the future of self-determination. *Remedial and Special Education, 36*(1), 20–23.

Wehmeyer, M.L., & Kelchner, K. (1995). *The ARC's Self-Determination Scale.* The ARC National Headquarters.

Wehmeyer, M. L., & Palmer, S. B. (2003). Adult outcomes from students with cognitive disabilities three years after high school: The impact of self-determination. *Education and Training in Developmental Disabilities, 38,* 131–144.

Woman, J. M, Campeau, P. I., DuBois, P. A., Mithaug, D., & Stolarski, V. S. (1994). *AIR Self-Determination Scale and User Guide.* Washington, DC: American Institutes for Research.

Workforce Innovation and Opportunity Act of 2014, Pub. L. No. 113-128, Stat. 129 (2014). https://www.govinfo.gov/content/pkg/PLAW-113publ128/pdf/PLAW-113publ128.pdf

Zirkel, S. (2008). The influence of multicultural educational practices on student outcomes and intergroup relations. *Teachers College Record, 110,* 1147–1181.

A

Transition Assessment Resources

Comprehensive Transition Assessment	Description/purpose	Cost*
TAGG Assessment https://tagg.ou.edu/tagg	Transition assessment and goals generator	Small cost
QuickBook of Transition Assessments https://www.ocali.org/up_doc/Quickbook_of_ Transition_Assessment.pdf	This book has information about a number of transition assessments, some of which are included	Free
Enderle-Severson Transition Rating Scales–Third Edition (Enderle & Severson, 2003) https://sdiprdwb.ku.edu/index.php	An informal assessment that looks at a number of transition domains	Small cost
Brigance Transition Skills Inventory (Curriculum Associates, 2010) https://www.curriculumassociates.com/programs/brigance	Formal assessment that helps students identify their goals	Prices range from $5.99 to $469
Transition Planning Inventory-3 (Clark & Patton, 2009) https://www.proedinc.com/Products/14865/tpi3-transition-planning-inventorythird-edition-complete-kit.aspx	Kit provides nine forms/assessment tools that can be used by students, family, and school personnel	$363 for kit
Supports Intensity Scale (American Association on Intellectual and Developmental Disabilities) https://www.aaidd.org/docs/default-source/sis-docs/sis_broch_2012_web.pdf?sfvrsn=86cdc812_2021) English and French language versions.	Assesses the supports an individual needs to function in various environments/settings. There is also an online option.	$150 (manual & 25 forms)
TEACCH Transition Assessment Profile–Second Edition (Mesibov et al., 2007) https://www.proedinc.com/Products/13708/ttapcv-teacch-transition-assessment-profile-computer-version.aspx	Designed for students with ASD	$125.00
Employability and Life Skills (Weaver & DeLuca, n.d.) https://www.proedinc.com/Products/13708/ttapcv-teacch-transition-assessment-profile-computer-version.aspx	Checklist to determine student skills. Family and Professional versions.	Free
Community asset mapping https://creately.com/usage/community-asset-mapping/	Provides a way to record the assets/strengths of a community	Free trial
Employment		
My Next Move O*NET Interest Inventory (U.S. Department of Labor, 2002) https://www.mynextmove.org/explore/ip	Online interest inventory	Free
Picture Interest Career Survey (Brady, 2007) https://www.paradigmeducation.com/products/picture-interest-career-survey-third-edition	Picture interest inventory. Can be accessed online or in hard copy.	$69 for online access code
Where R U Now? (U.S. Department of Education, n.d.) https://studentaid.gov/resources/prepare-for-college/checklists	Provides a range of resources to help your career search, map out a future, and set goals	Free
myFuture (U.S. Department of Defense, n.d.) https://myfuture.com/	Provides information about careers, education, and military options	Free
Virginia Education Wizard (Virginia Department of Education, n.d.) https://www.vawizard.org/wizard/home (Most states will have something like this either from the community college system or the state department of education.)	Provides information about apprenticeship programs, community college options, etc.	Free

Comprehensive Transition Assessment	Description/purpose	Cost*
Environmental-Job Assessment Measure (Waintrup & Kelly, 1999) https://risecondarytransition.org/project/environmental-job-assessment-measure Was developed for youth with emotional/behavior disorders, but it can be used with most transition-aged youth	Strengths-based assessment	Free
Armed Services Vocational Aptitude Battery (ASVAB; U.S. Department of Defense, 1999) https://www.officialasvab.com/	Armed services vocational aptitude battery	Free
Positive Personal Profile (TransCen, 2013) https://transcen.org/wp-content/uploads/2019/06/Blank-Positive-Personal-Profile.docx	A way to organize an individual student's interests and strengths related to employment	Free
Postsecondary education		
Student resources for going to college (Educational Credit Management Corporation, 2022) https://ecmc.org/studentseducators/student-resources/resources-guides They also provide resources in Spanish.	Provides a range of resources for students and parents about planning for college and finances	Free
College Navigator (National Center for Education Statistics, n.d.) https://nces.ed.gov/collegenavigator/ They also provide resources in Spanish	Resources for finding the right college for you	Free
Preparing for College (U.S. Department of Education, n.d.) https://studentaid.gov/resources/prepare-for-college/checklists Also provide resources in Spanish.	A series of checklists to help you prepare for college (from elementary through high school)	Free
College & Career Competency Framework: Needs Assessment (Erickson & Noonan, 2016) https://www.researchcollaboration.org/uploads/CCCNeedsAssessmentInfo.pdf	Provides information about the intra- and interpersonal skills needed for careers and college	Free
Foundational Skills for College and Career Learning Plan (Hart et al., 2017) https://thinkcollege.net/resource/campus-life-employment-supports/foundational-skills-for-college-and-career-learning-plan	Assesses skills needed to navigate college	Free
Independent living		
Adaptive Behavior Scale –Third Edition (Harrison & Oakland, 2015) https://www.pearsonassessments.com/store/usassessments/en/Store/Professional-Assessments/Behavior/Brief/Adaptive-Behavior-Assessment-System-%7C-Third-Edition/p/100001262.html Available in print, software, and online formats.	Assesses behavior skills	$103–$435 (kit)
Brigance Life Skills Inventory (Brigance, 1994) https://www2.curriculumassociates.com/products/detail.aspx?title=&partnum=11597.0	Assesses a range of transition skills, with a range of independent living and community participation areas	$39 for 10
Transition Behavior Scale (McCarney & Arthaud, 2012) https://www.hawthorne-ed.com/transition-behavior-scale-third-edition-complete-kit-details.html	Measures a student's readiness for transition to employment and independent living with a particular focus on behavior	$237 for kit; $50 for online

(continued)

Comprehensive Transition Assessment	Description/purpose	Cost*
Social Mapping and Planning for Community Membership (The Sam Houston State University Garrett Center, 2017) https://www.shsu.edu/dotAsset/4c8f98c7-0bd2-4dde-a151-c73397508ba4.pdf	Identifies activities student engages in now and identifies areas for growth	Free
Social Support Survey (RAND Corporation, n.d.) https://www.rand.org/health-care/surveys_tools/mos/social-support/survey-instrument.html	Identifies student needs related to social supports	Free
Ansell-Casey Life Skills Inventory (Nollan et al., 2000) https://www.casey.org/casey-life-skills/	Free tools that assess the independent living skills youth need to reach long-term goals	Free
Transition Health Care Checklist (Pennsylvania Department of Health, n.d.) https://www.health.pa.gov/topics/Documents/Programs/Infant%20and%20Children%20Health/The%20FINAL%20Transition%20May%209%202013.pdf	Helps the student identify health care needs	Free
Self-determination		
I'm determined project (Virginia Department of Education, 2021) https://www.imdetermined.org/quick-links	Provides resources that can help students with disabilities learn self-determination skills	Free
Choicemaker Curriculum (Martin et al., 2007) https://www.ou.edu/content/dam/Education/zarrow/transition-resources/curriculum/choicemaker/ChoiceMaker%20materials/ChoiceMaker%20Assessment%202016.pdf	Curriculum-based measure	Free
ARC Self-Determination Scale (Wehmeyer & Kelchner, 1995) https://www.ou.edu/education/centers-and-partnerships/zarrow/transition-resources/assessments	Validated measure of functional self-determination skills	Free
AIR Self-determination Assessment (Wolman et al., 1994) https://www.ou.edu/education/centers-and-partnerships/zarrow/transition-resources/assessments English, Spanish, and French versions.	Assesses both the capacity to be self-determined as well as opportunities to do so. Student, Teacher, and Family versions.	Free
Self-determination Inventory (University of Kansas, 2017) https://sdiprdwb.ku.edu/index.php Offers online audio version	Student or Adult, Teacher & Family versions. Asks questions about self-determination, making choices, goal setting and attainment, and decision making.	Free

*Costs listed were current at the time this chapter was written but are subject to change.

3

Student Self-Determination

Mayumi Hagiwara, Sheida K. Raley, Karrie A. Shogren, and Abdulaziz Alsaeed

DIGGING DEEPER: What Teachers Have to Say

My lifelong teacher has taught me the importance of inclusion and self-determination. She is not a teacher, researcher, or famous person by conventional standards. But she is my greatest mentor—my younger sister, Mikie, who was born with intellectual disability. She is incredibly personable and loves to chat with anyone. Mikie is always ready to help others when they ask, and she also asks if they need help. Growing up, she loved school because she could interact with all of the other students, including students without disabilities. Mikie always expressed her vision, which was full of her dreams. She wanted to work at a bakery. And she wanted to have a handsome boyfriend. However, school was not set up for students like her to learn, socialize, and thrive alongside peers without disabilities and to design and develop an inclusive life trajectory. Often, teachers and students without disabilities made cruel, ignorant comments to her. But Mikie was determined to go to school every day, although her determination for inclusion was never realized as she envisioned because of structural barriers and low societal expectations toward people with intellectual disability. After Mikie's graduation from a special education high school, these systemic and ableist barriers persisted into adulthood. Mikie has been working at a sheltered workshop for close to 20 years with no plan to measure or observe progress that would build to the future she once dreamed for herself. Now, she doesn't even talk about her future like she did before. So, I find myself asking, who or what took Mikie's dreams away?

My experiences as Mikie's sibling growing up in Japan led to my pursuit of a special education teaching certification and position in the United States. As I reflect on my teaching experiences, one in particular stands out. When I was a new elementary school teacher for students with extensive support needs, a White female special education teacher was showing me how she set up independent work by "meeting each student's needs." I noticed one African American female student was sorting objects by color and shape. The teacher explained, "You know, she needs to learn to sit and sort for her future workshop job." I was immediately struck by this response because it sounded exactly like Mikie's school experiences. I also felt powerless as a new teacher from culturally and linguistically diverse backgrounds about not being able to advocate for the student victimized by ableist ideas. The low expectations highlighted in this story portray how the views of people in positions of power (e.g., teachers) shape the future for students with disabilities and the critical importance of interrupting ableist structures that perpetuate misalignment of the goals and current supports for people with disabilities. Luckily, this particular student had a family who shared the same interests and preferences for her future goals.

All my life, Mikie has taught me that we were all born self-determined no matter what support needs we may have. This idea helped me to interpret the definition of self-determination as a dispositional characteristic and to understand that we each need support and opportunities to engage in self-determined actions to be the person we want to be. My sibling experience has laid a foundation for my teaching beliefs and philosophy, and my teaching experience has inspired me to design and implement self-determination instruction from a culturally sustaining lens. Continually searching for the answer to "Who or what took Mikie's dreams away?" early in my life has now shifted my focus to a different question: "How can we, as a society, support students with disabilities to prepare for and secure the life that they envision?" Universal design for transition (UDT), which effectively merges culturally sustaining pedagogy and self-determination offers multiple pathways to these answers.

Essential Questions

▶   How can educators best support transition-age students with disabilities from diverse cultural and linguistic backgrounds, including racially and ethnically marginalized youth?

▶   What are the three self-determined actions that make up self-determination as defined by Causal Agency Theory? What can educators do to facilitate each of these self-determined actions?

▶ What can educators do to empower *all* youth to identify, navigate, and dismantle racist, ableist, and other inequitable systems as they grow in their self-determination abilities, skills, and attitudes?

▶ Why is it so important to dismantle these systems?

As introduced in Chapter 1, UDT promotes student self-determination. Within the UDT framework, a focus on promoting self-determination centers the transition-age student's strengths, preferences, values, and beliefs as they engage in transition planning with support from family members, friends, school professionals, and others. In this chapter, we define self-determination and describe strategies for promoting self-determination with transition-age students from diverse cultural and linguistic backgrounds. Then, we introduce self-determination assessment and intervention approaches and provide practical guidance on ways to use self-determination assessment to inform self-determination intervention in culturally responsive and sustaining ways.

DEFINITION AND HISTORY OF SELF-DETERMINATION

Causal Agency Theory defines self-determination as a "dispositional characteristic manifested as acting as the causal agent in one's life" (Shogren et al., 2015a, p. 258). Self-determination develops over the life course as a person has opportunities, experiences, and supports to set and work toward goals driven by their individual, family, and community strengths, preferences, values, and beliefs. Causal Agency Theory defines three self-determined actions:

1. Volitional action or DECIDE (i.e., making conscious choices and decisions based on one's strengths, preferences, values, and beliefs)

2. Agentic action or ACT (i.e., taking action toward self-identified goals and identifying pathways to remove barriers)

3. Action-control beliefs or BELIEVE (i.e., feeling empowered to act based on one's beliefs in one's own abilities to DECIDE and ACT)

Self-determination has been recognized as important to advancing equity and inclusion for people with disabilities since the late 1960s and 1970s (e.g., Nirje, 1969, 1972). However, a strong focus on self-determination in secondary transition planning emerged in the 1990s when the Office of Special Education and Rehabilitative Services funded a series of projects to advance systemwide changes to promote a greater focus on self-determination in secondary education (Shogren & Ward, 2018). Over the past 3 decades, self-determination has been identified as a key value in the disability advocacy community (Wehmeyer et al., 2017) as well as in other cultural traditions. For example, the African American holiday Kwanzaa recognizes "the rights of African Americans to shape their own corporate destinies instead of having some other group (e.g., the majority culture) shape that destiny" (Wehmeyer et al., 2017, p. 12). As such, self-determined people not only act as causal agents in their own lives but also advocate for systemic change in their communities (Shogren et al., 2015a; Wehmeyer, 2014). Self-determination relates to and is incorporated in contemporary social justice movements, including Anti-Arab and Anti-Muslim Racism; Black Lives Matter; immigration advocacy; lesbian, gay, bisexual, transgender, intersex, queer/questioning, asexual, and more identities (LGBTQ+) rights; Stop Asian American Pacific Islander Hate; and the Me Too movement. These movements, in the context of an increasingly culturally and linguistically diverse population in the United States, have the potential to amplify opportunities for racially and ethnically marginalized students with disabilities to build abilities, skills, and attitudes associated with self-determination and engage in individual and collective advocacy.

Self-Determination and Transition Planning

The transition to adulthood is an opportune time for students with disabilities to be supported as they grow in their use of self-determined actions (i.e., DECIDE, ACT, and BELIEVE). For example, during the transition to adulthood, students have ample opportunities and experiences to build and apply self-determination abilities as they explore inclusive postsecondary education options, career pathways, community participation opportunities, and leadership within social justice movements. Furthermore, the transition to adulthood is a critical time to become more self-determined because self-determination is a predictor of positive postschool outcomes for students with disabilities (Mazzotti et al., 2021). Researchers have demonstrated that higher self-determination status when students exit high school leads to more positive postschool outcomes (e.g., competitive employment, community participation; Shogren et al., 2015b). However, although an array of research-based practices to promote self-determination for transition-age students with disabilities has accumulated over 3 decades (Algozzine et al., 2001; Burke et al., 2020), researchers consistently find that transition-age students and young adults with disabilities lack opportunities to build self-determination while in school, particularly in ways that are aligned with their cultural values and identities (e.g., Trainor, 2007). Furthermore, the lack of opportunities to build self-determination is more pronounced for racially and ethnically marginalized students with disabilities because opportunities, supports, and experiences to build self-determination during transition planning are often not available, accessible, or culturally and linguistically sustaining (Scott et al., 2021; Shogren et al., 2021).

Self-Determination and Culture

Although researchers suggest that people with disabilities and their supporters (e.g., family members, school professionals) value self-determination across the life course, how people perceive, express, and engage in self-determined actions differs based on cultural identities (Shogren & Wehmeyer, 2017a). Cultural identities shape the expression of self-determination as well as the opportunities and supports that students and their families value (Hagiwara et al., 2021; Wehmeyer et al., 2011). For example, researchers have suggested that a misalignment exists between how families understand and provide supports, opportunities, and experiences for self-determination at home and in the community and how school professionals operationalize and promote self-determination at school, leading to inequitable supports and opportunities for self-determination during transition planning (Dean et al., 2021; Shogren, 2012). For example, Scott and colleagues (2021) interviewed Black youth with intellectual and developmental disabilities and their families about opportunities for self-determination during transition planning. Both youth and families expressed that schools did not engage in family–school partnerships that respected and valued families' needs and concerns to promote self-determination in the transition planning process, particularly related to inclusion and starting transition planning early. Youth especially emphasized the importance of having teachers who understood and empowered them to use their voices to self-advocate (Scott et al., 2021). As such, there is a need to build communication about self-determination among students, families and teachers. Furthermore, ensuring openness to different ways to expressing and advancing self-determination is critical to challenge bias in special education services and supports. This is highlighted by the fact that teachers tend to perceive student's self-determination as lower than how students perceive themselves and that these disparities are greater when students identify with a race/ethnicity that is different from their teachers and when students have more extensive support needs (Shogren et al., 2020). Schools and school professionals' expectations for self-determination are critical to the opportunities and supports provided for students. In the following sections, we describe how school professionals can use self-determination assessment and intervention in culturally sustaining ways that recognize the intersection of multiple cultural identities (e.g., race/ethnicity, disability, family values and preferences) in the lives of all students.

SELF-DETERMINATION ASSESSMENT AND INTERVENTION DURING TRANSITION PLANNING

To effectively support transition-age students in building self-determination in culturally responsive and sustaining ways, it is imperative to note first that adolescence is a critical period when young people learn, enhance, and practice knowledge, skills, beliefs, and actions that enable them to navigate opportunities, experiences, and barriers that they encounter in their environment (Wehmeyer & Shogren, 2017). Also, "the ways in which young people are enacting race, ethnicity, language, literacy, and their engagement in culture is always shifting and dynamic" (Alim & Paris, 2017, p. 7). This will influence the development of self-determination over the life course but particularly during transition planning. This means that transition planning should be flexible, creating a natural context during adolescence for students to start acting as causal agents in their lives. According to the National Scientific Council on Adolescence (NSCA; 2021), "both agency and exploration support identity formation by allowing adolescents to try out different 'selves' and experiment with new roles within their peer groups, family, and community" (p. 10). However, for students with marginalized cultural identities, opportunities to act as causal agents and explore the world are significantly impacted by structural racism and ableism as well as others' explicit and implicit biases (NSCA, 2021). Therefore, instruction designed to promote self-determination needs to enable students to navigate and challenge structural inequities, address explicit and implicit bias, and advocate for individual and communal rights and high expectations for themselves and others, leading to improved outcomes (Aceves & Orosco, 2014; Hsieh et al., 2021).

Furthermore, opportunities, supports, and experiences to build self-determination must be designed, delivered, and evaluated intentionally to take students' multiple cultural identities into account and recognize that every student experiences cultural pluralism (Paris, 2012). In other words, it is critical to start by acknowledging the intersectionality of cultural and social identities within each student's life experiences, including race and ethnicity, family dynamics, languages, heritage, values, and beliefs. Planning for instruction designed to promote self-determination should start with considering how students can be successful not only within culturally dominant frameworks (e.g., existing school structures) but also in other cultural contexts. This is especially critical when students and families share culturally rooted expectations that may not align with dominant cultural values and practices. As described in Chapter 4, school professionals should collaborate with students, families (e.g., parents, siblings, extended family members), other school professionals, community support professionals, and other stakeholders that students and families value (e.g., neighbors, friends) to understand how self-determination is perceived across contexts and tap into authentic opportunities and supports for self-determination.

Self-Determination Assessments

Although the previous chapter discusses transition assessment in more depth, this section specifically targets self-determination assessment. A first step in supporting self-determination is using assessment tools that can do the following:

- Facilitate conversations with students to learn about their perceptions and experiences related to self-determination.

- Identify instructional needs to personalize interventions and supports based on a student's strengths, preferences, beliefs, and values influenced by cultural identities.

- Track the outcomes of self-determination interventions to establish their effectiveness.

Self-determination assessment should guide intervention planning and evaluation. It should be more than a step to "check off the list" within transition assessments. To this end, school professionals can partner with transition-age students and families to complete self-determination assessments and discuss ways to interpret and apply results to drive positive change.

A new set of self-determination measures was developed in 2017, called the Self-Determination Inventory System (SDIS; Shogren & Wehmeyer, 2017b). The SDIS includes SDI: Student Report (SDI:SR) for youth ages 13–22 with and without disabilities, SDI: Parent/Teacher Report (SDI:PTR) for family members and school professionals supporting youth, and SDI: Adult Report (SDI:AR) for people ages 18 and over with and without disabilities. Each measure includes 21 items. An overall self-determination score as well as scores for the self-determined actions defined by Causal Agency Theory (i.e., volitional action or DECIDE, agentic action or ACT, action-control beliefs or BELIEVE) are automatically calculated and provided to users. The SDI Report is provided at the end of the assessment and describes strengths and areas for growth across DECIDE, ACT, and BELIEVE, as well as specific recommendations on how people can strengthen self-determined actions across school, home, and community environments based on scores. The SDIS measures are completed online, allowing for embedded accessibility features (e.g., in-text definitions, audio playback) and the use of a customized, computer-scored slider scale to provide responses. Spanish and American Sign Language versions of the SDI:SR are also available within the SDIS. Please visit the Kansas University Center on

Developmental Disabilities Self-Determination website for more information and to take the SDI (https://selfdetermination.ku.edu).

Self-Determination Interventions

After completing self-determination assessments and reviewing strengths and areas of need for growth in self-determination, school professionals can partner with students and families to implement evidence-based interventions designed to promote self-determination in inclusive contexts in culturally sustaining ways. It is critical to emphasize that all self-determination intervention efforts should be guided by the student with disabilities and consider their cultural identity, values, and beliefs. All too often, intervention approaches are determined by people who have power to perpetuate structural inequalities even if positive intentions underlie their decisions. Therefore, centering the voices and experiences of students with disabilities in the intervention decision-making process is critical to promote student self-determination.

Using self-determination assessment results, such as the SDI Report, students and school professionals are well positioned to design and plan for self-determination instruction in culturally responsive ways. From the onset of planning for self-determination intervention, school professionals should be intentional about collaborating with students, their families, and other key supporters in students' lives to ensure that their strengths and assets in addition to their cultural identities, values, and beliefs are incorporated and respected.

The Self-Determined Learning Model of Instruction: Introduction and Phases

One evidence-based practice to promote self-determination in the context of transition planning (National Technical Assistance Center on Transition, 2017) is the Self-Determined Learning Model of Instruction (SDLMI; Shogren et al., 2019). The SDLMI pairs particularly well with the SDI as they are both aligned with Causal Agency Theory and associated self-determined actions (i.e., DECIDE, ACT, and BELIEVE). The SDLMI consists of a three-phase instructional process that focuses on self-regulated problem-solving skills as students set and work toward goals. It can be repeated each semester in school-based settings in order for students to benefit from multiple opportunities and experiences to build self-determination and establish and work toward new and different goals. It is important to note that students should be encouraged to identify goals that are important in their lives and their communities and that are related to social justice movements to challenge barriers introduced by systemic racism, ableism, and other forms of discrimination.

Each SDLMI phase presents an overall problem for students to solve with support from a trained facilitator (e.g., general education teacher, special education teacher, transition case manager): Phase 1, What is my goal? Phase 2, What is my plan? and Phase 3, What have I learned? (see Figure 3.1). The solution to the overall problem in each phase leads to the problem-solving sequence in the next phase. For example, in Phase 1, students are supported to identify a goal aligned with their interests, support needs, and vision for the future (e.g., applying for adult services or identifying an adult health care provider, identifying friendship networks, accessing postsecondary education or employment, participating in advocacy and social justice movements). Phase 2 follows the same steps as Phase 1, except that it targets developing an action plan for the goal set in Phase 1. In Phase 3, after implementing their action plan, students evaluate what worked, learning how to adjust their actions based on experiences,

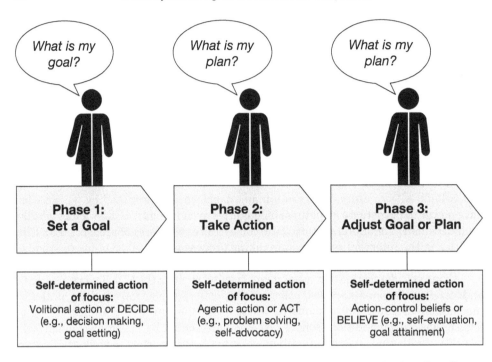

Figure 3.1. Self-Determined Learning Model of Instruction alignment with self-determined actions. (From Shogren et al. [2019]. Copyright 2022 Kansas University Center on Developmental Disabilities; adapted by permission.)

informing future goals as they cycle back to Phase 1 and work through the process again for their next SDLMI goal. When supporting students to evaluate their progress toward goals, trained facilitators need to be aware that the measure of success can be different depending on each student's and family's values, needs, and priorities (Achola & Greene, 2016).

Roles of the Facilitator in the Self-Determined Learning Model of Instruction Process Trained facilitators take on multiple roles in the SDLMI process: 1) the facilitator, who does what it takes to enable students to succeed by enabling students to grow and develop their self-determined actions; 2) the instructor, who delivers instruction that enables students to answer the questions and complete tasks; and 3) the advocate who lets students know they can succeed, removes barriers in the environment, and works with the student to achieve shared goals. Students also play multiple roles: 1) the self-directed learner, who actively engages in the process and, in so doing, more actively directs and initiates their learning; 2) the active learner, who acts in collaboration with the facilitator and grows in their direction over the learning process; and 3) the self-advocate, who communicates cultural values, interests, preferences, beliefs, and goals. It is important to remember that how each student defines and engages in these roles looks different based on their cultural values, preferences, and practices. Therefore, the partnership among trained facilitators, students, and families is critical to enact culturally sustaining practices within the three SDLMI phases. Such interpersonal dialogue and relationships "have a tremendous impact on the quality of teaching and learning" (Gay, 2018, p. 269). This dialogue and relationship can be further strengthened by school professionals understanding and incorporating culturally sustaining practices, such as promoting allyship and fostering a trusting relationship and sense of community among school professionals and students (Hsieh et al., 2021).

A PRACTICAL GUIDE TO PROMOTING SELF-DETERMINATION IN CULTURALLY SUSTAINING WAYS

This section of the chapter provides guidance about how educators can apply, in practice, the concepts and tools described previously and thereby promote students' self-determination and do so in a way that is culturally sustaining. This practical application occurs both within the assessment process and in day-to-day teaching as discussed in the following section.

Using the SDI:SR 3-2-1 Snapshot to Interpret Self-Determination Assessment

Relationships are key to supporting self-determination. It is important to make time for relationships to develop among students, families, and school professionals so that they can have intentionality in thinking, planning, and engaging in culturally responsive and sustaining supports for self-determination. Such relationship development—as with the development of self-determination—requires time and focused attention, especially for students with disabilities, who are often marginalized by societal biases and low expectations that limit their opportunities to act as causal agents. After transition-age students complete the SDI:SR, they can work through the SDI:SR 3-2-1 Snapshot (see Figure 3.2) with school professionals, peers, and families. The SDI:SR 3-2-1 Snapshot is designed to facilitate conversations with students and co-create a foundation for self-determination instruction by supporting students to interpret their results from the SDI:SR and identify next steps they can take to build their abilities, skills, and attitudes associated with self-determination. The SDI:SR 3-2-1 Snapshot includes three sections: 1) students identify *three actions* they can take to improve their self-determination, 2) students identify *two self-determination abilities and skills* they want to make stronger, and 3) students provide *one reflection* they had related to discovering or building their self-determination. School professionals using the SDI:SR 3-2-1 Snapshot with students with diverse support needs might consider providing specific accommodations, such as reducing the number of items, using visual supports, enabling audio-to-text applications, supporting students to answer with audio and/or video recordings, and changing font sizes and colors. In addition, when school professionals talk with students about what DECIDE, ACT, and BELIEVE mean to the students, these professionals should enable students to refer to personal/previous experiences as significant sources of knowledge and recognize students as experts in new learning with self-determination instruction (Fritzgerald, 2020; Gay, 2018).

Promoting Self-Determination in Daily Teaching

Throughout self-determination instruction, it is critical to remember to foster interpersonal dialogue, communicate high expectations, and discuss complex cultural identities, including privilege and marginalization (Hsieh et al., 2021), that influence student self-determination. School professionals also need to acknowledge that some students are excited and ready to engage in self-determined actions. In contrast, other

My SDI:SR on May 6 (*date*): **A self-determination 3-2-1 snapshot**

3 What are **3 actions** I can take this semester (*day/date*) **to improve my self-determination?**

DECIDE: What it means to me...

Decide means that when I set my mind to do something, I will be able to do it.

One **action** I can take to grow:

Decide what kind of goal I can set for completing and turning in assignments.

ACT: What it means to me...

Act means that I will actually do what I have decided to do, and I won't make excuses.

One **action** I can take to grow:

Try to have time (friends and hobbies) so I can focus.

BELIEVE: What it means to me...

Believe means being aware that sometimes I need the support of others who know me and my strengths. If I feel lost and worried sometimes, that that is okay.

One **action** I can take to grow:

Share my goal with others so they can encourage me.

2 What are **2 self-determination skills, abilities, and attitudes** (e.g., decision making, goal setting) **I want to make stronger?**

Problem solving

Thinking about different ways to get around a problem and the supports I need to get around barriers

One way I will **grow** in this skill:

Realize that there are people in my family and in my school who can listen, act as mirrors, and help me by talking through things.

Self-advocacy

Share my options with others

One way I will **grow** in this skill:

Remind myself that I can do anything. Think about the things that are important to me and that my family and I care about.

1 What is **one reflection** about discovering and developing your self-determination?

I've never really set goals for myself, but I think I can. My score in BELIEVE was the highest because my family has always believed in me, which I think has made me believe in myself.

Figure 3.2. *Self-Determination Inventory:* Student Report (SDI:SR) 3-2-1 snapshot example.

students might feel vulnerable sharing their strengths, preferences, and values and acting as causal agents, especially if they have not been empowered to do so. Relationship building and respecting students where they are is critical to supporting self-determination. Furthermore, school professionals should be engaging in frequent self-reflection about their biases, expectations, and privilege to "initiate, revise, revitalize, and validate" (Gay, 2018, p. 244) culturally responsive and sustaining teaching. Figure 3.3 provides self-reflection questions for school professionals to answer

Self-Reflection for Culturally Sustaining Self-Determination Instruction

Directions: Answer the following questions as a starting point to self-reflect on how to provide self-determination instruction in culturally responsive and sustaining ways. If possible, answer these self-reflection questions and discuss with colleagues who are also promoting self-determination to build a community of people supporting student self-determination across settings.

BEFORE Self-Determination Instruction

☐ What is my journey to becoming self-determined?

☐ How do I currently promote student self-determination?

☐ What do I know and not know about the cultural and linguistic backgrounds of students? What are my biases and expectations toward students' multiple cultural identities?

☐ What is my positionality as the instructor? What are current power dynamics in my classroom and with families?

DURING Self-Determination Instruction

☐ How am I fostering the development of DECIDE considering students' multiple cultural identities?

☐ How am I enabling students to ACT as they work toward their goals and use their action plans in ways that are aligned with their cultural and linguistic values, preferences, and practices?

☐ How am I promoting students' abilities related to BELIEVE by celebrating students' successes with them and their families?

☐ How am I acting as an ally to promote a culture of inclusion in my classroom using strengths- and assets-based approaches?

☐ How am I fostering interpersonal dialogue and a sense of community among students and key supporters in their family and community?

☐ How am I creating opportunities that invite students and their families to explore complex identities and critically discuss students' prior experiences and family backgrounds through analysis of power, opportunity, denial, and privilege?

AFTER Self-Determination Instruction

☐ How did I actively identify and address aspects of privilege and marginalization in my multiple social identities as I engaged in self-determination instruction?

☐ How did I facilitate the development of abilities, skills, and attitudes that enable students to be social critics and advance systemic reforms (e.g., changes in school or community practices)?

☐ How did I consistently communicate high expectations and provide appropriate supports aligned with students' goals, values, preferences, and strengths?

☐ How did I engage families and communities in my instruction?

Figure 3.3. Self-reflection questions for designing, implementing, and evaluating self-determination instruction.

before, during, and after self-determination instruction to ensure that instructional design and implementation are culturally responsive and sustaining. In addition, school professionals can follow practical tips and strategies listed in Table 3.1 when planning for and delivering self-determination instruction. Specifically, Table 3.1 provides 1) instructional design and strategies to promote partnerships with students and honor their diverse learning styles and 2) family–school partnership practices

Table 3.1. Tips and strategies for culturally sustaining self-determination instruction

Instructional Design and Strategies

- Use a variety of resources (e.g., books, articles, films, music, podcasts) to discuss how people engage in self-determined actions.
- Invite guest speakers from school and community who share cultural identities with students to talk about their experiences with self-determination (e.g., self-advocates in a local youth support group).
- Embed opportunities for students to work with peers or mentors to practice self-determined actions within authentic daily experiences and current events.
- Offer options for students to share and collaborate anonymously.
- Assist students to design or co-design self-monitoring tools based on their strengths, preferences, and values, and discuss how and when to monitor their progress (e.g., considering religious and cultural holidays).
- Enable students to explore community resources, including resources in the local community, to carry out their action plans and also generalize their action plans.
- Embed collaborative learning opportunities to enable students to identify what could keep them from taking action and what they can do to remove any barriers.
- Plan for community-based instruction for students to work with non-school supporters and carry out their action plans in a community of their choice.
- Support student self-reflection and celebrate together when they make progress toward their goals.

Family–School Partnerships Tips

- Learn about families' communication preferences (e.g., written correspondence, technology-based means of communication) to establish a line of communication.
- Create an accessible survey (digital, paper, in families' preferred languages) to understand families' perceptions and expectations for self-determination.
- Connect families with other families who have previously gone through self-determination instruction to hear about their successes, barriers, and suggestions.
- Share with families about the self-determination instruction (e.g., conference, back-to-school night) in families' preferred languages.

to communicate and build a supportive community for empowering student self-determination across environments.

Using the Self-Determined Learning Model of Instruction

We introduced the SDLMI previously, and integrating the model into instruction is another evidence-based way to promote student self-determination. After learning about and receiving training on the SDLMI (for more information, visit https://selfdetermination.ku.edu), facilitators can engage students in the three phases of the SDLMI to set goals for school and their transition to adulthood. The SDI:SR 3-2-1 Snapshot can provide a starting point for conversations about students' ideas for building their self-determination abilities to guide the process. Integrating the SDLMI over multiple semesters is beneficial for both students and facilitators, as is the use of materials that align with UDL.

As mentioned previously, the SDLMI is a cyclical process and the length of time needed for each phase can vary. This is why multiple semesters of working through the SDLMI to set and pursue goals can support students to feel more confident and also allow them to work toward complex or multifaceted goals related to challenging systematic barriers. Similarly, going through a cyclical process over multiple semesters can enable trained facilitators to grow in their confidence in designing, delivering, and evaluating culturally responsive and sustaining self-determination instruction. SDLMI facilitators learn to develop and customize materials based on their students' strengths and learning needs. These materials should also represent diverse people, cultures, and communities (Gay, 2018) and be provided in students'/families' languages with an option for students to write in the language they choose (Fallon et al., 2021). Importantly, materials should align with the UDL Guidelines (CAST, 2018). Figure 3.4 is an example of SDLMI materials that can support students as they engage in Phase 2, What is my action? School professionals should offer options of writing, typing, using a speech-to-text function, drawing, adding visuals, or audio/video recording when they support students to engage with materials. In addition, it is highly recommended that students develop a portfolio to record and showcase their development in self-determination over time.

Building and maintaining family–school partnership is a key element of culturally responsive and sustaining self-determination instruction. Trained facilitators should plan on communication strategies to stay connected with families about students' progress on the SDLMI (see Figure 3.5 for an example of the SDLMI

What Does Self-Determination Look Like in My Life?

Directions:
For each setting, fill out with your ideas. There are no right or wrong answers!

Setting	Self-determined actions *What are ways that you engage with self-determined actions in your life?*	Barriers *What barriers are keeping you from engaging with self-determined actions?*	Supports/ Opportunities *What supports and opportunities might help you overcome the barriers?*
At home	Ask my family about the different chores that need to be done around the house.	Sometimes, my siblings don't do the chores they are supposed to do. This feels unfair if I am the only one doing my chores.	Make a house-chore chart with my siblings and support each other to exchange chores when we need to.
At school	Ask my math teacher to give me resources to help me understand the problems on an assignment.	I get confused about which resources might be truly helpful to me, especially when there are several.	Ask the teacher to walk me through the resources so I can focus on the one that will help me the most.
At work	Monitor my progress toward completing the things I need to do.	When work gets too busy, it is hard to remember everything I am supposed to be doing.	Ask for tips to stay calm and organized from an experienced co-worker.
In the community	Join a community-based youth program to find opportunities to advocate for things I care about.	I am a bit nervous because I have never joined a program.	Ask friends to attend an event at the program together.

Figure 3.4. Self-Determined Learning Model of Instruction material for Phase 2 example.

Hello families and supporters!

This week, students are learning about the Self-Determined Learning Model of Instruction (SDLMI) and the roles that teachers and students play in using the SDLMI.

What is SDLMI?
Instructional model that provides supports and opportunities for students to set and go after goals that align with students' values, strengths, preferences, and interests. Students:
* Make **choices** and **decisions** about setting a goal
* Develop action **plans** for goals
* **Self-monitor** and **self-evaluate** progress toward goals
* **Adjust** the goal or plan

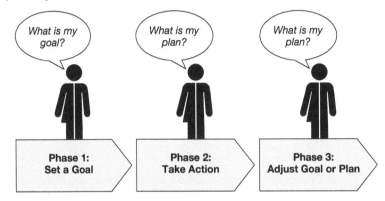

What types of goals do students set?
Students are encouraged to set **a short-term goal** that they can work toward within a semester or an academic year.
Goal areas are related to the transition domains:
* Inclusive postsecondary education
* Integrated community-based employment
* Inclusive community participation

What roles do students and teachers take?

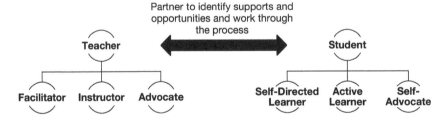

What can families and supporters do to support student self-determination at home and in the community?
* Ask what they are learning with the SDLMI.
* Talk about what setting a goal means in your family.
* Think about what these student roles look like within the family environment.

Please share your ideas, suggestions, and concerns to make the self-determined learning process more meaningful to all of us.

Figure 3.5. Self-Determined Learning Model of Instruction Family–School Communication Tool example.

family–school communication tool) and offer ways for families to provide feedback on students' progress using the family's preferred means of communication. It is equally important to modify communication strategies and frequency (e.g., daily, weekly, each SDLMI phase) based on students' and families' learning needs and preferences.

Reflection

Think back to Mikie's story presented at the beginning of the chapter. What inequitable systems interfered with her developing self-determination as a young adult? How could educators have worked with Mikie to facilitate self-determined actions in culturally sustaining ways that would help her become a causal agent in her life, navigating structural barriers and leading the adult life that she envisioned (e.g., working in a bakery, having a romantic relationship)?

WRAP-UP: SUPPORTING SELF-DETERMINATION

In summary, transition is a critical period for students with disabilities to learn, enhance, and practice knowledge, skills, beliefs, and actions so that they can be causal agents for their lives and work toward inclusive postsecondary pathways (e.g., education, career, community participation). It is important to start self-determination instruction early and to continue to support self-determination throughout the transition to adulthood. School professionals can leverage these opportunities and collaborate with students, families, other school professionals, and people in the community to tap into their strengths, assets, and personal and previous experiences to co-create culturally responsive and sustaining opportunities and supports for self-determination. When student self-determination is promoted in culturally sustaining ways, students are empowered to act as change agents to navigate opportunities, experiences, and barriers in their environment. Current social justice movements can enable youth to build individual and collective self-determination; they can also amplify opportunities for racially and ethnically marginalized students with disabilities to build abilities, skills, and attitudes associated with self-determination and for allies to recognize and challenge cultural bias. *All* youth can participate in dismantling racist, ableist, and other inequitable systems as they grow in their self-determination abilities, skills, and attitudes.

▶ **Tips for Supporting Self-Determination**

1. **Self-reflect before, during, and after self-determination instruction.** It is important to reflect on your own educational journey and identify privilege and marginalization in your multiple cultural identities to find a commonality with students. In addition, recognize students as significant sources of knowledge and experts in new learning with self-determination instruction.

2. **Plan the self-determination instruction schedule to allow flexibility for students.** Students can engage in each phase of the instruction (i.e., the SDLMI phases) by exploring culturally and linguistically authentic supports (e.g., people in their close community, books, films, music) and opportunities

(e.g., advocating for concerns affecting their school and home communities). School professionals also celebrate students' progress toward their goals based on the measure of success defined by students and families.

3. **Create ways for families to communicate and provide feedback.** Students' progress and feedback can be shared by using the family's preferred means of communication and modifying the communication strategies and frequency of communication (e.g., daily, weekly, each SDLMI phase) based on students' and families' preferences. Remember, some families may feel comfortable sharing feedback and constructive criticism, whereas other families may not feel comfortable directly sharing their suggestions and concerns with school professionals.

KEY RESOURCES: SELF-DETERMINATION

Print Resources

Burke, K. M., Shogren, K. A., Antosh, A. A., LaPlante, T., & Masterson, L. H. (2020). Implementing the SDLMI with students with significant support needs during transition planning. *Career Development and Transition for Exceptional Individuals, 43*(2), 115–121. https://doi.org/10.1177/2165143419887858

Institute on Community Integration. (2019). *Self-determination and supported decision-making for people with intellectual, developmental, and other disabilities.* University of Minnesota. https://ici.umn.edu/products/6sQ344H3QBu8KtJm3ogFlA

Raley, S. K., Burke, K. M., Hagiwara, M., Shogren, K. A., Wehmeyer, M. L., & Kurth, J. A. (2020). The Self-Determined Learning Model of Instruction and students with extensive support needs in inclusive settings. *Intellectual and Developmental Disabilities, 58*(1), 82–90. https://doi.org/10.1352/1934-9556-58.1.82

Raley, S. K., Hagiwara, M., Shogren, K. A., & Matusevich, H. (2022). Empowering transition-age students to use self-determination assessment to lead IEP goal development. *TEACHING Exceptional Children.* https://doi.org/10.1177/00400599 211066914

Shogren, K. A. (2013). *Self-determination and transition planning.* Paul H. Brookes Publishing Co.

Online Resources

I'm Determined

https://www.imdetermined.org/

This website offers tools (e.g., One-Pager, Good Day Plan, Goal Plan) and resources (e.g., videos of student-directed individualized education programs) for youth, educators, and families to engage in self-determination work. These tools are also available as a web app for anyone to access.

Self-Advocates Becoming Empowered (SABE)

http://www.sabeusa.org

SABE is a national organization of self-advocates.

Self-Determination at the University of Kansas

https://selfdetermination.ku.edu/

This website hosts the Self-Determination Inventory System and offers the implementation guides for the Self-Determined Learning Model of Instruction and Self-Determined Career Design Model. This website also shares research findings related to promoting self-determination.

REFERENCES

Aceves, T. C., & Orosco, M. J. (2014). *Culturally responsive teaching* (Document No. IC-2). University of Florida, Collaboration for Effective Educator, Development, Accountability, and Reform Center. http://ceedar.education.ufl.edu/tools/innovation-configurations/

Achola, E. O., & Greene, G. (2016). Person–family centered transition planning: Improving post-school outcomes to culturally diverse youth and families. *Journal of Vocational Rehabilitation, 45*(2), 173–183. https://doi.org/10.3233/JVR-160821

Algozzine, B., Browder, D., Karvonen, M., Test, D. W., & Wood, W. M. (2001). Effects of interventions to promote self-determination for individuals with disabilities. *Review of Educational Research, 71*(2), 219–277. https://doi.org/10.3102/00346543071002219

Alim, H. S., & Paris, D. (2017). What is culturally sustaining pedagogy and why does it matter? In D. Paris & H. S. Alim (Eds.), *Culturally sustaining pedagogies: Teaching and learning for justice in a changing world* (pp. 1–20). Teachers College Press.

Burke, K. M., Raley, S. K., Shogren, K. A., Adam-Mumbardo, C., Uyanik, H., Hagiwara, M., & Behrens, S. (2020). A meta-analysis of interventions to promote self-determination of students with disabilities. *Remedial and Special Education, 41*(3), 176–188. https://doi.org/10.1177/0741932518802274

CAST. (2018). *Universal design for learning guidelines version 2.2.* http://udlguidelines.cast.org

Dean, E. E., Kirby, A. V., Hagiwara, M., Shogren, K. A., Ersan, D. T., & Brown, S. (2021). Family role in the development of self-determination for youth with intellectual and developmental disabilities: A scoping review. *Intellectual and Developmental Disabilities, 59*(4), 315–334. https://doi.org/10.1352/1934-9556-59.4.315

Fallon, L. M., DeFouw, E. R., Berkman, T. S., Cathcart, S. C., O'Keeffe, B. V., & Sugai, G. (2022). Supports to improve academic outcomes with racially and ethnically minoritized youth: A review of research. *Remedial and Special Education, 43*(4), 237–254.

Fritzgerald, A. (2020). *Antiracism and universal design for learning: Building expressways to success.* CAST Professional Publishing.

Gay, G. (2018). *Culturally responsive teaching: Theory, research, and practice.* Teachers College Press.

Hagiwara, M., Shogren, K. A., & Lockman Turner, E. (2021). Examining perceptions about self-determination and people with disabilities: A meta-synthesis. *Journal of Developmental and Physical Disabilities.* https://doi.org/https://doi.org/10.1007/s10882-021-09823-8

Hsieh, B., Achola, E. O., Navarro, O., Reese, L., Keirn, T., Davis, S., & Moreno, J. (2021). Transforming educator practice through a culturally responsive and sustaining pedagogies rubric: Co-construction, implementation, and reflection. In E. Cain-Sanschagrin, R. Filback, & J. Crawford (Eds.), *Cases on academic program redesign for greater racial and social justice* (pp. 191–211). IGI Global.

Mazzotti, V. L., Rowe, D. A., Kwiatek, S., Voggt, A., Chang, W.-H., Fowler, C. H., Poppen, M., Sinclair, J., & Test, D. W. (2021). Secondary transition predictors of postschool success: An update to the research base. *Career Development and Transition for Exceptional Individuals, 44*(1), 47–64. https://doi.org/https://doi.org/10.1177/2165143420959793

National Technical Assistance Center on Transition. (2017). *Evidence-based practices and predictors in secondary transition: What we know and what we still need to know.* https://transitionta.org/wp-content/uploads/docs/EBPP_Exec_Summary_2016_12-13.pdf

Nirje, B. (1969). The normalization principle and its human management implications. In R. B. Kugel & W. Wolfensberger (Eds.), *Changing residential patterns for the mentally retarded*. President's Committee on Mental Retardation.

Nirje, B. (1972). The right to self-determination. In W. Wolfensberger (Ed.), *Normalization: The principle of normalization in human services* (pp. 176–193). National Institute on Mental Retardation.

Paris, D. (2012). Culturally sustaining pedagogy: A needed change in stance, terminology, and practice. *Educational Researcher, 41*(3), 93–97.

Scott, L. A., Thoma, C. A., Gokita, T., Bruno, L., Ruiz, A. B., Brendli, K., Taylor, J. P., & Vitullo, V. (2021). I'm trying to make myself happy: Black students with intellectual and developmental disabilities and families on promoting self-determination during transition. *Inclusion, 9*(3), 170–188. https://doi.org/10.1352/2326-6988-9.3.170

Shogren, K. (2012). Hispanic mothers' perceptions of self-determination. *Research and Practice for Persons with Severe Disabilities, 37*(3), 170–184. https://doi.org/10.2511/027494812804153561

Shogren, K. A., Anderson, M. H., Raley, S. K., & Hagiwara, M. (2020). Exploring the relationship between student and teacher/proxy-respondent scores on the Self-Determination Inventory. *Exceptionality*, 1–14. https://doi.org/10.1080/09362835.2020.1729764

Shogren, K. A., Raley, S. K., Burke, K. M., & Wehmeyer, M. L. (2019). *The Self-Determined Learning Model of Instruction: Teacher's guide*. Kansas University Center on Developmental Disabilities.

Shogren, K. A., Scott, L. A., Hicks, T. A., Raley, S. K., Hagiwara, M., Pace, J. R., Gerasimova, D., Alsaeed, A., & Kiblen, J. C. (2021). Exploring self-determination outcomes of racially and ethnically marginalized students with disabilities in inclusive, general education classrooms. *Inclusion, 9*(3), 189–205. https://doi.org/10.1352/2326-6988-9.3.189

Shogren, K. A., & Ward, M. J. (2018). Promoting and enhancing self-determination to improve the post-school outcomes of people with disabilities. *Journal of Vocational Rehabilitation, 48*(2), 187–196.

Shogren, K. A., & Wehmeyer, M. L. (2017a). Culture and self-determination. In M. L. Wehmeyer, K. A. Shogren, T. D. Little, & S. J. Lopez (Eds.), *Development of self-determination through the life-course* (pp. 159–168). Springer Netherlands. https://doi.org/10.1007/978-94-024-1042-6_12

Shogren, K. A., & Wehmeyer, M. L. (2017b). *Self-Determination Inventory: Student-Report*. Kansas University Center on Developmental Disabilities.

Shogren, K. A., Wehmeyer, M. L., Palmer, S. B., Forber-Pratt, A. J., Little, T. J., & Lopez, S. (2015a). Causal Agency Theory: Reconceptualizing a functional model of self-determination. *Education and Training in Autism and Developmental Disabilities, 50*(3), 251–263. https://doi.org/10.1007/978-94-024-1042-6_5

Shogren, K. A., Wehmeyer, M. L., Palmer, S. B., Rifenbark, G. G., & Little, T. D. (2015b). Relationships between self-determination and postschool outcomes for youth with disabilities. *Journal of Special Education, 53*(4), 30–41. https://doi.org/10.1177/0022466913489733

The National Scientific Council on Adolescence. (2021). *The intersection of adolescent development and anti-Black racism* (Council Report No. 1). https://developingadolescent.org/

Trainor, A. A. (2007). Perceptions of adolescent girls with LD regarding self-determination and postsecondary transition planning. *Learning Disability Quarterly, 30*(1), 31–45. https://doi.org/10.2307/30035514

Wehmeyer, M. L. (2014). Self-determination: A family affair. *Family Relations, 63,* 178–184. https://doi.org/10.1111/fare.12052

Wehmeyer, M. L., Abery, B. H., Zhang, D., Ward, K., Willis, D., Hossain, W. A., Balcazar, F., Ball, A., Bacon, A., & Calkins, C. (2011). Personal self-determination and moderating variables that impact efforts to promote self-determination. *Exceptionality, 19,* 19–30. https://doi.org/10.1080/09362835.2011.537225

Wehmeyer, M. L., & Shogren, K. A. (2017). The development of self-determination during adolescence. In M. L. Wehmeyer, K. A. Shogren, Little, T. D., & Lopez, S. J. (Eds.), *Development of self-determination through the life-course* (pp. 89–98). Dordrecht, The Netherlands: Springer. https://doi.org/10.1007/978-94-024-1042-6_7

Wehmeyer, M. L., Shogren, K. A., Little, T. D., & Lopez, S. J. (2017). Introduction to the self-determination construct. In M. L. Wehmeyer, K. A. Shogren, Little, T. D., & Lopez, S. J. (Eds.), *Development of self-determination through the life-course* (pp. 3–16). Dordrecht, The Netherlands: Springer. https://doi.org/10.1007/978-94-024-1042-6_1

4

Stakeholder Collaboration

Edwin Obilo Achola

DIGGING DEEPER: What Teachers Have to Say

As a Black male educator with a recent immigration history in North America, I have learned over the years to rely on asset-based relational pedagogies to uncover the roots of my difficulties navigating invisible cultural boundaries, particularly when collaborating with transition teams made up of diverse and globally dispersed members. It took me a few years to realize that the collaborative skills I had built over the previous decade in Kenya were not going to transfer easily to North America. Succeeding would depend on taking an entirely novel approach and making ongoing adjustments over an extended period. At the core of the novel approach are culturally sustaining approaches to collaboration.

Time and again, I find that even experienced and globally minded transition professionals struggle with building collaborative relationships, particularly when confronted with tasks involving families, students, and professionals from a vast array of cultural backgrounds and life experiences. Culturally sustaining (Alim & Django, 2017) approaches to collaboration represent asset-based relational models that transition professionals can rely on when serving youth from these communities. The framework reflects the cross-pollination of culturally sustaining pedagogy and universal design for transition (UDT). Specifically, this model honors culturally sustaining pedagogy's commitment to linguistic, literate, and cultural pluralism while also intentionally embedding principles of UDT.

Essential Questions

▶ What considerations should educators keep in mind for culturally sustaining collaborative practices and their alignment with UDT?

▶ How can special and general educators, families (including multigenerational ones), transition specialists, vocational rehabilitation (VR) specialists, faith-based communities, and other stakeholders critically reflect on and respond to cultural nuances during the transition process?

▶ What valuable information can families provide that educators will need in order to plan effectively for a student's transition?

▶ What barriers should educators be aware of that present challenges for implementing culturally sustaining collaborative practices?

This chapter begins with an overview of the purpose of collaborative service delivery models in transition planning, as well as their shortcomings. Next, we illustrate the need for culturally sustaining collaborative practices through the case studies of two students from different backgrounds—a young Cambodian-American woman and a young man of Kenyan and Scottish heritage. Their families have different aspirations for their children, different support needs, and different resources to turn to in their community; a culturally sustaining approach to collaboration is crucial to support these students and families effectively. The chapter then describes culturally sustaining collaborative approaches (CSCAs) to UDT in depth and explores the existing barriers to implementing CSCAs to UDT. It concludes by presenting possibilities for improving educational practices in this area.

COLLABORATIVE PRACTICE AS A SERVICE DELIVERY MODEL

Scholars have devoted a great deal of attention to collaborative service delivery models during transition planning, based on the assumption that these models will translate into positive postsecondary outcomes for students with disabilities. Specifically, scholars have identified that interagency collaboration as a service delivery model is an evidence-based predictor of improved education and employment outcomes for students with disabilities (Repetto et al., 2002; Test et al., 2009), and consider it a substantiated transition practice (Landmark et al., 2010; Lee & Carter, 2012). Interagency collaboration is commonly defined as the process by which professionals from different agencies and/or organizations try to work constructively together to positively impact children and families (Cooper et al., 2016).

Such collaborative service delivery models are intended to provide direct support to students and families, including support in accessing community resources necessary for youth with disabilities to be successful in postschool life (Blalock et al., 2003; Lehman et al., 2002). In addition, the reauthorized Workforce Innovation and Opportunity Act (WIOA, 2014) requires that transition stakeholders collaborate to develop strategies that will support the transition of youth with disabilities into the world of work, with 15% of funds dedicated to providing youth with preemployment transition services (Plotner et al., 2018).

In practice, however, collaborative service models have often fallen short of expectations, in part because of the compliance-driven approach favored by school-based transition personnel. Indeed, the Individuals with Disabilities Education Improvement Act (IDEA) of 2004 requires that schools "invite to the IEP [individualized education program] meeting a representative of any participating agency that is likely to be responsible for providing or paying for transition services" (34 CFR § 300.321 [b][3]). Unfortunately, in many school districts, this compliance-driven approach to collaboration has been described as exhausting and inefficient at best, and ineffective and anticollaborative at worst (Povenmire-Kirk et al., 2015). Povenmire-Kirk et al. further asserted that transition educators often contact only those agencies with which they are familiar and that they believe are likely to attend. When stakeholders are motivated primarily by the desire to remain in compliance with IDEA (2004), additional challenges can emerge, such as a lack of clarity regarding the roles of stakeholders (Shogren & Plotner, 2012), limited information on what factors contribute to enhanced partnerships, and poor communication.

The consequences of failing to collaborate effectively with key stakeholders can be profound. One likely result is abysmal transition outcomes for youth, especially those who live in traditionally marginalized communities. In addition, the lack of effective models of interagency collaboration may prevent schools from closing persistent opportunity gaps in transition planning. Consequently, in identifying the limitations and promise of collaborative service delivery models, particularly in the context of equity in transition planning, it is most useful to examine the intersections of collaboration, culturally responsive and sustaining pedagogy, and UDT. The case studies of Ana and Otieno, who have very diverse life experiences, will provide an opportunity to examine these intersections.

CASE STUDY: Ana

Looking to Family, Extended Family, and Community for Support

Meet Ana Chaya, a 15-year-old Cambodian-American girl who loves the visual and performing arts and spending time with her friends and family. Whereas Ana's stepfather was born and raised in southern California, her mother moved from Cambodia as an adult 17 years ago and has been living in Long Beach, California. Ana is currently in tenth grade and has a mild intellectual disability characterized by limitations in both intellectual functioning and adaptive behavior. Overall, managing Ana's care and education has been her stepfather's task. Ana's mother says (referring to herself) that she "makes decisions for the family but he does all the work." In addition, Ana's older sister and brother assume caregiving roles, especially when the parents are at work or out of town. Furthermore, Ana's extended family, including members of her faith community, live nearby and often provide support in a variety of ways, including picking her up from school. On occasion, Ana's aunt accompanies Ana's mother to individualized education program meetings. The family's support has been critical given the parents' busy work schedule: Ana's stepfather is an engineer at Boeing, and her mother is a critical care nurse. Ana's parents strongly believe in retaining their Cambodian identity while giving their children an opportunity to thrive in mainstream America. As a result, her parents often travel with the whole family to Cambodia on vacation, and they prefer to speak Khmer at home, even though every family member is fluent in both Khmer and English. In addition, Ana's parents have invested many resources to enable their children to gain access to the dominant American culture.

At the time of Ana's diagnosis, her parents had no prior experience caring for a child with disabilities. As a result, they had a difficult time accepting and responding to their daughter's condition. Furthermore, they (especially Ana's mother) struggled with feelings of shame and wondered whether friends and other members of the community would blame them for Ana's condition. What made it even more difficult for Ana's parents to accept her disability was that much of the terminology used by American teachers and medical professionals was new to them and did not align with what Ana's mother knew in Cambodia; moreover, because neither of them had any prior experience with the education of a child with a disability, they were unfamiliar with the special education system in the United States.

CASE STUDY: Otieno

Preparing for Adult Life in the United States and in Kenya

Next, meet Otieno Gor, a Kenyan-born 14-year-old multiracial boy who has a White father from Kenya and a Black mother from Scotland. Otieno's parents (Mr. and Mrs. Gor) met 18 years ago and moved to the United States as international students. After graduating from a university in Pennsylvania, the Gors moved to California and have remained undocumented (their student visas lapsed). Because of their undocumented status, Mr. and Mrs. Gor have had to work "under the table" running their own business in their community. A recent interview with the transition specialist revealed a number of aspirational, linguistic, familial, navigational, and resistant cultural assets (a form of cultural capital) relevant to Otieno's postschool goals. For example, his parents expressed an interest in supporting their son's racial socialization in preparation for his entry into the adult world. Racial socialization, often interpreted as the privilege and responsibility of raising children with culturally appropriate values, principles, and consciousness that prepare them to one day take on adult roles in society, is a process that is highly regarded among Kenyan immigrants.

Mr. and Mrs. Gor reported that they have access to a wide network of friends who are ready to offer Otieno employment opportunities, transportation, and other transition supports. All members of the family speak multiple languages and use a variety of communication skills—skills required for economic self-sufficiency in communities with large populations of immigrants.

Presently, Otieno attends a general education classroom full time, but he has had a long history of academic and behavioral challenges at school. After multiple prereferral interventions, Otieno was referred to be assessed for special education services. With consent from his mother, the school psychologist assessed Otieno and determined that he does, in fact, have an autism spectrum disorder, a diagnosis supported by evaluations from Otieno's pediatrician.

For Otieno's parents, this diagnosis has come as both a relief and a source of anxiety. On the one hand, it has given Mr. and Mrs. Gor a logical explanation for their son's struggles, confirming their belief that something was different about him. On the other hand, it has contributed to the palpable, overwhelming sense of anxiety they feel about Otieno's future: Mr. and Mrs. Gor plan to move to Kenya eventually, and they constantly worry that Otieno might not be able to assume his responsibilities as their oldest son and succeed in America, let alone adjust to life in Kenya. As with many immigrant families in the United States, Mr. and Mrs. Gor do not have blood relatives in the country, although they are well connected to members of their faith community—in the Gors' case, the Muslim community in Long Beach, California.

CULTURALLY SUSTAINING COLLABORATIVE APPROACHES AND UDT: OVERLAPPING FRAMEWORKS

Equitable access to learning for all students remains the central aim of CSCAs to UDT. In order to discuss the concept of CSCAs, first it is necessary to outline how universal design for learning (UDL) and UDT set the foundation for this approach. As stated previously, there is a great deal of overlap between UDL and UDT. Not only do the two frameworks share a principle of creating inclusive spaces for all people, but UDT is, in fact, based on UDL (Rose & Meyer, 2002). UDL focuses on addressing the academic needs of all students, using three characteristics: 1) multiple means of engagement, 2) multiple means of representation, and 3) multiple means of action and expression. To these characteristics, UDT adds the application to transition services for students with disabilities by blending academics and transition goals (Thoma et al., 2009). In doing so, UDT infuses the core elements of the transition planning process into academic lessons, including goal setting, assessments, and skill development, among others.

Similarly, CSCAs underscore pedagogical practices aimed at creating inclusive collaborative spaces for all young adults with disabilities. CSCAs also borrow from other core UDT principles (e.g., academic success) and emphasize cultural competence, critical consciousness, cultural pluralism, and asset-based approaches that are designed to promote the preservation of valued heritages from all communities. Table 4.1 illustrates the overlap between UDL, UDT, and CSCAs.

Within the field of transition planning, CSCAs have emerged from a long history of successful culture-centered teaching and learning practices anchored in the Ladson-Billings conception of culturally responsive pedagogy, which revolves around teaching that focuses on advancing student learning, developing cultural competence, and fostering critical consciousness (Ladson-Billings, 2021). To clarify, much like CRP, CSCAs foster the establishment of cooperative networks that allow learners of all backgrounds to learn how to negotiate both the academic and nonacademic demands of high school while demonstrating cultural competence. In this way, transition collaborators establish systems that allow learners to maintain their

Table 4.1.　Intersections of universal design for learning, universal design for transition, and culturally sustaining collaborative approaches

	UDL	UDT	CSCAs
1	Meet the academic needs of all students: All educators are required to understand their students' strengths and needs to provide learning opportunities for all (CAST, 2018).	Meet the academic and transition needs (blended approach): Remove instructional barriers and promote universal access to education pathway used to connect academic content and transition planning	Focuses on meeting both academic and nonacademic needs and highlights (a) preservation of heritage practices, (b) access to mainstream culture, (c) cultural pluralism, and (d) cultural competence
2	Multiple means of representation	Multiple life domains, multiple means of assessment, student self-determination, and multiple resources and perspectives for transition	Multiple adult outcomes
3	Multiple means of expression		Multiple transition pathways and processes: Indigenous and mainstream transition processes
4	Multiple means of engagement		Multiple stakeholders Asset-based assessments from multiple sources

Key: CSCAs, culturally sustaining collaborative approaches; UDL, universal design for learning; UDT, universal design for transition.

cultural integrity while accomplishing their postschool goals. For example, in applying CSCAs, the transition team supporting Otieno did the following (illustrated in Table 4.2):

- Established a community of collaborators, consisting of school-based transition personnel, adult service providers, leaders from his faith community, and members of his immediate and extended family

- Identified the cultural assets available within the family, student, and community

- Outlined both academic and nonacademic goals that have implications for postschool success

- Identified transition supports that address cultural competence and critical consciousness as well as preserve valued family heritage

Fostering Critical Consciousness

With their commitment to fostering critical consciousness, CSCAs call on transition practitioners to collaborate with individuals from a variety of backgrounds to prepare young adults to recognize and analyze systems of inequality and commit to taking

Table 4.2. Culturally sustaining collaborative approaches action steps for Oteino

CSCA step	Example	Action step and transition support
Establish a community of collaborators.	Special education teacher, administrator, school counselor, cultural liaison (paraprofessional), parents, siblings, representative from DACA legal services, Otieno's imam	Use a person- or family-centered approach as the primary collaborative framework. Address power dynamics that might impede the participation of some team members. Use multiple methods of engagement to facilitate the participation of all team members.
Identify cultural assets.	A wide network of friends ready to offer employment opportunities, transportation, and other transition supports Family aspirations about racial socialization Otieno's ability to speak multiple languages	Invite friends to participate. Address racial socialization as a transition goal. Recommend an ethnic studies course. Explore ideal career opportunities for multilingual individuals.
Outline both academic and nonacademic goals.	Otieno needs to pass Algebra 2. Otieno displays challenging behavior. Otieno is not documented. Otieno's family worries about racial socialization. Otieno's family would like to preserve their native language.	Translate all academic and nonacademic needs into annual transition goals. Identify on- and off-campus opportunities for Otieno to meet his transition goals. Ensure that all transition activities are research/evidence based as well as culturally responsive and sustaining. Ensure that all team members are involved in supporting Otieno in meeting his transition goals. Connect Otieno with DACA resources.

Key: CSCA, culturally sustaining collaborative approach; DACA, Deferred Action for Childhood Arrivals.

action against these systems. Research has shown that critical consciousness can be a gateway to academic motivation and achievement for marginalized students (El-Amin et al., 2017). Other scholars have noted that critical consciousness not only expands young people's commitment to challenging pervasive injustice (Ginwright, 2010; Watts et al., 2011) but also increases academic engagement (Carter, 2008; O'Connor, 1997). More important, critical consciousness about racism, in particular, has the potential to motivate Black students to persist in school and achieve in academics as a way to resist oppressive forces (Carter, 2008). Nonetheless, transition practitioners must not assume that learners are incapable of perceiving social inequities or that they are helpless in responding to such challenges. Whereas some young adults might pay little attention to social inequities in their communities, many others are attuned to the wide array of unjust structural forces operating in society and in their schools. Transition practitioners seeking to increase students' postschool success must directly address these relevant social forces by collaborating with knowledgeable partner agencies (e.g., antidiscrimination committees, civil liberties unions, Black Lives Matter) to 1) teach the language of inequality so that young adults with disabilities can better communicate and explain what they notice, 2) create space to examine inequality in the key transition domains (e.g., employment, education, and adult

Table 4.3. Critical consciousness action steps for Ana

Critical consciousness step	Action steps and transition supports
Teach the language of inequality.	Used direct instruction, creating lesson plans that included language of inequality
Create space to examine inequality in the key transition domains.	Showed all students historical and contemporary examples of resistance Invited guest speakers from multiple agencies to talk about identity and oppression as well as positive role models from similar backgrounds throughout history to provide relatable examples of resistance
Teach students how to take action.	Taught component skills linked to culturally congruent self-determination (e.g., self-advocacy, self-awareness) Created service-learning assignments that included group advocacy

living) and the myriad forces that sustain it, and 3) teach students how to take action. Table 4.3 illustrates how Ana's transition team addressed critical consciousness.

Establishing Multigenerational Networks

In addition, CSCAs emphasize the need to sustain cultural ways of being in communities of color by establishing multigenerational networks. Transition practitioners employing CSCAs use multigenerational collaborative networks to identify and preserve valued cultural heritages while providing access to the dominant culture. In doing so, the transition teams ensure postschool success in a pluralistic environment. In Ana's case, it was clear that her family was interested in preserving their native language and their Cambodian identity while giving their children an opportunity to thrive in mainstream America. With this in mind, the team took the following steps:

1. They set up a collaborative team composed of older and younger members of the family and other school-based partners.

2. They learned more about the elements of the family's Cambodian heritage and future aspirations that they would like to preserve.

3. They linked mainstream transition goals to the family's cultural heritage.

4. They identified and utilized school-based and community partners who were skilled at supporting Ana's goals.

5. They learned more about indigenous Cambodian transition practices that could be incorporated into the school-based transition process.

6. They developed and implemented a transition process that blended mainstream and nonmainstream practices and goals.

The benefits of CSCAs in transition are not limited to the success of students from multiple marginalized communities who have disabilities. Rather, just as with UDT, CSCAs support the success of young adults from a wide array of backgrounds, including those with multiple privileged identities. In particular, CSCAs' focus on learners from different backgrounds having access to cultural capital from a wide range of communities.

BARRIERS TO CHANGE

Calling on transition stakeholders to change current practices requires not only a deep understanding of the mechanisms by which CSCAs function but also consideration for the individual, organizational, and environmental barriers to these changes. These barriers include the following:

- Foremost, a perspective that is overly focused on school activities and on perceived deficits

- A lack of responsiveness to family values and cultural values, with these funds of knowledge being overlooked

- The difficulty and complexity of implementing culture-centered collaborative approaches

- Barriers at the system level

A School-Centric, Deficit-Oriented Perspective

The school-centric, deficit-oriented conception of collaborative practices presents perhaps one of the most persistent barriers. Many efforts initiated by schools to collaborate with families end up privileging school-centric activities, with little attention paid to nontraditional forms of collaboration that may occur outside of school walls (Lareau, 2000; Lawson, 2003). In fact, educators often prefer forms of collaborative relationships in which they join with school staff to define and delineate the ways in which families and other stakeholders can and should participate in the transition process (Lawson, 2003). For example, educators are more attuned to collaborating with individuals who represent institutions (e.g., general educators, transition specialists, and VR specialists) and are less likely to engage faith-based communities or members of multigenerational families (e.g., godparents and siblings) during the transition process. In addition, teachers do not often work with professionals outside of their staff to coordinate transition services as often as VR coordinators do (Shogren & Plotner, 2012).

It is important to note that many young adults from traditionally marginalized communities tend to have strong ties with faith communities. Collaborative relationships with such groups may allow for social–education capital exchange between school professionals and leaders in the community, increased opportunities for collective advocacy on behalf of youth, and opportunities to hire transition professionals with deeper cultural connections to students (from the community).

School-centric, deficit-oriented conceptions are perhaps anchored in two flawed assumptions:

1. That transitioning to adulthood begins at school and must be directed by school-based transition personnel and adult agency professionals

2. That transition planning is a formal process conducted primarily within institutional and legal boundaries applicable to all young adults regardless of their cultural backgrounds

The truth is that the process of preparing young adults to transition into adulthood exists in every community. There also exists a diverse—and unequal—spectrum of pathways into adulthood and resulting outcomes. In many nonmainstream communities, transitioning is an informal process frequently directed by trusted family and community members, which generally begins before the young adult turns 16 (the age mandated in IDEA 2004). Often, the transition process in nonmainstream communities begins at the onset of puberty—a time when youth encounter new relationships, privileges, responsibilities, and resources. Many young adults assume adult responsibilities early in life, such as working to support family and caring for siblings, and they learn about "adulting" through interactions with trusted family and community members, including leaders from faith communities. In some families, the transition process is initiated through a rite of passage ceremony, such as a quinceañera, whereas in others, young people transition into adult roles in response to the family's economic conditions or personal circumstances, such as pregnancy.

Scholars have long argued that flawed school-centric, deficit-oriented conceptions might be influenced by educators' perceptions regarding the student's and family's race, ethnicity, social class, and other markers of identity. For example, transition practitioners might adopt a deficit posture when they work with Latine families, based on the erroneous assumption that ethnically diverse families possess few transition-related resources when they enter school. In this case, the practitioners might treat Latine families primarily as recipients of supports rather than partners with assets to contribute. Similarly, the Latine family's response to efforts to initiate collaborative relationships might be influenced by their perceptions of and lived experiences with people in power. For instance, parents of color who have personally experienced educational inequality linked to race may be especially mindful of teachers' potentially negative expectations of their children's abilities, monitoring and intervening to shield their children from racial discrimination in schools (Cooper, 2003; Howard & Reynolds, 2008).

A Lack of Responsiveness to Family and Cultural Values

Unsurprisingly, recent evidence continues to show that existing service models are not always responsive to family or cultural values, creating barriers for many families of color who are trying to prepare their youth for transition (Povenmire-Kirk et al., 2015). For example, the student and family funds of knowledge (Moll, 1992) and community cultural wealth (Yosso, 2005) possessed by families of color are often ignored or devalued within educational institutions dominated by White, middle-class values and norms (Posey-Maddox & Haley-Lock, 2020). School-centric models of collaboration, operating under terms and conditions set by teachers and school staff, implicitly devalue students' and families' funds of knowledge and cultural wealth. Educators working with Otieno, for example, might fail to identify his cultural assets, such as his multilingualism, his connection to a wide network of individuals, and his aspirations for racial socialization, in part because the school-based teams rarely involve cultural brokers from the community.

Even worse, educators might perceive these cultural assets as deficits and consequently fail to identify future employment, education, and adult living opportunities linked to them. For instance, they might ignore the possibility that Otieno's ability to speak multiple languages could provide him with an advantage with employment opportunities that require such a skill. Educators implementing CSCAs, however, would create both postschool and annual employment goals that reflect multilingualism as a strength while still identifying opportunities available to monolingual youth.

The Complexity of Culture-Centered Collaborative Approaches

A final barrier to implementing culture-centered collaborative approaches such as CSCAs is the potentially arduous and complex nature of the task for transition professionals who lack the requisite training and work in communities different from their own. This is especially true for professionals who may be perceived as disconnected from the communities in which their students live and who may struggle to demonstrate attunement, authenticity, and power-sharing abilities with young adults and their families.

Attunement refers to the practitioner's ability to understand the varying lived experiences of students and families, through which practitioners can incorporate multiple perspectives, including nondominant ones. Attunement requires the practitioner to possess a level of cultural competency, especially when they step out of their own sociocultural identity. For example, a transition specialist who is less familiar with the daily realities of undocumented immigrant families like Otieno's may fail to identify and incorporate employment assets (e.g., entrepreneurships) available within such families and would instead focus on lack of documentation as a barrier to planning for employment. In doing so, the transition specialists not only demonstrate a lack of attunement, but also advance a deficit approach to transition planning.

Authenticity, on the other hand, is anchored in the assumption that practitioners can self-reflect, acknowledging that they themselves are cultural beings with biases and privileges. This allows families to see the practitioner as a human being attempting to do their best but who is bound to make decisions clouded by their limited worldviews. Authenticity further allows for dialogue to take place in a safe environment, because families can maintain their roles as valued members of the transition planning team. Table 4.4 illustrates attunement, authenticity, and power sharing.

Transition stakeholders are also called on to create a psychologically safe environment by recognizing power dynamics among all partners in the planning process and to redistribute power to allow all team members to contribute meaningfully. Practitioners must be aware of stakeholders who monopolize discussions and shift power to other participants either directly or indirectly. Sharing power during collaborative meetings allows educators to distribute time evenly among varying perspectives.

Lastly, many transition professionals have a limited understanding of the cultural subtleties that define how families in nonmainstream communities collaborate, such as a commitment to interdependence, an emphasis on emotional attachment, a relaxed attitude to certain social hierarchies, an attachment to faith communities, and the use of informal sources of information and natural supports. For example, Harry et al. (1999) asserted that culturally diverse parents are more comfortable using informal sources of information through personalized connections and conversational language. Similarly, natural supports, such as occasional check-ins by family members, assist students in acquiring and maintaining competitive employment (Carter et al., 2009; Frank & Sitlington, 2000).

System-Level Barriers

Many scholars have conceptualized schools as the center of a larger ecology, embedded within complex social contexts that intersect with the surrounding cultural, legal, and physical environments (Bronfenbrenner, 2005; Bryk et al., 2010). According to this perspective, the lack of CSCAs in schools is the product of an interplay

Table 4.4.   Indicators of attunement, authenticity, and power sharing

	Otieno	Ana
1. Attunement	In discussing adult living goals, a transition specialist includes a long-term goal focused on racial socialization and incorporates community-based resources (e.g., immigration advocates network) to support the achievement of the goal.	The transition specialist is aware of Ana's family history of marginalization and oppression and directs members of her ITP team to consider family history and thus begin the learning process.
2. Authenticity	The transition specialists who come from a different cultural community share their limited understanding of the cultural nuances of Otieno's community.	During Ana's ITP meeting, the transition specialist verbally states, "I have certain lived experiences that shape my worldview, so it is important for us to hear many perspectives."
3. Power sharing	The special education teacher leading Otieno's ITP meeting provides an alternative view of culturally sustaining transition activities, especially if no one in the meeting presents this perspective.	The special education teacher leading Ana's ITP meeting uses their own power to evenly distribute speaking time to varying perspectives.

Key: ITP, individual transition plan.

among several subsystems, such as the legal and policy frameworks at play (e.g., IDEA 2004); the characteristics of practitioners, schools, and students' families; and students' cultural context. These subsystems interact and influence each other reciprocally (Benbenishty & Astor, 2005) in ways that may negatively impact transition practitioners' ability to implement CSCAs. For example, the current legal framework (e.g., IDEA 2004) might encourage the use of potentially problematic mainstream approaches to family engagement, wherein decisions about children's education are centered on parents' choices. In particular, IDEA requires parental consent before the initial provision of special education and related services to children; in many families, however, parents play a peripheral role in making educational decisions regarding their children with a disability. In Ana's household, for example, decisions about her education are made by her mother and her mothers' sisters. If the school obtained consent from Ana's father without seeking input from Ana's mother and sisters, this could create a rift between Ana's life at home and life at school, even though the practitioner would be acting lawfully in obtaining consent solely from Ana's father. Educators must take on the work of addressing the rift between students' home and school lives because this reflects the structural inequities plaguing many urban schools (Ayers, 2014).

A child's life experiences at home and at school represent cultural contexts that are essential to postschool success. Consequently, educators must seek to build connections between and among these two critical spaces—home and school—that youth depend on. Unfortunately, the legal framework on which transition planning is built may hinder such connections, in part because the framework adopts an approach in which race and culture are not acknowledged. Merely ignoring race and culture serves to perpetuate and center White, mainstream worldviews that may conflict with some nonmainstream norms, with a readily noticeable impact on minoritized youth. For example, IDEA (2004) requires that schools begin providing transition services during the school year in which a child turns 16, highlighting employment, education, and independent living. Yet, for many young adults, the transition process often begins outside school at an age much younger than 16 and encompasses other priorities. In the case of Otieno, for example, he started to become an adult when he turned 13, at the onset of puberty: His parents began to assign him adult responsibilities, such as working at the family business after school, caring for his younger siblings who were taking virtual classes at home, helping his parents navigate institutional knowledge about how public schools work, and leading sermons as a youth leader in the local mosque. In addition, Otieno is expected to learn about navigating life as a young Black Muslim man living without documentation in the United States and to explore postschool training options that will prepare him to thrive in the family business. Some of his parents' concerns include the potential for discrimination based on his multiple marginalized identities and the need to ensure that Otieno is successful both in his immediate cultural environment and in the mainstream American context.

Clearly, IDEA's mandate does little to bridge the gaps between the cultural contexts of home and school. First, the age requirement ignores the fact the Otieno began his transition into adulthood much earlier in life. Consequently, educators working with him are less likely to build on the transition opportunities from which he has already benefited. Second, the heightened focus on postschool employment, education, and independent living likely overlooks other transition priorities that are closely tied to Otieno's identity and culture. For example, as a firstborn son, Otieno is expected to preserve the family business and pass it along to future generations—a priority educators are unlikely to incorporate into discussions of his transition to postschool employment. In addition, a culture- and race-neutral approach may fail to highlight the employment opportunities and challenges for a young Black Muslim youth such as Otieno. Educators may also ignore the opportunities available to Otieno as an interdependent member of his community, especially if they focus exclusively on preparing him to be independent, as defined in mainstream communities.

PRACTICE POSSIBILITIES

CSCAs are learned and, like learning in general, require training and support from all stakeholders, including the institutional infrastructure required to establish and sustain long-term change, such as supportive policies and administrative support. Moreover, CSCAs are sequential processes that take time, passing through a series of stages of development. Therefore, stakeholders should not expect their initial efforts at implementing CSCAs to be ideal. With that in mind, the following suggestions for stakeholders to enhance their capacities, complementing those covered previously in this chapter, are offered.

All stakeholders must be cognizant of how mainstream race-evasive attitudes manifest themselves in institutional practices, relational behaviors, and policies. This will allow stakeholders to 1) draw attention to potentially problematic practices, behaviors, and policies; 2) develop equity-oriented solutions; and 3) monitor their progress toward effectively implementing CSCAs. For example, an institutional practice that requires outside agencies to be invited to transition planning meetings may be based on the assumption that, to be successful, all young adults with disabilities must depend on different agencies throughout their postschool lives. Whereas this may be true for many young adults from White, middle-income families, youth from diverse communities tend to rely more on the network of family members, who often serve as lifelong support systems. All stakeholders collaborating with families are expected to assume the role of an *ally:* "a person who is a member of the dominant or majority group who works to end oppression in his or her personal and professional life through support of, and as an advocate for, the oppressed population" (Washington & Evans, 1991, p. 195). Thus, the related term *allyship* reflects the adoption and expression or performance of an ally identity by a member of a dominant group (Anzaldua, 2000).

Finally, although it may sound appealing to focus on micro-level changes, such as those that take place within a class, it is the systemic, multidirectional changes that are most desirable. Micro-level changes may not persist over time, in part because they often depend on a few committed individuals and are rarely codified in institutional policies and practices.

Reflection

What does it mean to collaborate with a student's family and community in a way that is culturally sustaining? Why is it crucial for educators to make a conscious effort to do this—and to be aware of barriers they will likely encounter in trying to implement CSCAs to UDT?

Culturally sustaining collaborative relationships between families, communities, and transition professionals are anchored asset-based approaches that affirm and respect the sociocultural realities of all students. Such collaborative efforts use students' and family's cultural knowledge, prior experiences, and frames of reference as the basis on which to establish effective relationships. More important, the professionals who establish culturally sustaining relationships view schools as places where the cultural ways of being in communities of color are sustained rather than eradicated. In doing so, the professionals avoid assimilative practices (collaborative practices aimed at transmitting the dominant culture) that are often counterproductive and harmful to students and families. The effects of the assimilative practices include loss of identity, homesickness, and even mental illness.

WRAP-UP: CULTURALLY SUSTAINING, COLLABORATIVE APPROACHES TO UDT

In sum, CSCAs to UDT seek to foster student success in transition planning by taking into account equity considerations that are often missing in "business-as-usual" transition programs. As with other culturally responsive approaches, CSCAs likely benefit students from marginalized backgrounds as well as their peers from dominant communities. In other words, CSCAs are not pedagogical practices reserved just for Black and youth from other underrepresented minority groups. Rather, they represent universal practices and attitudes that foster equitable transition outcomes for all students with disabilities. To achieve this aim, CSCAs 1) highlight cultural assets relevant to postschool outcomes, 2) cross-pollinate culturally sustaining pedagogy principles and UDT, 3) bridge the gap between home and school cultures, 4) foreground indigenous transition processes that already exist within families and communities, and 5) emphasize equity-oriented practitioner attitudes and skills (e.g., attunement, authenticity, power sharing).

▶ **Tips for Collaborating in a Culturally Sustaining Way**

1. **Take time to learn about resources and supports that exist in different communities.** Remember, government agencies are not the only valuable source of support for students transitioning into adulthood. Think about the supports that Ana and Otieno and their families relied on. What similar resources might exist within the communities to which your students belong, such as cultural or faith communities?

2. **Practitioners should use their privileges linked to their dominant identities to support families and young adults with disabilities.** The stakeholders should also engage in thoughtful dialogues about privilege with people of other backgrounds and self-reflect to understand privilege.

3. **Attentive stakeholders should identify such race-neutral practices and incorporate an equity-oriented approach that involves outside agencies and family members, especially siblings of youth with disabilities.** Recognizing the cultural context of sibling relationships throughout the life cycle gives practitioners a broader perspective for understanding individual needs (Watson & McGoldrick, 2011).

REFERENCES

Alim, S. H., & Django P. (Eds.). (2017). *Culturally sustaining pedagogies: Teaching and learning for justice in a changing world.* Teachers College Press.

Anzaldua, G. E. (2000). Allies. In M. Adams, W. J. Blumenfeld, R. Castaneda, H. W. Hackman, M. L. Peters, & X. Zuniga (Eds.), *Readings for diversity and social justice* (pp. 475–477). Routledge.

Ayers. (2014). Critical discomfort and deep engagement needed for transformation. *Democracy & Education, 22*(2).

Benbenishty, R., & Astor, R. A. (2005). *School victimization embedded in context: Culture, neighborhood, family, school and gender.* Oxford University Press.

Blalock, G., Kochhar-Bryant, C. A., Test, D. W., Kohler, P., White, W., Lehmann, J., Bassett, D., & Patton, J. (2003). The need for comprehensive personnel preparation in transition and career development: A position statement of the division on career development and transition. *Career Development and Transition for Exceptional Individuals, 26,* 207–226.

Bronfenbrenner, U. (Ed.). (2005). *Making human beings human: Bioecological perspectives on human development.* SAGE.

Bryk, A. S., Sebring, P. B., Allensworth, E., Easton, J. Q., & Luppescu, S. (2010). *Organizing schools for improvement: Lessons from Chicago.* University of Chicago Press.

Carter, D. J. (2008). Cultivating a critical race consciousness for African-American school success. *Educational Foundations, 22*(1–2), 11–28.

Carter, E. W., Swedeen, B., & Trainor, A. A. (2009). The other three months: Connecting transition-age youth with disabilities to meaningful summer experiences. *TEACHING Exceptional Children, 41*(6), 18–26.

CAST. (2018). *Universal design for learning guidelines version 2.2.* http://udlguidelines.cast.org

Cooper C. (2003). The detrimental impact of teacher bias: Lessons learned from the standpoint of African American mothers. *Teacher Education Quarterly, 30,* 101–116.

Cooper, M., Evans, Y., & Pybis, J. (2016). Interagency collaboration in children and young people's mental health: A systematic review of outcomes, facilitating factors and inhibiting factors. *Child: Care, Health and Development, 42*(3), 325–342. https://doi.org/10.1111/cch.12322

El-Amin, A., Seider, S., Graves, D., Tamerat, J., Clark, S., Soutter, M., Johannsen, J., & Malhotra, S. (2017). Critical consciousness: A key to student achievement. *Phi Delta Kappan, 98*(5), 18–23. https://doi.org/10.1177/0031721717690360

Frank, A. R., & Sitlington, P. L. (2000). Young adults with mental disabilities-does transition planning make a difference? *Education and Training in Mental Retardation and Developmental Disabilities, 35,* 119–134.

Ginwright, S. (2010). *Black youth rising: Activism and racial healing in urban America.* Teachers College Press.

Harry, B., Rueda, R., & Kalyanpur, M. (1999). Cultural reciprocity in sociocultural perspective: Adapting the normalization principle for family collaboration. *Exceptional Children, 66*(1):123–136. https://doi.org/10.1177/001440299906600108

Howard, T., & Reynolds R. (2008). Examining parent involvement in reversing the underachievement of African American students in middle-class schools. *Educational Foundations, 22,* 79–98.

Individuals with Disabilities Education Improvement Act (IDEA) of 2004, Pub. L. No. 108-446, 20 U.S.C. §§ 1400 *et seq* (2004).

Ladson-Billings, G. (2021). I'm here for the hard re-set: Post pandemic pedagogy to preserve our culture, *Equity & Excellence in Education, 54*(1), 68–78. https://doi.org/10.1080/10665684.2020.1863883

Landmark, Ju, S., & Zhang, D. (2010). Substantiated best practices in transition: Fifteen plus years later. *Career Development for Exceptional Individuals, 33*(3), 165–176. https://doi.org/10.1177/0885728810376410

Lawson, M. A. (2003). School–family relations in context parent and teacher perceptions of parent involvement. *Urban Education, 38*(1), 77–133.

Lareau, A. (2000). *Home advantage: Social class and parental intervention in elementary education.* Rowman & Littlefield.

Lee, G. K., & Carter, E. W. (2012). Preparing transition-age students with high-functioning autism spectrum disorders for meaningful work. *Psychology in the Schools, 49*(10), 988–1000. https://doi.org/10.1002/pits.21651

Lehman, C. M., Clark, H. B., Bullis, M., Rinkin, J., & Castellanos, L. (2002). Transition from school to adult life: Empowering youth through community ownership and accountability. *Journal of Child and Family Studies, 11,* 127–141.

Moll, L. C. (1992). Bilingual classroom studies and community analysis: some recent trends. *Educational Researcher, 21*(2), 20–24.

O'Connor, C. (1997). Dispositions toward collective struggle and educational resilience in the inner city: A case analysis of six African-American high school students. *American Educational Research Journal, 34*(4), 593–629.

Plotner, A. J., Mazzotti, V. L., Rose, C. A., & Teasley, K., (2018). Perceptions of interagency collaboration: Relationships between secondary transition roles, communication, and collaboration. *Remedial and Special Education, 41*(1), 28–39. https://doi.org/10.1177/0741932518778029

Posey-Maddox, L., & Haley-Lock, A. (2020). One size does not fit all: Understanding parent engagement in the contexts of work, family, and public schooling. *Urban Education, 55*(5), 671–698. https://doi.org/10.1177/0042085916660348

Povenmire-Kirk, T., Diegelmann, K., Crump, K., Schnorr, C., Test, D., Flowers, C., & Aspel, N. (2015). Implementing CIRCLES: A new model for interagency collaboration in transition planning. *Journal of Vocational Rehabilitation, 42,* 51–65.

Repetto, J. B., Webb, K. W., Garvan, C. W., & Washington, T. (2002). Connecting student outcomes with transition practices in Florida. *Career Development for Exceptional Individuals, 25,* 123–139.

Repetto, J. B., Horky, S. C., Miney, A., Reiss, J., Saidi, A., Wolcott, L., & Jaress, J. M. (2012). Expanding transition to address the needs of students with invisible chronic illness. *Career Development and Transition for Exceptional Individuals, 35,* 4–13. https://doi.org/10.1177/0885728811423653

Rose, D. H., & Meyer, A. (2002). *Teaching every student in the digital age: Universal design for learning.* ASCD.

Shogren, & Plotner, A. J. (2012). Transition Planning for Students with Intellectual Disability, Autism, or Other Disabilities: Data from the National Longitudinal Transition Study-2. *Intellectual and Developmental Disabilities, 50*(1), 16–30. https://doi.org/10.1352/1934-9556-50.1.16

Test, D. W., Mazzotti, V. L., Mustian, A. L., Fowler, C. H., Kortering, L., & Kohler, P. (2009). Evidence-based secondary transition predictors for improving postschool outcomes for students with disabilities. *Career Development for Exceptional Individuals, 32,* 160–181.

Thoma, C. A., Bartholomew, C. C., & Scott, L. A. (2009). *Universal design for transition: A roadmap for planning and instruction.* Paul H. Brookes Publishing Co.

Washington, J., & Evans, N. J. (1991). Becoming an ally. In N. J. Evans & V. A. Wall (Eds.), *Beyond tolerance: Gays, lesbians, and bisexuals on campus* (pp. 195–204). American College Personnel Association.

Watson, M. F., & McGoldrick, M. (2011). Practice with siblings in a cultural context. In J. Caspi (Ed.), *Sibling development: Implications for mental health practitioners* (pp. 59–81). Springer Publishing Company.

Watts, R., Diemer, M., & Voight, A. (2011). Critical consciousness: Current status and future directions. *New Directions for Child and Adolescent Development, 134,* 43–57.

Workforce Innovation and Opportunity Act of 2014, Pub. L. No. 113-128, Stat. 129 (2014). https://www.govinfo.gov/content/pkg/PLAW-113publ128/pdf/PLAW-113publ128.pdf

Yosso, T. J. (2005). Whose culture has capital? *Race, Ethnicity and Education, 8*(1), 69–91.

II

Culturally Sustaining
UDT Across Domains

5

Employment Supports

Amber Brown Ruiz, Genna Kieper, Holly N. Whittenburg, and Marcus Poppen

DIGGING DEEPER: What Teachers Have to Say

We begin this chapter by sharing our collective experiences and perspectives on the importance of employment support for youth and young adults with disabilities. Amber has worked as a vocational rehabilitation (VR) counselor with transition-age youth caseloads and taught career development courses for Pre-Employment Transition Services (Pre-ETS). Genna is a fourth-year doctoral student in educational psychology whose research focuses on naturalistic learning within work environments for students with disabilities. Holly has worked as a community-based job coach, a special education teacher and administrator, and a research coordinator for two federal grants focused on improving employment outcomes for transition-age students who are on the autism spectrum. For the entirety of his career, Marcus has worked to support youth and young adults with disabilities to gain access to employment. These diverse experiences inform our perspectives on education and employment.

The long-term purpose of school is to prepare students for a career or, under the Individuals with Disabilities Education Act (IDEA; 1997, 2004), to become economically self-sufficient. We have observed many high school students picking up jobs to make financial ends meet, to develop new skills, or just to be engaged in an activity. In our experience of supporting students with jobs and long-term career goals, many were already working on skills and career paths based on their talents and community-related opportunities. We have worked with culturally and linguistically diverse (CLD) students with disabilities who pursued passions in different areas, such as exploring national parks during the summers; developing skills in graphic design and art; working as DJs, hair stylists, and barbers; supporting their parents' shops; working with younger children in their churches' nurseries; starting their own businesses; and many more who were active members of their communities. There are also other students who have not had as many opportunities to explore their passions, so classroom discussions about career and employment discovery through the universal design for transition (UDT) framework can benefit them. In academic areas such as math, science, history, and English, there are places to leverage student experiences so they can connect to the world of work—for example, teaching about income and cash flow in math; discussing unions and labor laws, and how they impact us today, in history; discussing career pathways in science; and teaching about email communication and proper grammar and mechanics for applications and cover letters in English. As we think about careers and universally designed and culturally sustaining employment, we reflected that by the time students make it to their final years in high school, they have a background and history that can and should be validated and understood to support student growth. We should become better at using their academic and community interests to support them in building careers.

Essential Questions

▶ What practices and supports from culturally sustaining pedagogy (CSP) can help to ensure that students from CLD backgrounds are ready to enter the workplace and maintain employment?

▶ What role do federal policies play in supporting equity in employment?

▶ What steps should educators follow to conduct employment-related transition assessments and planning?

▶ How can educators help students acquire work experiences—and ensure that they have the on-the-job supports and resources they need?

▶ How can educators support students' self-determination and advocacy, and future planning, through career development and work experiences?

I n the workplace and during employment training, many concepts such as professionalism and career development have historically been centered around practices and workplace cultures for White people. Although many industries have evolved to become more inclusive because of civil rights policies, many areas of improvement still exist for employment-related equity, especially for students from CLD backgrounds. In this chapter, we discuss how CSP and supports can ensure that students from CLD backgrounds are ready to enter the workplace and maintain employment. Relevant approaches include coordinating and adequately preparing youth and stakeholders through the use of culturally sustaining practices and holding individuals accountable for career development efforts that fully consider culture and community.

Based on the framework discussed in Chapter 1, culturally sustaining practices are used to hold practitioners accountable for actions that impact the growth and development of marginalized people. UDT is another part of the framework used in Chapter 1 specifically to support CLD students with disabilities during transition. Figure 5.1 provides an overview of how the chapter will cover culturally sustaining practices and UDT for employment. In this chapter, we aim to combine both concepts to better support employment outcomes for youth from multiple marginalized identities (e.g., CLD students with disabilities).

CASE STUDY: Ciara

Introducing Mrs. McDowell, Ms. Dunnaway, and Ciara

Mrs. McDowell is a high school physics and Advanced Placement chemistry teacher who is the advisor for many of the school's Science, Technology, Engineering, Art, and Math (STEAM) extracurricular programs. She has been teaching at the high school for 3 years. She graduated from a Historically Black University, Jackson State University, with a degree in chemical engineering. After working in pharmaceuticals for a while, she retired and decided to come back to her hometown to help prepare students in her community for STEAM-related careers.

This year, she learned that Ciara, a Black female student with a significant hearing loss and dyslexia who is served with an individualized education program (IEP), will join her Physics I class. Before this year, Mrs. McDowell had never taught a student with an IEP or who needed accommodations. She will be working with Ms. Dunnaway, Ciara's special education case manager, to navigate Ciara's transition goals.

Ciara is excited to be in Mrs. McDowell's physics class because she heard from her older sister that the class takes a lot of field trips for science-related events and has a team that makes it to the robotics competition every year. Ciara loves tinkering and hopes to have a career in engineering, specifically robotics or the automobile industry, but she is also interested in child care because she's been babysitting her neighbor's daughter for 6 years. She is open to exploring options. Ciara became interested in robotics and cars after spending a lot of time with her dad, who collects and fixes trophy-worthy cars and enjoys operating remote-controlled cars.

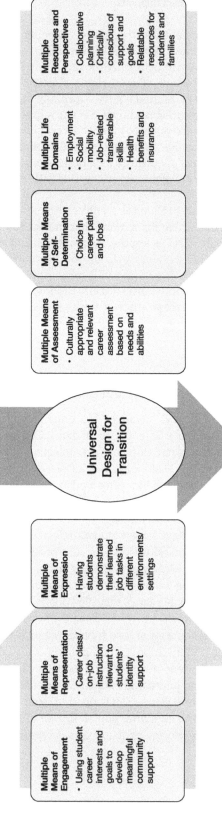

Figure 5.1. Overview of culturally sustaining practices and universal design for transition for employment. (Source: Scott & Bruno, 2018.)

EMPLOYMENT POLICIES AND EQUITY

Legal standards and antidiscrimination policies for employment are included in Title VII of the Civil Rights Act of 1964. The basic purpose of Title VII is "protection against employment discrimination based on race, color, religion, national origin, and sex." The policy was created to address discrimination (Civil Rights Act, 1964), but culture is often left out of the conversation. Appearance and language are assumed characteristics under Title VII, but the legal standard does not technically protect against those categories, which are often sociocultural. Policies that address issues of discrimination directly covered by Title VII in the workplace include Creating a Respectable and Open World for Natural Hair (CROWN Act, 2019) and The Religious Freedom Restoration Act (RFRA, 1993). The CROWN Act is state-specific legislation that is active in 12 states because Black people with locs, afros, and other curly/coily styles felt discriminated against because of their hair choices. The RFRA protects people who wear cultural or religious garments, such as hijabs and turbans. These policies and their roots highlight the issues that CLD students with disabilities entering the workplace may face (Clark, 2018). The circumstances that gave rise to these policies also highlight many of the issues related to employment outcomes of people of color with disabilities. For instance, Black (15.2%) and Hispanic (13.9%) people with disabilities have higher unemployment rates compared to White people with disabilities (9.2%; U.S. Bureau of Labor Statistics, 2022).

It is essential for transition professionals to learn more about the discrimination that their students may face in order to better plan and provide services to support their career goals and employment. Under the Workforce Innovation and Opportunity Act (WIOA, 2014), various employment services can be provided, and if delivered using a UDT framework, these services can be provided in group settings or across life domains for employment. These WIOA services are called Pre-Employment Transition Services (Pre-ETS), which focus on training, development, and work-based learning. These are coordinated services provided by VR agencies and may sometimes be provided in classroom or group setting for students with disabilities (Federal Register, 2016). State VR agencies are required to ensure the coordination and delivery of these services to all potentially eligible students with disabilities in their states who may need them (WIOA, 2014). This is important because when transition services are coordinated and delivered in inclusive classroom settings, students with disabilities are more likely to have access to more resources and information about employment and career pathways. Furthermore, inclusion is one of the strongest predictors of postschool employment success (Mazzotti et al., 2021). This emphasis on training, development, and job placement is vital for students, but the reality of student issues goes beyond just the job—it is about understanding equity and equity-based practices when providing those services for CLD students with disabilities, thus highlighting the need for culturally sustaining practices, in addition to UDT.

CASE STUDY: Ciara, *continued*

Maintaining High Expectations When Planning

Ciara's IEP team had to advocate for her to enroll in Mrs. McDowell's physics class. Her family and other IEP members worked with Ciara to explore her interests and identify potential classes that would fit into her schedule. Some members of her IEP team and Mrs. McDowell had reservations about allowing Ciara to be in the class because their expectations for her were lower than they should have been, but everyone was reminded of Ciara's career goal of being an engineer and agreed to her enrolling in the class. Ciara has clearly demonstrated her capacity to meet expectations in areas of her interests, and she has so far passed all of her math and science classes. However, she has yet to pass the biology state assessment that is required before graduation. To become a more supportive teacher, Mrs. McDowell works with Ciara's special education case manager, Ms. Dunnaway, to learn more inclusive strategies, such as UDT. Mrs. McDowell and Ms. Dunnaway used assessments that were relevant to the physics class and also to Ciara's career development. Mrs. McDowell asked all of her students about their career interests and learned that they were more interested in the class when the physics course content and instructional activities were tailored to their postschool career interests.

TRANSITION ASSESSMENTS AND PLANNING: MULTIPLE MEANS OF ASSESSMENT

Conducting transition assessments and using them to plan is an in-depth, multistep process. There are formal and informal transition assessments to support the direction of the planning process. When conducting assessments for career and employment interests, the Virginia Commonwealth University Center on Transition Innovations (2021) lists five steps:

1. Gather existing data.
2. Identify assessment needs and assess.
3. Analyze data.
4. Determine and coordinate transition services.
5. Instruct and evaluate.

Steps 1, 2, and 3 are ways that transition assessments are developed and used, whereas Steps 4 and 5 are part of the planning process.

Assessing Student Needs and Strengths

A number of steps can be taken to support the employment and career goals of CLD students with disabilities, and this support starts with assessing their needs and strengths (Carter et al., 2009).

Step 1: Gather Existing Data   The team can gather existing data in many ways, including in a more exploratory manner or through established methods of the team or district. Some existing data may come from IEPs—formal assessments, observations, classroom supports, or discussions. Career awareness activities can be offered as a means to gather observational data. Various career awareness activities in group settings could include career fairs, field trips, and career discovery classes with guest speakers and potential mentors who discuss relevant jobs and career pathways. In these activities,

- students can explore their community to identify their interests, passions, or dreams; or

- the transition team learns more about the student's life and interests inside and outside of the classroom and uses that information to build on their ideas about the future to create career pathway ideas or employment opportunities.

Mrs. McDowell helped her physics students explore their interests and dreams by incorporating more community partners into the classroom and becoming more informed about the students' passion for science. She noticed that the students who were more engaged in her class were more likely to want a career in science. Through her weekly student check-ins, when the class had open discussions about the physics lessons that week, she was able to gather data that were correlated with students' grades and interests. She saw more of Ciara's potential to be successful in applied physics, and she learned that Ciara would need more support with theoretical physics concepts.

Step 2: Identify Assessment Needs and Assess   The second step is to identify assessment needs and then assess. To do this, the team will think about the student's assets and identify or develop assessments that target those assets; they will also learn about barriers in a non-deficit–oriented manner emphasizing components of culturally sustaining practices and UDT. The Virginia Commonwealth University Center on Transition Innovations (2021) lists three basic questions that represent appropriate strength-based assessments and tools:

1. Where is the student presently?

2. Where is the student going beyond high school (employment, further education/training, living arrangements)?

3. How does the student get there? (p. 8)

For example, teams could create an informal interview to discuss the hopes and dreams of the youth, which focuses on skills and supports for the student and not on their inability to do certain activities. In Ciara's case, members of her IEP team asked Ciara questions about her interests, goals, strengths, and support needs by framing the latter inquiry in a positive way. Rather than asking Ciara what her weaknesses are, IEP members asked her what she needs in order to learn best, at what tasks she has to work harder to achieve, and for what tasks she most often asks for help. Framing inquiry in this way allows Ciara to consider what she can do to overcome obstacles rather than focusing on the obstacles themselves.

The team should be mindful of the small steps students can take toward their goals and reassess their interests after each step or experience to see if anything has changed. In addition, it is important that transition assessments are culturally relevant and acknowledge each student's background as being a central part of their identity. Understanding the distinction between employment and careers can also help support student development. Employment for students is about jobs that can be done in the present, whereas careers are types of jobs over time that inform students' life work. As Ciara is working through her career interest choices, work experiences can help her clarify her career interests. She is more interested in exploring engineering, but she also has an interest in and experience with child care. The physics class can help her explore topics that will be important in a variety of careers. Mrs. McDowell recognizes that all of her students are being challenged with exploring different career options, such as medicine, music, and software development. Sometimes, the decision to select a career is culturally driven. Mrs. McDowell realizes that her own career decision to retire from the pharmaceutical industry was culturally driven because her parents were teachers and her family had a deep commitment to supporting their community. Mrs. McDowell uses surveys and open-ended test questions to gauge these interests in her students. She is able to bring in other professionals and create more applied field trips for her classes and extracurricular activities for students.

Step 3: Analyze Data   The third step is to analyze the assessment data so the student and their team can make informed decisions about what additional instruction and support the student may need. For example, after information about the students' preferences, interests, strengths, and needs have been collected, the team could meet both to review this information and to ensure that the student and their team are all on the same page. If the student says they are interested in working in a science lab and their teacher says they can only get a job bagging groceries, the team should decide to move forward with the student's interest to guide the additional instruction and support they receive. After the data are reviewed and everyone is on the same page about the student's preferences, interests, strengths, and needs, the planning can begin!

Collaborative Planning

Collaboration is a natural part of the transition planning process. For the employment domain, this is most apparent in the final two steps of this process.

Step 4: Determine and Coordinate Transition Services   The next step is to determine and coordinate transition services. Speaking with the student, family members, service providers, and other stakeholders is how we as professionals learn more about ways to best serve the student. We learn about the resources and social and cultural capital that each person brings to the planning process (Achola & Greene, 2016). For example, the family may have social and cultural capital that can assist the student in navigating spaces with people who feel familiar to them, and the transition professionals' knowledge of financial and service-related resources could help with the overall support of the family. During Ciara's coordinating process, the team was unaware of her father's connection to the mechanic community there. Eventually, the team was able to find out more about the family's background. Ms. Dunnaway and other adult service providers were able to support Ciara's accommodation needs in the classroom and at work, and Mrs. McDowell was able to support her career learning needs using UDT. The best use of these resources and capital is led by the fundamental principle of *what is in the best interest of the student.* The goal of collaboration when working with transition professionals and other team members is to best serve the student.

Use Varied Means of Communication Based in Equity   In addition to navigating spaces, the team must understand how to work with the family by gaining more information about their preferred communication preferences and family structure. The best way to gain this information is by, quite simply, asking families about their preferences, respecting those preferences, and building rapport over time. The individuals themselves know their needs and preferences, so teachers should avoid making assumptions.

Communication is about having formal and informal ways of connecting with members to discuss team and student goals. In UDT, this means focusing on providing a variety of ways to communicate. Currently, technology makes communication accessible through email, texts, and web-based case management systems. As a team, stakeholders should create a communication plan based on communication preferences for informal/quick updates and have set times for formal meetings. Equity-based communication during the planning for students is about also understanding different communication styles and appreciating cultural communication styles, assets, and comfort levels. Communication for students and their families is about having a sense of belongingness in a space. Communication with professionals is about ensuring that the team has been able to create that space for students and families.

Reflect Critically About Communication   Although communication is key to building trusting relationships, critical reflection should also be used to evaluate the effectiveness of communication and create awareness among the team. Critical reflection aligns with concepts related to CSP and serves the purpose of acknowledging ways, no matter how small, to make systemic changes or reframe personal thinking to better serve students. Members of a team must be conscious of goals, students, and environment to provide resources and perspectives during career development.

Achola (2019) suggested that the best way to be critically reflective and plan resources for students is to build a diversity-informed resource map. (For a list of steps in this process, see Figure 5.2 below; Table 5.1 provides an example.) A diversity-informed resource map is a terrific way to learn more about the community, local businesses, and organizations, and it can include a list of all potential partners and resources. Based on a student's needs and results from their transition assessments, the team can tailor a diversity-informed resource map to identify mentors, community services, transportation, and potential jobs. The map can list names of resources, descriptions, supports, contacts, and activities. Transition teams can collect this information using informal assessments. Many places and people, such as universities and local libraries and community partners, may be able to assist in identifying the individuals and resources needed to develop a diversity-informed resource map.

Step 5: Instruct and Evaluate   The last step is to instruct and evaluate. Employment-related instruction is needed that allows students to explore opportunities that match their interests. A way to provide instruction that is aligned with UDT and is culturally sustaining is to promote inclusive and relevant experiences as much as possible by including team members who are involved in students' lives.

Many people are involved with a student's transition from school to adult life. The individuals involved in the plan may include stakeholders such as the student, family members, teachers (e.g., special educators, general educators, case managers), transition specialists or coordinators, VR counselors, school administrators, and other related service providers, in addition to employers and community members. Collaborative planning and communication, such as career conversations with the other science teachers for Ciara or conversations with current employers and mentors about her overall skill development, are essential to the success of the student. Evaluations of the team's progress must also be completed periodically to determine whether the plan is effective or if it needs to change.

---

1. Assess student and family assets, needs, and challenges.
2. Develop partnerships with other service professionals in schools and adult service agencies based on needs for professional services or employment.
3. Assess community assets, needs, and challenges.
4. Develop partnerships with community-based stakeholders.
5. Map resources with stakeholders based on student goals.

Figure 5.2.   Steps to develop a diversity-informed resource map. (Sources: Achola, 2019; Crane & Mooney, 2005.)

Table 5.1. Diversity-informed resource maps

Community partner name	Description	Populations served	Supports offered	Contact information	Alignment with student goals and activities
Pine Crest Educational Center	Forestry and conservation center	Community Student learners LGBTQ+ friendly	Community garden	Emily Dotson (223) 473-9912 director@pinecrested.com	Internship opportunity to learn more about park, sustainability, and forestry services and food-to-table–related resources
American Job Center	Government assistance center for employment	Unemployed individuals People with disabilities	Access to internet, telephones, and career counseling	Anita Jones (301) 234-4422 AJjones35@ajc.gov	Internet access for students/families without these resources outside of school hours to complete employment-related activities
The Referral Group	Grant-writing group that supports different community projects	Black and Indigenous businesses and entrepreneurs	Leadership and financial management course and supports Start-up funds for small businesses	Kayla Greene (901) 123-2233 Kayla.greene@thereferral.com	For students interested in learning more about self-employment and growing their businesses
State College Language Learning Resource Center	Resource center for ELLs and those who support ELL students	ELL students ELL teachers and support staff	Volunteer student translators Language and communication classes/support groups	Joan Lattimore (901) 335-5045 lattimorej@go.sc.edu	For families needing translators during meetings or community social supports

Sources: Achola, 2019; Crane & Mooney, 2005.

Note. Fictional names are modeled after community resources. *Key:* ELL: English language learner; LGBTQ+, lesbian, gay, bisexual, transgender, intersex, queer/questioning, asexual, and more identities.

CASE STUDY: Ciara, *continued*

Supporting the Student in Obtaining Work Experiences

The physics students in Mrs. McDowell's class typically are high school seniors who are on track to graduate and attend college. The students are working on their college applications and are applying to scholarships. Mrs. McDowell knew that the colleges and scholarships that her students are applying for are competitive and grades alone are not enough to stand out to colleges and scholarship committees. She also knew through Ciara's meeting that relevant work experiences for students are achievable during high school. Mrs. McDowell allowed time during her class to explore different jobs or extracurricular activities related to science that students could do for extra credit. This challenged students to think more consciously about their career path. Mrs. McDowell was also thinking about equity-based supports. She knew that some students may not have the personal and professional connections needed to obtain work experiences, so she provides mentoring and has students assist in planning physics experiments or conduct research for the robotics team.

Ciara and her transition team agreed for her to have a work-based learning experience at a local mechanic shop whose owner is a friend of Ciara's dad. The experience allowed Ciara to explore different components of cars and how to install those components. Mrs. McDowell has also been a great mentor to Ciara by using her network to help build Ciara's understanding about different engineering jobs. In the spring, Ciara will be applying for a summer internship at a car manufacturer based on Mrs. McDowell's recommendation. Ciara will also continue to babysit for pay and to learn how to manage her own money.

DEVELOPING CULTURALLY SUSTAINING WORK EXPERIENCES: MULTIPLE LIFE DOMAINS

Work experiences in high school encompass a range of activities, including internships, part-time employment, summer work, and apprenticeships (Mazzotti et al., 2021; WINTAC, 2016). Considering ways to develop UDT-aligned, meaningful work experiences for students from CLD backgrounds is a critical task for educators and other service providers involved in transition, because participation in work experiences during high school is associated with improved employment outcomes postschool for students with disabilities generally and CLD students with disabilities specifically (Balcazar et al., 2018; Mazzotti et al., 2021; Wehman et al., 2014).

Key Ideas to Keep in Mind

As special educators and other service providers seek to create work-based learning experiences for CLD students with disabilities, it can be helpful to remember two key ideas. First, in keeping with UDT and culturally sustaining practices, be sure to *focus on the student's personal interests, goals, and dreams, while also considering family and community values and beliefs, as you work collaboratively to develop work experiences.* This focus helps ensure that work experiences are meaningful to students and supports them in identifying and progressing toward their career goals inside and outside of the classroom. Second, *be mindful of how implicit bias can quietly enter the work experience development process.* Unconscious acceptance of implicit cultural assumptions within transition planning (e.g., tracking students into specific internships based on their gender, racial/ethnic background, or other identity markers; making assumptions about students' career goals based on these same factors) can lead to inequities within the work experience process (Achola, 2019).

Strategies for Developing Work Experiences

Transition teams can use several strategies to develop work experiences that incorporate culturally sustaining practices. First, special educators and other service providers can tap into the social networks (e.g., school, home, community) of students and their communities to identify possible work experience placements. Family, clergy members, and community business leaders may be willing themselves, or may know others who would be willing, to hire a student as an employee or intern. Second, using the diversity-informed resource map, transition team members can research local businesses whose work aligns with student interests and whose corporate values indicate a strong commitment to diversity, equity, and inclusion. Special educators or service providers can seek out information about companies by reviewing their webpages and social media accounts and by talking to members of the student's community about their experiences with the organization. Third, transition team members can work to connect students with professional mentors within their fields of interest. If available, mentors who reflect students' cultural and personal backgrounds can be valuable assets for helping students to envision themselves within the field and in building personal professional relationships (Brown Ruiz & Scott, 2021). Mentors can also be effective allies in developing work experiences for students of color with disabilities in their own organizations.

CASE STUDY: Ciara, *continued*

Self-Advocating for Needed Supports

At the mechanic shop, Ciara has been having a hard time hearing her supervisor over the loud tools. All year, Ciara has been gaining self-advocacy skills through many parts of her transition process, such as getting into her physics class and explaining to her transition team that she wants to explore engineering more while continuing to work in child care. So, when the problem started, Ciara was able to let her supervisor know about the issue, and they decided to go to the transition team to get help with ideas. The team developed a visual light system to use that Ciara was trained on, and the system also worked for her co-workers, who always had a problem hearing in the shop as well.

ON-THE-JOB PRACTICAL SUPPORTS AND NEEDS: MULTIPLE RESOURCES AND PERSPECTIVES

As with other students, CLD students with disabilities often require various supports when at their place of employment. Although it is important for students to advocate for themselves, the responsibility of developing these supports and resources does not fall on them alone. Job coaches, employers, and other systems of support can apply UDT and CSP in developing supports that allow CLD students with disabilities to carry out their necessary job duties—while feeling confident and competent and contributing to shared goals in the workplace just like every other employee. Some of these resources can be developed for any new employee and used on a need basis, but some may require more collaborative work with the student, employer, and other individuals involved in supporting the student on the worksite (e.g., VR coaches, job coaches, employment coordinators).

Examples of beneficial on-the-job supports for people with disabilities to develop and use include job duty lists, prompting and visual or technical supports, natural supports, and transportation.

Job Duty Lists

Job duty lists outline every essential or nonessential activity the employee may engage in during a given work shift. An overall job duty list is beneficial for any new employee, but people with disabilities may require more detailed, comprehensive job duty lists that include approximate times for each duty, reminders to check in with advisors, breaks, and protocols for arrival and departure from the job site. When used universally, job duty lists can inform other new employees of step-by-step instructions that may have been forgotten. The subtle reminders of a job duty list are one way in which CLD students with disabilities can develop independence.

Prompting and Visual or Technical Supports

Prompts, ranging from fully restrictive to least restrictive, include full physical prompts (hand over hand), model prompts (showing an example), gestures (pointing at a clock), and verbal prompts ("Look at the clock") and can assist in helping CLD students with disabilities know when transitions are occurring, how to transition, and where things may be located at a worksite.

Visual supports may include compensatory materials such as labeling specific areas for each job duty or visual schedules with photos to reduce the amount of reading necessary to complete work duties. Visual supports allow for instruction and prompting to happen even when students are not receiving direct support from another person. Using photos from the actual worksite cues students into seeking these items, spaces, or tasks without being prompted by another person and allows students to build competencies in troubleshooting and familiarizing themselves with their surroundings rather than being told what to attend to.

Assistive technology is any item, piece of equipment, or product system designed to increase, maintain, or improve the functional capabilities of CLD students with disabilities (IDEA, 2004) and should be made readily available on request to allow individuals with disabilities to have full autonomy in the workplace. These supports allow CLD students with disabilities to maintain employment; however, it is important to note that, at times, workplace modifications may be made to revise the employee's training plan and determine what is limiting success.

Natural Supports

Natural supports present another mode of supporting employment for people with disabilities. These natural workplace supports are most often found through coworkers, who provide immediate support to the employee when workplace issues arise that are not accounted for in any of the supports discussed previously. Natural workplace supports can provide social networks for employees with disabilities that create a safe space for learning, asking questions, and developing appropriate

---

Purpose: Supporting the transition goal of self-determination and self-advocacy by working with students on the importance of identity and belongingness and employers on providing natural supports in the workplace.

Learning Objectives:

1. Speak directly to the individual using accessible language.

2. Remain mindful of student needs for support in the workplace.

3. Remember that individuals with disabilities are adults and deserve to be treated as such.

4. Maintain open communication with people with disabilities and ask questions about their preferences for communication.

5. Provide a sense of agency to students in the workplace—this will empower them more.

Evaluation and Reflection Questions:

1. In what ways have we confronted our own biases?

2. In what ways have we coped with the complexity of racism and microaggressions?

3. How can we become better at encouraging the employer/natural supports and students?

4. How do we deal with difficult conversations about organizational changes and developing more supportive workplace polices?

5. How can we improve the way we support employer/natural supports and students?

Figure 5.3. Agenda for communication workshop and transition team reflection to address barriers or challenges in the workplace. (Sources: Kieper, 2021; Kieran & Anderson, 2019.)

workplace conduct skills. In addition to the mentors mentioned previously, natural supports for CLD students with disabilities are people in the workplace who have the cultural competency and capacity to support CLD students—for example, same-race job coaches or informed employers and co-workers. Communication workshops are a great way to encourage natural supports, which not only inform employers and their staff about disabilities but also build understanding of cultural competency (see Figure 5.3).

Transportation

Transportation and travel to and from the worksite can often present a barrier to successful work experiences. This is especially true in rural areas where traditional public transportation may not be readily accessible. Many communities provide a form of rideshare transportation service specifically designed for people with disabilities or other conditions that may impact their ability to navigate to necessary locations in the community. The National Aging and Disability Transportation Center (https://www.nadtc.org/) provides additional resources to promote the availability and accessibility of transportation options for people with disabilities. Public transportation may serve as a resource in navigating to and from the worksite. Methods of supporting CLD students with disabilities may include transportation training given directly to the individual, training on technology required to navigate public transit in a given community, and a connection to the transportation agency to provide support in ensuring people with disabilities are arriving at their correct destination. Even though transportation looks different in each community, resources are available to address this often-complex barrier.

CASE STUDY: Ciara, *continued*

Putting Self-Determination and Self-Advocacy Into Action

As a part of Pre-ETS, Ms. Dunnaway teaches her students about self-determination and advocacy. Ciara learns how to advocate for herself and understands that her field of interest is a male-dominated field and that Black women are not well represented. Also, even though Ciara's dad knows the owner of the mechanic shop, the owner still has trouble connecting with her and understanding how to work with her. Ciara typically likes to style her hair with 26-inch long thick braids, and her supervisor sees this as a hazard at work but does not want to feel like he is disrespectful toward her. Ciara wears her hair in this style to cover her hearing aid and feel more feminine. The team hosted a communication workshop to discuss how to work with a CLD student with a disability and offered resources for the employer. Ciara was also able to advocate to keep her hair the way she styles it but opted to tie it up when working around the machines.

Mrs. McDowell used the communication workshop in her class to teach all of her students about discrimination practices versus safety in the workplace, and the importance of having CLD students in STEAM. She hosted Black and Latine engineers and researchers from her professional network to talk with the students about their fields and how they navigated their careers. One of the engineers used examples of how artificial intelligence was not registering darker skin tones because some creators and engineers lacked the knowledge about darker complexions.

ADDRESSING BARRIERS OR CHALLENGES THROUGH SELF-DETERMINATION AND ADVOCACY

In the workplace, CLD students with a disability may face numerous barriers. Whether the issue is ableism or racism, the physical, stereotypical, and communication barriers can be difficult to navigate. Specific factors that contribute to work outcomes of people of color with disabilities include differences in cultural values, priorities, and expectations; inequitable access to resources; and discrimination (Lindsey et al., 2021). Strategies to address barriers or challenges in the workplace include the following:

- Improving the knowledge of employers and other natural workplace supports about the intersecting identities of students with disabilities (Fabian et al., 1993; Lövgren et al., 2017)
  - In practice: Facilitate discussions between students and employers about their backgrounds; provide students with scripts to begin bridging gaps with their co-workers to build rapport.
- Confronting biases (Fabian et al., 1993; Sabat et al., 2014)
  - In practice: Speak directly with employers and others in the workplace about common biases and urge them to reflect on their own biases in a shared safe space.

- Affirming student identity and belongingness (Sabat et al., 2014)
  - In practice: Ask students questions about themselves, build rapport with them over time, and show interest in their daily routines, family dynamics, and stylistic choices.

- Empowering students to make informed choices and identify discriminatory practices (Sabat et al., 2014)
  - In practice: Engage in discussion with your students about what discriminatory practices look like and what they do not look like; equip students with the tools to confront these biases and reiterate that you are a safe person with which to discuss these occurrences.

The responsibility of addressing barriers and challenges cannot be fulfilled by students alone. Marginalized students from CLD backgrounds need allies to support them and equip them with the skills and language to advocate for themselves. Increasing employer knowledge about disabilities has been seen to positively impact the work experience of a person with a disability (Fabian et al., 1993). Workshops and training—such as a communication workshop (mentioned previously)—can also be a time to discuss how the transition team, employers, and people providing natural support reflect on and combat negative biases by being reminded of student assets and strengths. The team can help grow strengths and build employment skills by empowering the student to understand their identity and building their sense of belongingness. It is important to discuss with students how those differences in identity should not make a person feel less than human. Students need tools to identify discriminatory practices and non-examples of discriminatory practices and have discussions with a transition team member or mentor on how to differentiate between the two. When engaging in these discussions with students, allow them the space to attempt to identify these practices through examples (e.g., written, video, or graphic examples of discriminatory behaviors), provide feedback and insight about how you may identify these practices, and instruct students on how to respond if/when they experience discrimination in the workplace. When issues of discrimination are addressed with both students and employers, risks for discrimination could be lowered.

CASE STUDY: CIARA, *continued*

Preparing for Graduation

For Ciara's last IEP meeting, the transition team worked with her to help her understand her options when she graduates. With the support of her team and teachers, she passed her biology state test, got a B in her physics class, gained experience working on cars, and was selected to be a high school summer intern for a car manufacturer. Before graduation, she learned that her hearing was getting worse and she would need to get better hearing aids. After meeting with the VR counselor, Ciara learned more about how her adult benefits could help her afford her hearing aids after she graduates. She was even able to get benefits counseling.

Ciara is excited to graduate and head to college. She has a lot to do to prepare, but she has a great support system. Mrs. McDowell connected Ciara with a mentor from her sorority at one of Ciara's university choices who is also studying engineering. Ciara's guidance counselor and IEP team talked about financial aid options and supported Ciara and her parents in completing the FAFSA (Free Application for Federal Student Aid), taking the SAT/ACT, and discussing other postsecondary options as well.

FUTURE PLANNING: EMPLOYMENT, PUBLIC BENEFITS, AND ADVANCED CAREER DEVELOPMENT

As students and their families begin to envision life after high school, it is important that they have up-to-date and accurate information about how postschool employment can potentially affect important benefits (e.g., health insurance, Social Security). Fears about losing benefits and associated services can be a disincentive to employment, especially for students who may have struggled to be approved for benefits in the first place or who rely on benefits for household income or medical services (Kregel, 2012). In response to these and similar issues, the Social Security Administration (SSA) developed a series of work incentives to help Social Security recipients with disabilities keep critical benefits while also working. These incentives may include personalized benefits counseling, retaining Medicaid eligibility up to a given salary threshold, being able to save earnings/income for expenses related to specific vocational goals, and excluding certain work-related expenses in benefit calculations (e.g., transportation, uniforms) (Brooke & McDonough, 2008).

It is imperative that special educators and other service providers understand the perspectives on benefits of students and families and that they work collaboratively with students and families to ensure they have the resources and knowledge needed to make informed decisions. Transition teams can incorporate information on benefits planning into their own transition processes by taking several steps:

1. Learning more about SSA benefits through online resources

2. Talking with students and families during transition meetings about the benefits they receive and questions they may have about benefits and employment

3. Connecting those who receive public benefits to organizations who can provide expert advice and planning services (typically through state VR agencies or Centers for Independent Living)

It is also important for families and students with disabilities to consider health care work accommodations and benefits, such as Family Medical Leave (FML), Employee Assistance Programs (EAP), and wellness programs. Under the Family Medical Leave Act (FMLA, 1993), employees are entitled to job protections for major family and medical reasons. FML is in place to make sure employees with public sector jobs and private sector jobs with 50 or more employees can maintain their jobs for at least 12 weeks (FMLA, 1993). In general, people with disabilities and families with children with disabilities often face hardships due to the pressure of attending work while seeking serious medical attention (Parish &

Cloud, 2006). FML can cover some of the time off for needed medical necessities if a person has depleted paid time off and sick leave. In most cases, if an employee works full time in a company with more than 500 people, that company can also offer EAP and wellness programs as a supplement to health insurance (Masi, 2020; U.S. Department of Labor, 2016). EAP is a group of short-term services that range from mental health support, work stress supports, end-of-life planning, and financial counseling (Masi, 2020). Wellness programs are preventive health care services that were typically developed with the goal of lowering health care costs over the long term. FML, EAP, and wellness program policies can vary from company to company, but if a student or family member is a full-time worker at a company that offers these benefits, they should be informed of these resources if they ever run into issues regarding their health and employment.

Finally, students and their families may want to consider opportunities for additional vocational training or postsecondary education after they leave high school, because postschool vocational training and college/university participation are associated with improved employment outcomes for students with disabilities (Cimera et al., 2018; Whittenburg et al., 2019). However, it can be difficult to navigate these application processes and figure out ways to pay for vocational training or postsecondary education, especially for first-generation students and their families. Transition teams can support students and their families through these processes in several ways. First, they can connect students and families with school guidance counselors and state VR agency representatives, who can explore options and discuss funding avenues with them. In some cases, VR counselors may be able to offer tuition assistance to students with disabilities who qualify for services. School guidance counselors can point students toward private, local, and state-level scholarships to help offset the costs of vocational training or postsecondary education. Second, special educators can help students and families complete enrollment applications and FAFSA forms. These often-lengthy forms can be confusing and complicated, particularly if students and families have not encountered them before. Finally, it can be helpful to connect CLD students with disabilities and their families with other students and families from similar backgrounds and communities who have gone on to further training or education after high school. Talking with others who have gone through these processes successfully can help dispel fears, provide strategies and approaches for navigating unfamiliar systems that do not mirror kindergarten through Grade 12 education, and offer opportunities for mentorship and support to students and families alike.

Reflection

Think about the different ways to support employment that are described in this chapter. Then, identify a student you work with who is preparing to transition to work after high school. What concrete steps can you take to assess their skills, interests, and needs and begin coordinating to plan employment opportunities? What supports might this student need at the type of job they are seeking? What factors related to culture and equity will you need to think about when helping this student plan for their adult work life?

WRAP-UP: EMPLOYMENT

CLD students, including students of color, and their families deserve quality equity-based employment services and employers who accept and support them. Equity-based practices to reach team goals require support from others to provide services and hold each other accountable for any bias and uncertainties about moving forward with service plans. Accountability and awareness are a process of communication and critical reflection to understand the lives of students and the systematic barriers that they may face when obtaining employment.

▶ **Tips for Supporting Employment**

1. **Continue to practice and understand how to build your relationship with the community.** To get started, see "Module 16b: Building Relationships with the Community" in the professional development series created by Project READY: Reimagining Equity & Access for Diverse Youth, available at the following link: https://ready.web.unc.edu/section-2-transforming-practice/16b/

2. **Create diversity-informed resource maps.** Diversity-informed maps can be created as a class assignment for students, and field trips and guest speakers can be planned from information on these maps. To get started,

   - use Google Maps to research community resources: https://www.google.com/maps

   - engage with local chambers of commerce: https://www.uschamber.com/co/chambers

   - work with a local library for resources, information, and books on student career interests: https://www.worldcat.org/libraries

   - consider virtual field trip options: https://www.discoveryeducation.com/community/virtual-field-trips/

3. **Understand students' language and history to make changes in your classroom.** To get started, see "Module 18: 'Leveling Up' Your Instruction with the Banks Framework" in the professional development series created by Project READY: Reimagining Equity & Access for Diverse Youth, available at the following link: https://ready.web.unc.edu/section-2-transforming-practice/module-18-leveling-up-your-instruction-with-the-banks-framework/

REFERENCES

Achola, E. O. (2019). Practicing what we preach: Reclaiming the promise of multicultural transition programming. *Career Development and Transition for Exceptional Individuals, 42*(3), 188–193.

Achola, E. O., & Greene, G. (2016). Person–family centered transition planning: Improving post-school outcomes to culturally diverse youth and families. *Journal of Vocational Rehabilitation, 45*(2), 173–183.

Balcazar, F. E., Awsumb, J., Dimpfl, S., Langi, F. G., & Lara, J. (2018). Jobs for Youth program: An intervention to improve transition outcomes of former dropout minority youth. *Career Development and Transition for Exceptional Individuals, 41*(3), 166–174.

Brooke, V., & McDonough, J. T. (2008). The facts ma'am, just the facts: Social Security disability benefit programs and work incentives. *TEACHING Exceptional Children, 41*(1), 58–65. https://doi.org/10.1177/004005990804100107

Brown Ruiz, A., & Scott, L. A. (2021). Guiding questions for a culturally responsive framework during preemployment transition services. *TEACHING Exceptional Children, 53*(5), 369–375.

Carter, E. W., Trainor, A. A., Sun, Y., & Owens, L. (2009). Assessing the transition-related strengths and needs of adolescents with high-incidence disabilities. *Exceptional Children, 76*(1), 74–94.

Cimera, R. E., Thoma, C. A., Whittenburg, H. N., & Ruhl, A. N. (2018). Is getting a postsecondary education a good investment for supported employees with intellectual disability and taxpayers? *Inclusion, 6*(2), 97–109. https://doi.org/10.1352/2326-6988-6.2.97

Civil Rights Act of 1964, Pub. L. No. 88-352, 78 Stat. 241 (1964). https://www.govinfo.gov/content/pkg/STATUTE-78/pdf/STATUTE-78-Pg241.pdf

Clark, L. (2018). Beyond bias: Cultural capital in anti-discrimination law. *Harvard Civil Rights-Civil Liberties Law Review, 53*(2), 381–444.

Crane, K., & Mooney, M. (2005). *Essential tools: Community resource mapping.* University of Minnesota, National Center on Secondary Education and Transition.

CROWN Act of 2019, H.R. 5309, 116th Cong. § 2 (2019).

Fabian, E. S., Edelman, A., & Leedy, M. (1993). Linking workers with severe disabilities to social supports in the workplace: Strategies for addressing barriers. *Journal of Rehabilitation-Washington, 59,* 29–29.

Family and Medical Leave Act (FMLA) of 1993, Pub. L. No. 103-3, 5 U.S.C. §§ 6381 *et seq.,* 29 U.S.C. §§ 2601 *et seq.* (1993).

Federal Register. (2016). Preamble Pre-employment Transition Services (§361.48(a)). Final VR Regulations at 81(161), 55693-55694. https://www.govinfo.gov/content/pkg/FR-2016-08-19/pdf/2016-15980.pdf

Individuals with Disabilities Education Act Amendments (IDEA) of 1997, Pub. L. No. 105-17, 20 U.S.C. §§ 1400 *et seq.* (1997).

Individuals with Disabilities Education Improvement Act (IDEA) of 2004, Pub. L. No. 108-446, 20 U.S.C. §§ 1400 *et seq.* (2004).

Kieper, G. (2021). Communication Workshop for ROAR Community Partners [PowerPoint Slides]. WSU ROAR program, Washington State University.

Kieran, L., & Anderson, C. (2019). Connecting universal design for learning with culturally responsive teaching. *Education and Urban Society, 51*(9), 1202–1216.

Kregel, J. (2012). Work Incentives Planning and Assistance Program: Current program results document the program's ability to improve employment outcomes, reduce dependence on benefits, and generate cost savings for SSA. *Journal of Vocational Rehabilitation, 36*(1), 3–12. https://doi.org/10.3233/JVR-2012-0577

Lindsay, S., Varahra, A., Ahmed, H., Abrahamson, S., Pulver, S., Primucci, M., & Wong, K. (2021). Exploring the relationships between race, ethnicity, and school and work outcomes among youth and young adults with disabilities: A scoping review. *Disability and Rehabilitation, 1*–20. https://doi.org/10.1080/09638288.2021.2001056

Lövgren, V., Markström, U., & Sauer, L. (2017). Towards employment: What research says about support-to-work in relation to psychiatric and intellectual disabilities. *Journal of Social Work in Disability & Rehabilitation, 16*(1), 14–37. https://doi.org/10.1080/1536710X.2017.1260516

Masi, D. A. (2020). The history of employee assistance programs in the United States. *Journal of Employee Assistance, 50*(4), 30–33.

Mazzotti, Rowe, D. A., Kwiatek, S., Voggt, A., Chang, W.-H., Fowler, C. H., Poppen, M., Sinclair, J., & Test, D. W. (2021). Secondary transition predictors of postschool success: An update to the research base. *Career Development and Transition for Exceptional Individuals, 44*(1), 47–64. https://doi.org/10.1177/2165143420959793

Parish, S. L., & Cloud, J. M. (2006). Financial well-being of young children with disabilities and their families. *Social Work, 51*(3), 223–232.

Religious Freedom Restoration Act of 1993, 42 U.S.C. §§ 2000b b-2000b b-4 (1993).

Sabat, I. E., Lindsey, A. P., Membere, A., Anderson, A., Ahmad, A., King, E., & Bolunmez, B. (2014). Invisible disabilities: Unique strategies for workplace allies. *Industrial and Organizational Psychology, 7*(2), 259–265. https://doi.org/10.1111/iops.12145

Scott, L. A., & Bruno, L. (2018). Universal design for transition: A conceptual framework for blending academics and transition instruction. *The Journal of Special Education Apprenticeship, 7*(3), 1.

U.S. Bureau of Labor Statistics. (2022). Persons with a Disability: Labor Force Characteristics 2021 News Release. Economic News Releases. https://www.bls.gov/news.release/archives/disabl_02242022.htm

U.S. Bureau of Labor Statistics, Department of Labor. (2016). Employer-provided quality-of-life benefits, March 2016. *The Economics Daily.* https://www.bls.gov/opub/ted/2016/employer-provided-quality-of-life-benefits-march-2016.htm

Virginia Commonwealth University Center on Transition Innovations. (2021). *Transition assessment process: A guide for developing postsecondary goals and transition services.* https://centerontransition.org/publications/download.cfm?id=161&fbclid=IwAR2ssE5ri1s1ptweB6UXdbOXYOc55v30sGeb6xva144inX5WZCiWQaW1C-c

Wehman, P., Sima, A. P., Ketchum, J., West, M. D., Chan, F., & Luecking, R. (2014). Predictors of successful transition from school to employment for youth with disabilities. *Journal of Occupational Rehabilitation, 25*(2), 323–334. https://doi.org/10.1007/s10926-014-9541-6

Whittenburg, H. N., Cimera, R. E., & Thoma, C. A. (2019). Comparing employment outcomes of young adults with autism: Does postsecondary educational experience matter? *Journal of Postsecondary Education and Disability, 32*(2), 159–172.

Workforce Innovation and Opportunity Act of 2014, Pub. L. No. 113-128, Stat. 129 (2014). https://www.govinfo.gov/content/pkg/PLAW-113publ128/pdf/PLAW-113publ128.pdf

Workforce Innovation Technical Assistance Center (WINTAC). (n.d.). *CRP Pre-ETS guidebook: Strategies for community rehabilitation providers to collaborate on Pre-ETS.* http://www.wintac.org/topic-areas/pre-employment-transition-services/resources/crp-guidebook#section6

6

Postsecondary Education

Lauren P. Bruno, Kathryn M. Abrams,
Katherine R. Brendli Brown, and Donald D. McMahon[1]

DIGGING DEEPER: What Teachers Have to Say

As an undergraduate, I was told that, often, a teacher doesn't know what to do during their first year—you just need to survive to the next year. I got my degree in special education and graduated with a cohort of 22 women and one man, all White. I never thought much of it, given that we were all just passionate about teaching. Our college was located in a rural community, and the students we taught during our program were predominantly White, with a small number of Spanish-speaking children of farmers. My Spanish was never great, but I seemed to get by. After graduation, I got a teaching position at a school about 2 hours away, where the student population was 82% non-White, Hispanic; 7% Middle Eastern; and 11% White. I entered my first year full of optimism.

My first day was . . . well, not what I expected. I had never felt like the minority before, but there I was, a White, non-Hispanic, cisgender woman, in a classroom where not one person looked like me or sounded like me and where I also heard words that were unfamiliar.

During the first few weeks of school, I felt disconnected from my students. They made references to things I didn't know or understand, such as favorite foods or

[1] Chapter 6 is informed by the authors' experiences working with students in the Washington State University ROAR (Responsibility Opportunity Advocacy Respect) program based at Washington State University in Pullman, Washington.

hair maintenance tips I had never heard of. No one ever raised their hand to ask or answer a question, nor did any student stay after class. My students did not seem comfortable with me, and I couldn't understand what I was doing wrong!

Thankfully, I was soon assigned a mentor who gave me exercises about recognizing my own implicit biases and emphasized the importance of building positive relationships with my students and their families. My mentor also shared with me the difference between a safe space and a brave space and strategies on how I could foster a brave space within my classroom (e.g., acknowledging my own privilege and presuming positive intentions) so that my students can feel comfortable, and not threatened or defensive, while learning together in my classroom. Finally, even though I had heard of universal design for learning (UDL), my mentor also shared with me the elements of universal design for transition (UDT), such as emphasizing the need for multiple resources and perspectives so I could effectively connect with families and connect families with local agencies to better support their young adult's transition out of high school.

I began reading more about culturally responsive transition planning and how to create realistic and meaningful goals—including goals that honor the families' cultural values and what they want for their child. Prior to transition meetings, I began helping my students create their own presentations to share what was important to them and what they wanted to achieve after high school, using their preferred communication method. In the meetings, often held over the weekend when my students' family members were available outside of work hours, I emphasized the students' diversity as their strengths and focused on their preferences, interests, and needs.

One day, when I asked some of my students about the possibility of attending college, I had a few students speak up. One wanted to go because her siblings did it. Another just wanted the "college experience" and also believed he would need college to get his dream job of becoming a video game designer. However, even though multiple students wanted to go to college, many of these same students also explained why they couldn't. A few had been told by former teachers, family members, and even peers that college would never be a realistic option for them . . . because of their disability. Among the rest, the majority either did not want to go or had never considered education after high school, because some would have been first-generation college students.

I wanted to tell them all, "Of course you can go to college if you want to" and "Always set the bar high, because you can and will make meaningful contributions to this world!" I began using the UDT framework to determine how I could help students prepare for college. But what about my students with more significant intellectual disabilities, who weren't on a regular diploma track? What was I supposed to tell them?

I confided in a childhood friend whose brother had an intellectual disability and autism. I found out he had just started college last semester. My friend told me about programs affiliated with colleges and universities that give people with intellectual disabilities opportunities to participate in postsecondary education (PSE) and engage in academic courses, clubs, and organizations with nondisabled peers.

A few weeks later, I started having representatives from different colleges come in to talk to my students, and in my second year of teaching, I volunteered to co-host a college night, where a variety of colleges were represented, including those with online options and inclusive higher education programs. My priority was to educate my students and their families early on about the different diploma options, how different options impact the likelihood of college admission, and possible college and career opportunities. I then learned from my mentor about different in-school experiences in high school, such as being included in general education and setting goals to increase the likelihood of attaining successful outcomes like college and employment. I realized that using the UDT framework not only promotes inclusive education but also gives students the tools and instruction they need to be successful.

Essential Questions

▶ What are the various PSE options for students with disabilities?

▶ What specific tools, resources, and supports can be used when planning for college for students with disabilities?

▶ How can educators use the UDT framework to enhance students' knowledge and skills to plan for and prepare for PSE opportunities?

Enrollment in PSE can significantly benefit young adults, especially those with disabilities who have historically experienced poor postschool outcomes. Historically, people with disabilities have earned lower wages, have less economic independence, and have lower enrollment in PSE. Despite legislative changes in recent decades that have supported greater access to PSE for all students, including those with disabilities (e.g., the Higher Education Opportunity Act, 2008), they are also less likely than people without disabilities to earn a bachelor's degree or higher, 15% versus 32%, comparatively (Cornell Disability Statistics, 2018).

The term *postsecondary education* refers to any education after high school, including 4-year colleges and universities, 2-year programs, trade or technical schools, and/or community college (Individuals with Disabilities Education Improvement Act [IDEA], 2004). Definitions of each of the following types of programs are in Table 6.1. Research suggests that students with disabilities who participate in PSE of any kind have increased employment options (Cimera et al., 2018), are more likely to live independently (Ryan et al., 2019), and are more likely to participate in their community after graduation (Lee & Morningstar, 2019). In fact, PSE participation—regardless of whether a student earns a degree or certificate—broadens the scope of employment options for students with disabilities (Grigal & Papay, 2018).

This chapter begins by providing an overview of policies that support students' transition into PSE. Next, we discuss recommendations for supporting students with

Table 6.1.   Definitions of postsecondary education options for students with disabilities

Option	Definition
4-Year colleges and universities*	An institution authorized primarily to award bachelor's (or higher) degrees, such as a college or university
2-Year colleges*	A collegiate institution offering courses only through the first 2 years of college instruction and granting an associate's degree or a certificate or title
Vocational-technical schools and programs*	A technical or vocational school that primarily provides vocational education to individuals who have completed or left high school and who are available for study in preparation for entering the labor market, including students seeking an associate degree or certificate through a course of vocational instruction offered by the school
Community college*	Two-year schools that provide affordable postsecondary education as a pathway to a 4-year degree
Inclusive postsecondary education programs	Programs that provide access to people with intellectual disabilities to postsecondary education

*Open to all students with a disability as identified under the Individuals with Disabilities Education Improvement Act (2004) or Section 504 of the Rehabilitation Act (1973).

disabilities, including culturally and linguistically diverse students, in accessing information and resources they need to plan for PSE. The final sections of the chapter discuss this preparation in relation to the UDT framework. We discuss these concepts as they apply to the case study of Julia, a young woman preparing for transition, whose story is revisited throughout the chapter.

POLICIES SUPPORTING TRANSITION TO POSTSECONDARY EDUCATION

At the level of federal policy, several measures have been enacted that support students with disabilities in transitioning to higher education. These include IDEA (1990, 1997, 2004), the Higher Education Opportunity Act (HEOA, 2008), and the Workforce Innovation and Opportunity Act (WIOA, 2014). Details of each piece of legislation are discussed in the sections that follow.

The Individuals with Disabilities Education Act

As noted previously, changes to federal legislation have increased college/university enrollment for students with disabilities in recent decades. For starters, IDEA (1990), formerly known as the Education for All Handicapped Children Act (1975), has been the centerfold in terms of education policy for students with disabilities in the kindergarten through Grade 12 (K–12) settings since 1990. Yet, it was not until the 1997 reauthorization of IDEA that special education policy mandated services that focused on transition from high school to PSE, independent living, and/or employment for students with disabilities. With the IDEA reauthorization in 2004, transition planning must begin when a student with a disability turns 16 years old (formerly age 14), and per Indicator 13, transition services must be provided and should consider PSE as an outcome. To complete a holistic and compliant transition plan, educators must include measurable goals in the areas of employment and PSE in addition to employment and independent living (if appropriate); use age-appropriate transition assessments, invite outside agencies (i.e., state vocational rehabilitation agencies) to learn about the supports they can provide for enrollment in PSE, and connect transition plans with annual individualized education program (IEP) goals (Prince et al., 2013). By including all of these required transition pieces, practitioners, educators, students, their families, and other stakeholders can be involved in the transition process to enhance overall outcomes for the students. This is critical because Indicator 14, added to the reauthorization of IDEA in 2004, which measures students' postschool outcomes, and students' enrollment in PSE within 1 year after leaving high school, is one of the indicators being tracked.

Despite the mandates for transition planning, students from historically marginalized backgrounds experience disparities in postsecondary degree enrollment and attainment. Thus, increasing the representation of students of color in higher education, particularly students of color with disabilities, requires educators to take further action to ensure that transition planning is culturally responsive, sustained, and holistic. One way to do this is through the use of the UDT framework.

The Higher Education Opportunity Act of 2008

Another critical piece of legislation that empowers individuals with disabilities to gain access to PSE opportunities is HEOA, which was enacted in 2008 as a reauthorization of the Higher Education Act of 1965. The overarching purpose of this policy is to strengthen the educational resources of colleges and universities to provide assistance to individuals with disabilities to participate in PSE, including programs for young adults with intellectual and developmental disabilities. The first critical piece was the authorization of the creation of comprehensive transition and postsecondary (CTP) programs for students with intellectual and developmental disabilities with a focus on academic, social, employment, and independent living supports (Shanley, 2010/2011). In addition, students enrolled in a CTP program were also made eligible for certain kinds of federal financial aid.

The HEOA not only provides opportunities for students with disabilities to access higher education but also provides a greater focus on transition planning and enhancing transition planning in prekindergarten through Grade 12. Secondary special educators can learn about various college programs and can offer information and resources to students and their transition planning teams (e.g., family members, extended family, community agency partners). Vocational rehabilitation professionals can also offer support or address topics related to transitioning to PSE. Parents and families can also encourage the development of opportunities for students with disabilities at institutions by offering to share information, serve in advisory capacities, and bring resources from other networks or their community to planning meetings. This is a critical component because when parents expect their children to attend PSE institutions, they are more likely to achieve PSE (e.g., Chiang et al., 2012; Doren et al., 2012; Papay & Bambara, 2014). Wagner et al. (2014) found that when controlling for socioeconomic status and parent expectations (among other mediators), African American students were more likely than their White peers to graduate from high school and participate in PSE (e.g., a 4-year college or university) or training (e.g., career technical education programs).

The Workforce Innovation and Opportunity Act of 2014

Another policy that has impacted the lives of individuals with disabilities is the WIOA. Signed into law in 2014, this act replaces the Workforce Investment Act of 1998. WIOA's priority is to serve individuals who are most at risk; this can be determined by different factors, including disability status, income, and school enrollment status. The purpose of the law is to help individuals who are seeking employment to gain the education, training, and support services needed in order to be successful within the labor market. This law also matches employers to the workers with the appropriate skill set to compete within the global economy (U.S. Department of Labor, n.d.).

In addition, it is important to note that WIOA (2014) seeks to minimize racial/ethnic disparities. This is critically important because historically marginalized populations (e.g., racially and culturally diverse students) are often underrepresented in PSE. To illustrate, 73% of students with intellectual and developmental disabilities enrolled in PSE programs are White (Grigal et al., 2016), and 42% of students enrolled in traditional college/university programs are also White, with a majority of students identifying as Asian (59%; de Brey et al., 2019). Therefore, WIOA now requires localities to report on the racial and ethnic characteristics of their participants; based on planning and performance accountability systems, traditional systemic barriers to obtaining resources, services, and opportunities will be minimized, thus enhancing the access to postsecondary enrollment for individuals from historically marginalized backgrounds.

Some of the specific services that are included within WIOA and individualized to youths' goals and assessments are tutoring, paid and unpaid work experiences, occupational skills training, leadership development, counseling, and other support services. These services are based on each individual's goals and assessments. Services provided under WIOA, through state divisions of vocational rehabilitation services, can also help students prepare for and enroll in PSE.

SUPPORTING ACCESS

It is important to understand the variety of PSE options so families can start planning as early as possible for their child's life after high school. For instance, does the student want to obtain a specific degree or certificate, or enroll in an inclusive PSE program? Determining what type of program would be a good fit for the student to reach their goals is a critical first step. In addition, it is important to consider whether there is a specific university that a student wants to attend because of 1) alumni in their family, 2) their race/ethnicity, 3) their religious affiliations, or 4) an interest in sports (i.e., Division I, II, III sports) or the arts.

Begin Planning Early

These conversations need to begin early, and parents/guardians and family members need to be considering these options well before the student enters high school. Ideally, this is a conversation that begins in elementary school and carries throughout their schooling when discussing their goals and eventually beginning their transition plan. During the transition process, within the IEP, case managers should discuss postschool goals and possible college options with students and their families, caregivers, and support networks—that is, they should seek multiple resources and perspectives—to gauge their interest level. Therefore, it is critical that transition specialists, case managers, and/or special educators be familiar with the PSE options and programs to highlight what services can be provided in the different settings (i.e., inclusive PSE programs, traditional university experiences, junior colleges, vocational schools, and the job force).

Table 6.2. Preparing for college checklist for all students

Time period	Preparation
Elementary	• Do your best in school. • Have fun. • Read a lot. Parents can help instill an interest in reading at an early age by reading to their child regularly.
Junior high/ Middle school	• Begin thinking about college as an important part of your future. • Talk with family and friends about ideas. • Begin saving for college. • Take interesting classes to prepare for high school and determine your interests. • Ask family members, teachers, or community members to help you identify what classes to enroll in for high school. • Do your best in school. • Develop strong study habits. • Get involved in school activities and the community (e.g., religious groups, sports, music, art, cultural groups). • Speak with adults in your community (e.g., family, friends, teachers, counselors, relatives) about their job and what education they needed for it.
High school	• Begin exploring the FAFSA website (https://studentaid.gov/h/apply-for-aid/fafsa). • Take challenging classes in core academic subjects and your interest areas. • Stay involved in school or community-based activities that are interesting or important to you. • Talk to your counselor and family about education after high school and ask questions. • Take necessary college admissions exams and research admission requirements (check application requirements too). • Explore careers and identify the schooling/career pathway needed to obtain that career. • Visit and explore college and career planning websites to understand options; this includes talking to your teacher and family about available options.

The U.S. Department of Education (n.d.-a) provides students with a college preparation checklist that begins as young as elementary school. Specific skills for college planning are presented in Table 6.2. As you read through the case study of Julia later in this section, you will see that she began thinking about and planning for college during middle school, a crucial time to start to think about your future. However, for students with disabilities, it is important to be mindful of student goals, the training or education that is needed to achieve those goals, and if education or training is in the students' interest. Moreover, student and family members must also be aware of the different high school diploma options offered by the school, because some types of diplomas are not accepted by community colleges or universities. This is typically addressed in IEP meetings when discussing students' academics and their transition out of high school. Ensuring that families have a full understanding of the options, and the requirements to meet those options, is necessary.

Examine a Variety of Options

Often, the options that first come to mind are 2- or 4-year colleges and universities requiring, at minimum, a regular high school diploma for admission and from which a student graduates with a degree in a particular area of study. However, many other education and training opportunities can also be of great interest to students and align with their transition goals. For example, young adults with intellectual disabilities may desire to apply to inclusive PSE programs offered at colleges and universities across the country. In addition, culturally and linguistically diverse students may wish to apply to a school that focuses on educating students from the same cultural or linguistic background or to a school that has a large population of students from the same background.

Options for Students With More Significant Disabilities   Inclusive PSE programs may receive the recognition of CTP program under the Higher Education Opportunity Act (2008). A CTP program for students with intellectual disabilities means a degree, certificate, or non-degree program that is offered by a college or career school. These programs are designed to support students with intellectual disabilities who want to continue academic, career, and independent living instruction to prepare for gainful employment. CTP programs require students with intellectual disabilities to participate, for at least half of the program, in regular enrollment in credit-bearing or audit courses with nondisabled students and internships or work-based training with nondisabled individuals. In addition, students typically participate in inclusive campus and community activities, and these programs also offer academic advising and a structured curriculum.

Minority-Serving Institutions   Although access to college for students with disabilities is important, understanding college options specific to culturally and linguistically diverse students with disabilities is also important. For instance, Black students who want PSE might consider enrollment in one of the Historically Black Colleges and Universities (HBCUs), which are as defined under the Department of Education. They were originally established with their primary mission being the education of Black Americans. HBCUs provide inclusive campus communities for traditionally underrepresented minorities.

Others include Hispanic Serving Institutions, which are accredited, postsecondary, higher educational institutions with at least 25% total full-time enrollment of Hispanic undergraduate students. Hispanic Serving Institutions include 4-year and 2-year public and private educational institutions. There are also Tribal Colleges and Universities and Asian American and Pacific Islander Serving Institutions. Recognizing and understanding the missions of these universities can help educators better guide, educate, and connect students and families with resources that may align with their values, culture, and ethnicity.

CASE STUDY: Julia

Using Early Interests to Begin Planning

Meet Julia, a Native American high school student who was diagnosed with autism when she was 3 years old. Julia, who was raised by her grandparents, and the rest of her family live in a small rural community near the native lands of the Colville tribe. She and her family are members of the Confederated Tribes of the Colville Reservation in Washington state, located in the inland Pacific Northwest. Julia's Native American heritage has inspired her creativity and her love of art. In her words, "My autism has prevented me from understanding emotions until I learned that emotions are colors. Native American art is filled with colors and set patterns. Drawing my culture on paper both calmed me and allowed me to express my emotions. I fell in love with drawing and was inspired to try other styles of illustrations." Her passion is art, and she uses this as a means to express herself, her heritage, and her experiences. In Julia's words, "Since I live on the Native Lands, I'm able to see problems drugs, alcohol, unemployment, and poverty cause. Suicide is a common escape. I try to help by drawing Native American–themed suicide prevention illustrations with the message that people matter. I don't know if they help others, but they have helped me be at peace with what I've seen." While Julia was working on a project in high school, Julia's ninth-grade art teacher talked to her about their college experience. Julia then began to get curious and asked her grandparents about college and whether she could go. Her grandparents explained that college can help students get a degree and further themselves in their careers. They had concerns about her attending college because she has a disability, was working on meeting her IEP goals, and was still developing her interpersonal relationship skills. However, knowing this was becoming a dream and goal of Julia's, they decided to open a special financial account to start saving money for this potential opportunity. They began to inquire with her IEP case manager about college opportunities for Julia. Due to Julia's ability levels, they determined enrollment in an inclusive PSE program would be best. The case manager found a checklist of skills Julia would need to be successful within the inclusive PSE program (see Figure 6.1).

Understand Barriers to Enrollment

Julia's grandparents had some concerns about how her disability might impact her college experience. Many students with disabilities face barriers to enrollment. Two common barriers are financial barriers and barriers related to independent living skills and self-advocacy.

Financial Barriers   Cost, whether it be in an inclusive PSE program or a traditional 2- or 4-year college, often creates barriers for many students seeking enrollment in inclusive PSE programs. This is also true for students with disabilities enrolling as traditional students in PSE programs as well. One criticism of CTP programs is that many require families to pay out of pocket for most of the cost of tuition—which is the same as, or similar to, regular tuition rates for degree-seeking students. Research suggests that household income is strongly related to college enrollment, and students with disabilities from low-income backgrounds experience an even greater gap in access to PSE (Madeus et al., 2014). One resource to which educators can direct students that supports enrollment in PSE is Federal Student Aid (also known as Free Application for Federal Student Aid [FAFSA]; U.S. Department of Education, n.d.-b). The FAFSA website (https://studentaid.gov/h/apply-for-aid/fafsa) also provides students and their families with checklists for academic and financial preparation, including other financial aid opportunities to pay for college. These include the following:

- Grants and scholarships: Financial aid that does not have to be repaid, including Federal Pell Grants (students in CTPs have access to these as well), which can award as much as $5,815 to each low-income student per year (HEOA, 2008)

- Work study: A program that allows students to earn money for their education

- Low-interest loans: Aid that allows students to borrow money for their education; loans must be repaid with interest.

Preparation Skills Checklist for Students
in an Inclusive Postsecondary Education Program

☐ Be comfortable spending nights away from home

☐ Independence with health and grooming (e.g., shower daily, use deodorant, take own medication)

☐ Independent living skills:

    ☐ Clean and organize your room and complete chores and tasks around the house

    ☐ Manage money

    ☐ Buy things that are needed for yourself and the apartment

    ☐ Prepare and cook meals

☐ Independence in navigating the campus and community using a map and the bus system

☐ Willingness to make new friends and/or initiate appropriate relationships with other students and peers

☐ Ability to use technology for academic purposes

☐ Organization skills for time management and class assignments

☐ Basic math skills and know how to use a calculator

☐ Have prior work or volunteer experience

☐ Complete tasks in those work-related experiences

☐ Develop daily schedule for time management

☐ Willingness to meet other people and learn how to work with them

☐ Learn and practice social skills that you are comfortable with

☐ Practice building a resume and cover letter

Figure 6.1. Preparation skills checklist for students in an inclusive postsecondary education program.

Another potential barrier for some students and families is developing the independent living skills the student will need at college, especially if they plan to move out of the family household and into a dormitory or apartment. These include everyday skills such as the following:

- Using maps and transportation
- Using a college meal plan or planning and preparing one's own meals
- Doing laundry
- Keeping one's living space neat and clean

- Managing one's daily schedule (including sleep/waking times)

- Getting along with roommates/housemates

- Advocating for one's own needs

Learning and using these skills can be an adjustment for any young adult living apart from their family for the first time, including young adults with disabilities. This was another concern Julia's grandparents had about her making the transition into college.

CASE STUDY: Julia, *continued*

Teaching Independent Living and Self-Advocacy Skills

After reviewing the preparation skills checklist (Figure 6.1), Julia's grandparents still had concerns about her college readiness. Because Julia lived in a small town, opportunities to learn some of these skills, such as using a bus system, were not available to her. Her grandparents stated, "Although she does well in most of her inclusive high school courses, Julia has a hard time with some specific independent living tasks. So, we are worried about her living on her own in an apartment with other students. It is a lot of responsibility to run a household and complete the tasks to maintain this. Some of the specific things we are worried about are her navigating around town or to new locations, advocating for herself when she needs help, and keeping up with household tasks." Her special education teacher assured her grandparents that these were skills they could work on in the classroom while also making sure Julia was getting the academic instruction she needed.

This included working with Julia on her self-determination and utilizing multiple resources and perspectives (e.g., gaining input from her other teachers, grandparents, art teacher). It also involved inviting representatives from a variety of community agencies, including the Division of Vocational Rehabilitation, to start Julia in group Pre-Employment Transition Services to receive instruction in self-advocacy to help with disability disclosure. The teacher and family also wanted to ensure that she would attend a university that would help her stay connected to her Native American heritage.

Design Transition Programming to Support Enrollment

Research suggests that designing and evaluating transition programs in alignment with predictors (i.e., in-school experiences that predict specific postschool outcomes) of postschool success may support the attainment of outcome areas, such as enrollment in PSE. There are currently 23 predictors of postschool success (Mazzotti et al., 2020). Among these predictors, the research shows that in addition to grandparents and family members, educators also play a critical role in supporting students to reach their postschool goals, including supporting students' potential aspirations to participate in PSE. By understanding students' goals, educators can help families better understand what is needed (e.g., a specific diploma type) or what would support (e.g., aligning transition programs with predictors) the students in achieving their goals. In particular, educators' curriculums, expectations, and use of technology influence enrollment in PSE (Madeus et al., 2014), which aligns with principles of UDL and the UDT framework.

Next, it is important to know what about a university is important to the student and their family. Questions teachers and families should consider address the characteristics of the college/university. Questions that you can ask students include the following:

- Do you want a large or small university (e.g., community college, small private college, liberal arts school, technical school)?

- What type of setting/community do you want for your choice of university (e.g., urban, suburban, rural) and what are the transportation options in the area?

- What do you want your living arrangements to be (e.g., commuter, residential, apartment, dorm)?

- How accessible is the campus?

- What types of courses do you want to take and are they available at your preferred university?

- What types of supports will you need to be successful?

- What specific groups, clubs, and networks are there that support diverse students (i.e., race/ethnicity, first generation, gender/sexual orientation, disability)?

- What groups must be available for you to feel connected and supported as you make the transition to college?

Because students may not know these answers right away, it will be important to allow students to explore college websites, understand campus resources, and research programs that may be good for them. By allowing students to explore these topics on their own, it can help them become more independent and self-directed when making their decisions. As Julia's story illustrates, it is important to incorporate the whole team into the decision-making process, tour campuses, and acquire a clear understanding of what a program offers.

CASE STUDY: Julia, *continued*

Finding the Right Program and Preparing for Transition

By the time Julia was a junior in high school and preparing to attend college, she was working closely with her parents, IEP case manager, and guidance counselor to identify postsecondary programs that might align with her needs and goals. After independently searching and identifying three programs, Julia and her family planned to tour the programs and campuses and then apply to the program that seemed like the best fit. Julia stated that her favorite campus was one where she received a prompt email from the program with directions on how to sign up for a tour. Julia and her family made the drive to the college campus and were feeling anxious but excited for the opportunity.

Julia and her family were greeted by one of the program staff when they entered the building where the program was housed. When she first entered the building, one part that struck Julia immediately and made her feel connected to the university was the Native American Student Center; she later learned her classes would be in the same building. The tour, which was led by current students in the program, began, and it included a stop at the Native American Student Center. Julia was able to meet the staff member who runs the center. Knowing this was an important part of her heritage and identity, the family appreciated this specific tour stop and conversation.

Julia then attended one of the PSE program's specific courses. During the class, Julia learned about specific skills that students use when they are on the job or in their internships. After the class, a few of the students led Julia and her family to the students' apartments. They showed her the laundry room, where they get their mail, and the inside of an apartment. This helped Julia's family feel more comfortable about the transition to college. Julia liked that there was a lot of space in the living room and that she would have her own room. After visiting the student apartment, Julia enjoyed some down time with her family, and they had lunch in the community.

The last part of the tour included a social event put on by the PSE program. The students and peer allies met and played board games, listened to music, and ate snacks together. Julia chose to play a card game with some of the other students. She left the campus tour feeling excited to apply and enroll in college.

A few months later, Julia learned she had been accepted into the program. Julia was really excited that she got into college. In her acceptance letter, the staff told her that she would be able to take art classes because that is what she liked to do.

Julia still had some questions and approached her teacher about them. She said, "Someday I would like to be an artist and sell my work to authors or the newspaper. However, I am also kind of nervous to go to college. Some questions that I have are:

- Can I join clubs on campus that have to do with art?
- Are there other campus organizations for Native American students?
- How do the buses on campus work?
- If I get sick, what should I do?
- What types of events are on campus where I can meet people with interests similar to mine?"

Although Julia's case manager did not have all of the answers, she knew she could help Julia in certain areas. Her case manager began doing more research about opportunities for Julia to get connected within the campus community. Julia's case manager knew about and recognized how important Julia's Native American heritage was to her. Therefore, she visited the college website and put together a list of resources and opportunities for Julia to get connected with other Native American students on the campus through various student organizations as well as other on-campus resources and support for academics and employment opportunities. This helped Julia and her family know what else to ask about and search for when she arrived on campus. Julia's teacher also knew that writing and art are important to her. Therefore, she began helping Julia improve her writing skills by using technology and reporting on current events in her social studies class.

PREPARING STUDENTS USING THE UDT FRAMEWORK

The planning considerations discussed throughout this chapter can all be addressed using a UDT framework for preparing students for PSE. Preparation informed by this framework addresses multiple life domains, uses multiple means of assessment, fosters student self-determination, and includes multiple resources and z.

Multiple Life Domains

When beginning to research or explore PSE options, transition teams should be aware of different types of programs that are designed differently to meet different student needs and ability levels. These various types of programs might differ in terms of length (2-year vs. 4-year), campus type (residential vs. commuter), and outcomes (certificate vs. degree). All of these options create different opportunities for the students attending the programs. By understanding them, students and their families can determine which option would be best when preparing for the rigor of multiple life domains—not just education and employment, but also community living as well as social inclusion and engagement.

For many students, PSE serves as a starting point to following their goals for their career. Therefore, to ensure a complete and integrated transition, there are a few other things to determine and keep in mind. With the student's future life goals in mind, stakeholders can inquire with the student about which program would align with these goals. Once the student is clear about what their goals are, the student, with family and/or school support, can use college search website features (e.g., College Board, Think College [https://thinkcollege.net]) to narrow down the program of choice. These filters can help students and families make decisions based on the alignment of the students' future goals across a variety of areas. Search features include filters based on the following:

1. Location (filter by state)

2. Program features:

   a. Serves students in high school

   b. Offers financial aid

   c. Offers housing

   d. Is not limited by schools/districts

3. Disability categories served

4. Public or private institution

5. Type of school

6. Length of program

This will help students ensure that they are on the correct trajectory to reach their life goals. For instance, if a student wants to ultimately live independently with their family's support, it would be important to select programs or universities that have on- or off-campus housing, rather than a commuter campus where the student may still need to live at home. In addition, it is important to consider whether the student will be working during college when determining their class schedule and involvement in extracurricular activities.

Multiple Means of Assessment

Collecting information about students using unbiased, personalized assessments allows PSE programs and transition experts to move beyond compliance but understand assessment data through an equitable lens. Data can be harmful when it reinforces untrue and negative stereotypes about students (Toldson, 2021). It is also important to collect data through multiple sources, such as 1) interviews with students, family members, and/or teachers; 2) observations of students across settings; 3) completion of interest inventories, positive personal profiles, or life skills inventories; and/or 4) use of formal assessments (e.g., Self-Determination Inventory System [Shogren & Wehmeyer, 2017], BRIGANCE Transition Skills Inventory–2 [Curriculum Associates, n.d.], Adaptive Behavior Assessment System, Third Edition [Harrison & Oakland, 2013]). When collecting the data, it is also important to hold students to high expectations and push them beyond their limits while also listening to their goals without minimizing them. This focuses on the students' assets, supports meaningful engagement, and practices sociopolitical awareness. Research suggests that data use can lead to increased student learning and achievement (e.g., Lai et al., 2014; McNaughton et al., 2012; Poortman & Schildkamp, 2016; Van Geel et al., 2016).

Transition teams ideally will apply multiple means of assessment to a PSE student and keep the UDL guidelines in mind. While doing so, they can also foster self-determination. Following is a practical example of how multiple means of assessment can increase student self-determination by putting the student in charge and setting high expectations for their success. Incorporating multiple means of assessment based on the student's strengths empowers the student's knowledge within the setting. Self-determination is discussed further in the next section.

CASE STUDY: Julia, *continued*

Planning Assessments That Foster Self-Determination

Julia is now enrolled in the PSE program to which she applied and was accepted. She is very confident in her art skills but is nervous to audit a university-level course in art history. Previously, in high school, writing was not one of her strengths, so looking at the syllabus for the course is overwhelming for her. Staff within the program provide modifications to the assessments that incorporate Julia's drawing skills, but they also require her to explain what she has drawn using speech-to-text software. This not only empowers her to show what she is learning through her art, but also it asks her to explain more to her professor about how and why she chose to draw what she did.

Student Self-Determination

Student self-determination is woven into the goals and philosophies if many PSE programs. Self-determination is the ability to make choices, solve problems, set goals, evaluate options, take initiative to reach one's goals, and accept consequences of one's actions (Rowe et al., 2015). Within self-determination is goal setting. A review of the predictor literature (Mazzotti et al., 2016) found two quality exploratory studies (Carter et al., 2012; Chiang et al., 2012) with enough evidence to establish goal setting as a predictor of post-school education and employment. Although considered a component of self-determination, in the Test et al. (2009) review, goal setting was also used to define students' level of self-determination in high school.

Families and school teams can prepare students for PSE programs by supporting them in gaining some of the skills they would need to be successful in that setting. Figure 6.1, shown previously in this chapter, addresses independent living skills to prepare for college, which could be woven into the student's IEP goals, tracked, and monitored by school staff. These skills could also be reinforced in the home. Mastering them allows for students to become more independent and confident in their skills before attending college. Another way students can become more self-determined is to have an awareness of their disability, strengths, preferences, and identity. Students can do this by becoming involved within their community and seeking out groups/clubs that interest them. This could seem like a daunting task on a college campus. Therefore, it is important for students to build relationships with PSE staff and get them involved, so the staff can help them get more connected on the campus.

Multiple Resources and Perspectives

After collaborating with the student to understand their PSE goals and narrowing down their college search, counselors and other stakeholders can support the student in reaching out to the programs to learn more. Some programs have generic information available online whereas others may need to be contacted directly. The student could request more information or a campus tour, or the student could ask to be connected with students in the program to learn more about their individual experiences. Families may also want to inquire with their local vocational rehabilitation services in their area, as well as other disability services that are available to them. School counselors may also be able to support students in their PSE journey by contacting the PSE programs to learn more about specific skills students need upon entry to the program, or how the admissions process works. Counselors and case managers should also be aware of the groups, clubs, and networks available on the college campus that can support students with diverse backgrounds. Connecting the prospective student with the college's cultural centers and programs would provide an important resource for the student who is weighing their postsecondary options.

Supports and resources will likely look different for the student in college as compared to a K–12 experience. To prepare for this change, access to campus resources may be beneficial. Following are some of the campus resources that stakeholders might want to inquire about with PSE staff to ensure their needs may be met and can fully enjoy an inclusive education experience:

- Health services

- Disability services

- Tutoring services

- Library

- Student life

- Recreational centers

- Technology services

In addition, for students from historically underrepresented backgrounds, it is imperative to identify additional resources and supports that can be used to feel connected to a larger campus community. Some of these include the following:

- Multicultural student affairs

- Centers for equity, inclusion, and diversity

- Sororities or fraternities

- Student organizations

Many of these services are available to students on a college campus. Before enrolling or applying to a PSE program, students and their families may want to inquire about the PSE program's connection to these on-campus services. Once on campus, engaging with these services and clubs may help students increase their self-determination, advocacy, and cultural awareness.

Technology Supports for UDL

PSE programs do not just focus on students learning academics, but a wide variety of domains, such as independent living, employment, social skills, and technology. Technology is one useful tool that individuals who attend PSE programs can individualize based on their needs across all of these domains and use to be successful in these educational settings. With mobile devices, tablets, and assistive technology tools, students in PSE programs can use accessibility features and customizations to meet their PSE and life goals. Table 6.3 intertwines the UDL guidelines and specific technology tools that students could use to support their learning needs within inclusive environments to promote a positive and successful transition to PSE. These are just a few of the examples of how technology can assist students to reach their goals within the PSE program and beyond.

Reflection

Consider the recommendations in this chapter for how to support a student who is pursuing PSE. Then, identify a student with whom you work who has disabilities. Where are they in the process of planning for secondary education—just beginning to identify interests and future goals, well along in their high school education, or preparing to transition into PSE within the next year? What concrete steps can you take to identify PSE options that align with this student's and family's aspirations (which may include a desire to stay connected with a specific culture, as in Julia's case)? How can you help the student and family learn more about potential programs? What supports might this student need in a PSE setting?

Table 6.3. Inclusive postsecondary education needs matched to universal design for transition guidelines

Engagement	Representation	Action and expression
Recruiting interest • Use a person-centered planning approach to identify students' interests/wants for inclusive course options, internship opportunities, and social activities. • Minimize distractions in transition activities by teaching students to utilize technology features, such as "Do not disturb" mode on their personnel devices. • Help students to understand why the transition skills you are teaching match to their authentic personal goals. Allow students to explore, experiment, and have opportunities to use their imagination to help them understand the value of these transition skills.	**Perception** • Know and understand how to use accessibility features on devices (e.g., phones/computer). • Teach students to use text-to-speech tools to listen to course readings. • In higher education, information in some classes is presented only once. A critical means of providing options for perception includes making sure students can revisit, review, and relearn critical information when necessary. Try to create supports and systems that allow students to be in control of replaying information "just in time" exactly when they will need it (e.g., recording lectures).	**Physical action** • Students engage in exergaming opportunities with their same-age peers. • Increase access to assistive technologies (ATs) such as "Read Write," which allows students alternatives to typing and/reading large sections of text and provides options for the speed of content. • Provide and teach various methods for using AT to provide supports for their full participation in transition and independent living activities (teach multiple navigation supports using technology to increase community independence). • Ensure that AT tools are sustaining the language and culture of the student at home and in educational settings.
Sustaining effort and persistence • Use a variety of technology tools to allow students to engage with course content. In addition to readings, consider podcasts, videos, and self-directed learning modules. • Build communities that meet in person or virtually to connect about transition challenges and to celebrate transition skill successes (e.g., employment or recipe clubs). • Vary demands and resources used to teach and support employment-related tasks. Examples include direct peer supports, video models, audio prompts, or printed task analysis to help a student work independently.	**Language and symbols** • Embed Grammarly (https://www.grammarly.com) onto your browser to help with editing and writing. • Install and use a visual thesaurus. • Use a Lucidchart (https://www.lucidchart.com/) to create graphic organizers/mindmaps.	**Expression and communication** • Allow students to use multiple technology tools to express and demonstrate their content mastery, such as an interactive whiteboard app. • Students can illustrate/draw what they know on a topic and record their explanation. • For example, in an Introduction to Ecology class lesson on nonpoint source pollution, the student can draw what they know about how nonpoint source pollution enters the water cycle and then use it as a volunteer or internship opportunity to help with community cleanup.
Self-regulation • Optimize motivation for independent living and employment tasks with checklists, rubrics, and guides that students can use when they are struggling. • Provide same-age peers who mentor, coach, or provide models of successfully completing transition skills. • Help student reflect on the importance of transition skills to achieve their personal goals (e.g., "I'm watching this YouTube video on how to make this meal so I can work on living on my own").	**Comprehension** • Have students use text-to-speech tools to listen to the assignments in the course's learning management system (e.g., Canvas, Blackboard, Moodle). • For assignments and help providing work experiences, use video models to help provide supports (video with task analysis on how to complete an activity). • Select AT tools that support transfer and generalization of skills.	**Executive function** • Digital assistants on mobile devices, such as SIRI, Alexa, and Google Assistant, can allow students to quickly set reminders and prompts for where to go and when, and to provide reminders for working on assignments. • Use scaffolds for organization and goal setting with technology tools such as OneNote (Windows), Reminders (iOS), or Tasks (Google). • Provide scaffolded templates for course assignments that help the student understand the steps of the assignment/project.

Source: McMahon & Smith (2012).

WRAP-UP: PREPARING FOR POSTSECONDARY EDUCATION

Preparing for life after the K–12 learning experience is not an easy task. There can be much uncertainty and hesitation for individuals with disabilities, not to mention additional barriers for historically marginalized individuals. Understanding and utilizing UDT, with the use of technology, can provide individuals who seek PSE a better understanding of the options available to them after their K–12 experience. The positive outcomes for individuals with disabilities after attending a PSE program are promising in terms of gaining employment and living independently. By learning a wide variety of life and academic skills, setting goals, increasing self-awareness, and collaboration with stakeholders, individuals with disabilities can lead purposeful, meaningful, and successful lives.

▶ **Tips for Preparing Students for Postsecondary Education**

1. **Know the different options for PSE and which are appropriate for students to meet their goals.** Consider not only the student's career goals but also goals related to their personal interests (e.g., Julia's interest in art) and to other life domains, such as independent living in the community and social life. Be aware of any goals students have for building or strengthening connections to their culture.

2. **Know what degrees/credentials are needed to obtain employment in the area the student is interested in pursuing after college.** Research this subject so you can provide the student and family with up-to-date, specific information.

3. **Engage and share information with families about postsecondary options starting early.** Ideally, these discussions begin in middle school or early in the student's high school years. Maintain ongoing communication about the student's strengths, interests (career and otherwise), and areas where the student and the family expect to need supports.

4. **Bring in guest speakers and connect with PSE programs throughout the country to share information with students.** Guest speakers might include students and staff from PSE programs.

5. **Connect students' academic and transition goals with skills needed for enrollment in PSE.** By reaching out to PSE programs to understand eligibility criteria, students and their case managers can develop IEP goals that would lead them to the path of inclusive PSE programs.

   Table 6.4 lists resources for supporting students in pursuing PSE.

Table 6.4. Resources for supporting students in pursuing postsecondary education

College search tools	
College Board https://www.collegeboard.org/	A comprehensive website that provides a variety of services that include scholarship applications, research, advocacy, college planning, and college and career search tools
Think College https://thinkcollege.net/	A national organization dedicated to developing, expanding, and improving inclusive higher education options for people with intellectual disability
Preparing for college	
College Board's Big Future https://bigfuture.collegeboard.org/	Big Future helps students plan for college and careers—with chances to earn scholarships.
Grammarly https://app.grammarly.com/	A cloud-based typing assistant that reviews spelling, grammar, punctuation, clarity, engagement, and delivery mistakes. Grammarly can help students who are preparing college essays.
Federal Student Aid (U.S. Department of Education) https://studentaid.gov/	The Free Application for Federal Student Aid (FAFSA) form can be used to apply for financial aid for college and learn more about preparing for college.
Mapping Your Future http://mappingyourfuture.org/collegeprep/	Plan for college now and learn how to be a successful college student.
NTACT resources	
NTACT: The Collaborative—Postsecondary Education https://transitionta.org/topics/postsecondary-education/	Provides tools and resources for successful transition planning to postsecondary education, including a transition guide and toolkit
NTACT: The Collaborative—Diversity, Equity, and Inclusion https://transitionta.org/topics/dei/	Resources to ensure that teachers are meeting the needs of all learners, including students from traditionally underrepresented backgrounds
Professional organizations	
Council for Exceptional Children, Division on Career Development and Transition https://dcdt.org/	An international professional educational organization whose members are dedicated to shaping policies and practices that impact the quality of career development and transition services of youth with exceptionalities

REFERENCES

Carter, E. W., Austin, D., & Trainor, A. A. (2012). Predictors of postschool employment outcomes for young adults with severe disabilities. *Journal of Disability Policy Studies, 23*(1), 50–63. https://doi.org/10.1177/1044207311414680

Chiang, H.-M., Cheung, Y., Hickson, L., Xiang, R., & Tsai, L. (2012). Predictive factors of participation in postsecondary education for high school leavers with autism. *Journal of Autism and Developmental Disorders, 42,* 685–696.

Cimera, R. E., Thoma, C. A., Whittenburg, H. N., & Ruhl, A. N. (2018). Is getting a postsecondary education a good investment for supported employees with intellectual disability and taxpayers? *Inclusion, 6*(2), 97–109.

College Board. (2022a). *BigFuture.* https://bigfuture.collegeboard.org

College Board. (2022b). *College starts here.* https://www.collegeboard.org

Cornell Disability Statistics. (2018). *American Community Survey data.* https://www.disabilitystatistics.org/reports/acs.cfm?statistic=9

Curriculum Associates. (n.d.). *BRIGANCE Transition Skills Inventory–2.*

de Brey, C., Musu, L., McFarland, J., Wilkinson-Flicker, S., Diliberti, M., Zhang, A., Branstetter, C., & Wang, X. (2019). *Status and trends in the education of racial and ethnic groups 2018* (NCES 2019-038). U.S. Department of Education. National Center for Education Statistics. https://nces.ed.gov/pubsearch/pubsinfo.asp?pubid=2019038

Doren, B., Gau, J. M., & Lindstrom, L. E. (2012). The relationship between parent expectations and postschool outcomes of adolescents with disabilities. *Exceptional Children, 79*, 7–23.

Education for All Handicapped Children Act of 1975, Pub. L. No. 94-142, 20 U.S.C. §§ 1400 *et seq.* (1975).

Grigal, M., Hart, D., Smith, F. A., Domin, D., & Weir, C. (2016). Think College National Coordinating Center: Annual report on the transition and postsecondary programs for students with intellectual disabilities (2014–2015). University of Massachusetts Boston, Institute for Community Inclusion.

Grigal, M., & Papay, C. (2018). The promise of postsecondary education for students with intellectual disability. *New Directions for Adult and Continuing Education, 2018*(160), 77–88.

Harrison, P. L., & Oakland, T. (2013). *Adaptive Behavior Assessment System, Third Edition.* WPS.

Higher Education Reform and Opportunity Act (HEOA) of 2008, P.L. 110-315, 114th Cong.

Individuals with Disabilities Education Act (IDEA) of 1990, Pub. L. No. 101-476, 20 U.S.C. §§ 1400 *et seq.* (1990).

Individuals with Disabilities Education Act Amendments of 1997, Pub. L. No. 105-17, 20 U.S.C. §§ 1400 *et seq.* (1997).

Individuals with Disabilities Education Improvement Act (IDEA) of 2004, Pub. L. No. 108-446, 20 U.S.C. §§ 1400 *et seq.* (2004).

Lai, M. K., Wilson, A., McNaughton, S., & Hsiao, S. (2014). Improving achievement in secondary schools: Impact of a literacy project on reading comprehension and secondary school qualifications. *Reading Research Quarterly, 49*(3), 305–334.

Lee, H., & Morningstar, M. E. (2019). Exploring predictors of community participation among young adults with severe disabilities. *Research and Practice for Persons with Severe Disabilities, 44*(3), 186–199.

Madeus, J. W., Grigal, M., & Hughes, C. (2014). Promoting access to postsecondary education for low-income students with disabilities. *Career Development and Transition for Exceptional Individuals, 37*(1), 50–59.

Mapping Your Future, Inc. (2022). *Prepare for college.* http://mappingyourfuture.org/collegeprep/

Mazzotti, V. L., Rowe, D. A., Kwiatek, S., Voggt, A., Chang, W-H., Fowler, C. H., Poppen, M., Sinclair, J., & Test, D. W. (2020). Secondary transition predictors of postschool success: An update to the research base. *Career Development and Transition for Exceptional Individuals,* 1-18. https://doi.org/10.1177/2165143420959793

Mazzotti, V. L., Rowe, D. A., Sinclair, J., Poppen, M., Woods, W. E., & Shearer, M. L. (2016). Predictors of post-school success: A systematic review of NLTS2 secondary analyses. *Career Development and Transition for Exceptional Individuals, 39*(4), 196–215. https://doi.org/10.1177/2165143415588047

McMahon, D., & Smith, C. S. (2012). Universal design for learning: Implications and applications in UT Knoxville FUTURE Program. *Think College Insight Brief,* Issue No. 14. University of Massachusetts Boston, Institute for Community Inclusion.

McNaughton, S., Lai, M. K., & Hsiao, S. (2012). Testing the effectiveness of an intervention model based on data use: A replication series across clusters of schools. *School Effectiveness and School Improvement, 23*(2), 203–228. https://doi.org/10.1080/09243453.2011.652126

National Technical Assistance Center on Transition (NTACT). (n.d.-a). *Diversity, equity, & inclusion.* https://transitionta.org/topics/dei/

National Technical Assistance Center on Transition (NTACT). (n.d.-b). *Postsecondary education.* https://transitionta.org/topics/postsecondary-education/

PACER National Parent Center on Transition. (n.d.). *The Workforce Innovation and Opportunity Act (WIOA).* https://www.pacer.org/transition/learning-center/laws/workforce-innovation.asp

Papay, C. K., & Bambara, L. M. (2014). Best Practices in Transition to Adult Life for Youth With Intellectual Disabilities. *Career Development and Transition for Exceptional Individuals, 37*(3), 136–148. https://doi.org/10.1177/2165143413486693

Poortman, C. L., & Schildkamp, K. (2016). Solving student achievement problems with a data use intervention for teachers. *Teaching and Teacher Education, 60*, 425–433. https://doi.org/10.1016/j.tate.2016.06.010

Prince, A. M. T., Katsiyannis, A., & Farmer, J. (2013). Postsecondary transition under IDEA 2004: A legal update. *Intervention in School and Clinic, 48*(5), 286–293.

Rehabilitation Act of 1973, Pub. L. No. 93-112, 29 U.S.C. §§ 701 *et seq.* (1973).

Rowe, D. A., Mazzotti, V. L., & Sinclair, J. (2015). Strategies for teaching self-determination skills in conjunction with the common core. *Intervention in School and Clinic, 50*(3), 131–141.

Ryan, J. B., Randall, K. N., Walters, E., & Morash-MacNeil, V. (2019). Employment and independent living outcomes of a mixed model post-secondary education program for young adults with intellectual disabilities. *Journal of Vocational Rehabilitation, 50*(1), 61–72.

Shanley, J. (2010/2011, Fall/Winter). *Federal legislation increasing high education access for students with intellectual disabilities.* Impact Feature Issue on Postsecondary Education and Students with Intellectual, Developmental and other disabilities. https://publications.ici.umn.edu/impact/23-3/federal-legislation-increasing-higher-education-access-for-students-with-intellectual-disabilities

Shogren, K. A., & Wehmeyer, M. L. (2017). *Self-Determination Inventory.* Kansas University Center on Developmental Disabilities.

Test, D. W., Mazzotti, V. L., Mustian, A. L., Fowler, C. H., Kortering, L. J., & Kohler, P. H. (2009). Evidence-based secondary transition predictors for improving postschool outcomes for students with disabilities. *Career Development for Exceptional Individuals, 32*, 160–181. https://doi.org/10.1177/0885728809346960

Toldson, I. A. (2021). Developing a higher education completion agenda for Black students (Editor's commentary). *Journal of Negro Education, 90*(1), 1–5.

U.S. Department of Education. (n.d.-a). *College preparation checklist. https://studentaid.gov/resources/prepare-for-college/checklists*

U.S. Department of Education. (n.d.-b). *Federal student aid.* https://studentaid.gov

U.S. Department of Labor. (n.d.). *Workforce Innovation and Opportunity Act.* https://www.dol.gov/agencies/eta/wioa

Van Geel, M., Keuning, T., Visscher, A. J., & Fox, J. P. (2016). Assessing the effects of a school-wide data-based decision-making intervention on student achievement growth in primary schools. *American Educational Research Journal, 53*(2), 360–394.

Wagner, M. M., Newman, L. A., & Javitz, H. S. (2014). The influence of family socioeconomic status on the post–high school outcomes of youth with disabilities. *Career Development and Transition for Exceptional Individuals, 37*(1), 5–17.

Workforce Innovation and Opportunity Act of 2014, Pub. L. No. 113-128, Stat. 129 (2014). https://www.govinfo.gov/content/pkg/PLAW-113publ128/pdf/PLAW-113publ128.pdf

7

Community Living

Ashley J. Mliler, LaRon A. Scott, and Colleen A. Thoma

DIGGING DEEPER: What Teachers Have to Say

In my former role as an interim principal at a unique urban middle school, together with our student success team we designed a unique curriculum that, without our knowing it, exemplified an equity-focused universal design for transition (UDT) model. Our curriculum was designed to teach critical academic skills while also incorporating multicultural applications and connections to real-life situations that were relevant to the needs of the community, family, and students. Thanks to our independent school model, we had the autonomy to plan and facilitate unconventional community engagement experiences, on site and off site, that built on students' academic skills while widening their life experiences and outreach with community representatives. We had opportunities such as hosting guest speakers, including college administrators from Historically Black Colleges and Universities (HBCUs), at daily morning meetings. It was written in school enrollment policies that families were equal partners and contributors. As interim principal, I spent a few hours every week walking the local neighborhood, talking to residents, making home visits to the parents and relatives of our students, and organizing daily parent visits to observe their child and volunteer in classrooms.

A universal design for learning (UDL) approach was paramount for our teachers in planning day-to-day content-focused lessons. The model offered teachers critical autonomy and flexibility to shape their instruction to include 1) multiple ways for students to acquire the knowledge or skills and 2) a range of options for students to engage with and express their learning. This helped teachers to meet the various student needs and suit instruction to their backgrounds, aspirations, and available resources. We applied a UDT approach to create the link between the academic content taught in our core classes and the transition from school to postschool success. For example, students had science lessons centered around oxygen, hydration, and necessary nutrients for vegetation health, and then they applied these lessons in our school garden, beehive, and chicken coop. In those settings, students learned to harvest fruits, vegetables, and livestock that supplied our school kitchen for school and family take-home meals. Academic instruction combined with community enrichment opportunities provided our students with multiple means for them to demonstrate what they knew and practice the skills they learned across varying settings and adults in their community.

Preparing students with disabilities for community living is a key component of transition planning. Unfortunately, students with disabilities from culturally and linguistically diverse (CLD) backgrounds, especially those from racially minoritized communities, face more barriers and challenges on their quest for quality adult life. Most transition frameworks provide a broad range of community living services without considering racially minoritized and other CLD students with disabilities or linking them to culturally responsive and sustaining practices, supports, and services. Students with disabilities, especially students from racially and culturally minoritized groups, undocumented Americans, and English language learners, must learn how to do the following:

• Identify and articulate their community living aspirations with self-awareness of their strengths and needs, understanding how their aspirations differ or overlap with their family's.

• Identify their physical and emotional "needs" to align with community resources, including health care, transportation access, recreation and leisure opportunities, and so forth.

• Determine the role they see for themselves in the community, as well as the function their family members will play in future community living environments.

• Learn about and strengthen their self-determination skills that align with their family, cultural, and racial values.

• Identify and obtain the support, resources, and/or personnel needed to acquire and sustain their desired level of living independence.

• Afford what they want, including knowledge on how they can acquire and sustain financial independence and resources that help them throughout phases of their lives.

• Anticipate potential barriers and obstacles relevant to their culture, race, and community living environment, and how to apply self-determination skills to navigate and overcome those challenges.

• Obtain the assistance needed in learning to use universally designed spaces and technology while working toward their community living goals.

If we, as educators, are to improve the community living outcomes for students with disabilities from marginalized groups, they must leave their secondary experience with the aforementioned knowledge from a functional curriculum that included real-life experiences. This requires planned efforts from key stakeholders to design a culturally sustaining curriculum that balances functional and academic skills with community based-learning experiences where students can apply those skills in the community setting with and without adult supervision. Getting these critical components of a well-balanced transition curriculum to coalesce presents challenges within a traditional secondary general education curriculum focused primarily on core subjects tied to state standards mandated to meet district and state requirements to graduate. It can be especially daunting for schools to balance a functional curriculum with real-world experiences with guided support, serving CLD students in school with restrictive budgets and limited resources.

Researchers (Cimera et al., 2018; Whittenburg et al., 2019) have reported that youth with disabilities from minority groups continued to fall behind in terms of indicators of a quality adult life compared with their peers of similar age without disabilities. For example, Eilenberg and colleagues (2019) reviewed 40 research articles and found that CLD transition-age youth outcomes across education, health and safety, employment, and other transition areas (e.g., community living) were more adverse than outcomes for White students on the autism spectrum. Similarly, the National Longitudinal Transition Study-2 (2005) data, which tracked students ages 13–16 from secondary school into their adult lives, found that among other factors, minority status, specifically for African American and Hispanic youth, was an added predictor of poor life outcomes across all transition domains including independent living compared to their White peers. What, then, can special education teachers, families, general education teachers, transition coordinators/specialists, and agency providers do to provide equitable transition services to support a more racially and ethnically diverse population of youth with disabilities to be successful after exiting school?

At its core, UDL allows for fluidity in how teachers present new material, engage their students, and provide choice for them to express their learning growth. Minor customizations to UDL lessons are driven by students with significant and/or pervasive needs. With growing diversity in our classrooms and ongoing current events that highlight social and racial injustice, special education professionals are driven now more than ever to go beyond traditional "supports," "instruction," and "services" to meet the needs of their CLD students with disabilities. In this chapter, we discuss community living with the viewpoint of CLD students and families, including the following:

1. Culturally appropriate UDT assessments to understand student skills and abilities in relation to their community living aspirations and preferences

2. Culturally appropriate UDT supports that enable a student and their family to identify and find their preferred community living options

3. Ways of connecting students and their families to community/neighborhood resources

MULTIPLE MEANS OF ASSESSMENT

Where one lives is a highly personal decision driven by both necessity and personal preferences. Apart from the initial attractiveness of a specific living area, or the familiarity a student feels toward it, the student and their transition team must also consider the student's health needs; transit access; and proximity to local companies, resources, activities, and relevant work opportunities when selecting a place for the student to live. Before the team can envision and plan for a culturally sustaining UDT curriculum that supports students in transitioning to adult community living, they must understand the student's community living aspirations and preferences. They can accomplish this by initiating a systematic community living–focused transition assessment plan.

In Chapter 2, we learned about the targeted focus of administering transition assessments. Applying those recommendations to the transition domain of community living, teams should target administering assessments around the following aims:

1. Identifying students' preferences and interests for their postschool community living goals

2. Identifying the skills necessary for the student to accomplish their community living goals

3. Identifying discrepancies between student abilities and the necessary community living skills identified to meet their goals (the student's "needs")

4. Using that information to target the supports, services, and instruction necessary for individual students

Therefore, understanding the student's community living aspirations and preferences in the near and distant future is a central starting point.

Step 1: Gather Information From the Student

Figure 7.1 provides a sample student questionnaire for a student to identify their ideal living environment and compare the components they value in it to their current living environment—its features and what they have access to, feel, and enjoy. This example aids the team in understanding the students' aspirations related to their ideal community living environment. This understanding of the student's ideal living environment is focused on how they want to feel there, what they want to access there, what features exist in this environment, what activities and/or experiences they want to enjoy there, and what people and/or animals they want to have there. The form shown in Figure 7.1 can be adjusted to accommodate the students' disabilities—for example, the team can add lines for the student to write their responses or members can conduct the questionnaire verbally for the student to verbalize their responses rather than writing them. The team can also tailor prompts to fit the students' cultural backgrounds to ensure that they feel the exercise is approachable and that they have a positive experience with identifying their independent living preferences. (A reproducible copy of this form is provided with the other online resources for this book available at the Brookes Download Hub.)

After the team understands the student's ideal postschool living aspirations, they should identify the skills and knowledge the student would need to meet these aspirations. Assessment tools can assess the student's living skills and knowledge. Table 7.1 provides a list of transition assessment tools along with the community living components skills assessed and where to access a copy of each tool.

Step 2: Gather Information From the Student's Family

A student's decisions about where to live and what role to take in that community setting may also reflect others' preferences or expectations, including those of

RESOURCE 7.1

Community Living Aspirations

Name: _____ Grade: _____ Date: _____

Describing My Ideal

Directions: Complete the sentences.

After high school in my ideal community living environment...

1. ...it's important that I feel...

2. ...I want access to...

3. ...the following features would be included...

4. ...I want to enjoy the following activities and/or experiences...

5. ...the following would be included if it were up to my parent(s)/guardians/caregivers...

6. ...the following people and/or animals would be with me (if at all)...

Universal Design for Transition: The Educators' Guide for Equity-Focused Transition Planning, Second Edition by LaRon A. Scott and Colleen A. Thoma. Copyright © 2024 by Paul H. Brookes Publishing Co. All rights reserved.

(page 1 of 3)

(continued)

Figure 7.1. Community Living Aspirations worksheet.

Figure 7.1. *(continued)*

RESOURCE 7.1: Community Living Aspirations *(continued)*

Describing the NOW

Directions: Complete the sentences.

1.   I would describe my current living environment as…

2.   I enjoy the following in my current community and/or living environment…

3.   In my local community and/or living environment, I least enjoy….

(page 2 of 3)

RESOURCE 7.1: Community Living Aspirations *(continued)*

Present vs. Future Aspirations

Directions: Compare your current living environment to your ideal living environment by completing the table below. Use the details you outlined previously when describing where you live now and your aspirations for your ideal living environment. Add rows as needed.

Where I live NOW	My ideal living environment
I feel...	I want to feel...
1.	1.
2.	2.
3.	3.
I have access to...	I want access to...
1.	1.
2.	2.
3.	3.
It has features including...	I want features including...
1.	1.
2.	2.
3.	3.
I enjoy...	I want to enjoy...
1.	1.
2.	2.
3.	3.
People and/or animals I have with me...	People and/or animals I want with me...
1.	1.
2.	2.
3.	3.

Table 7.1. Community Living Transition Assessment Tools

Assessment tool	Community living areas assessed on this tool	Link

The Life Skills Inventory Independent Living Skills Assessment Tool developed by the Division of Children and Family in 2000	• Money management/consumer awareness
	• Food management
	  ◦ Personal appearance and hygievne
	  ◦ Health
	  ◦ Housekeeping
	  ◦ Transportation
	  ◦ Educational planning
	  ◦ Job-seeking skills
	  ◦ Job maintenance skills
	  ◦ Emergency and safety skills
	  ◦ Knowledge of community resources
	  ◦ Interpersonal skills
	  ◦ Legal skills
	• Pregnancy prevention/parenting and child care
		Transition Assessment Database Can be accessed through this link (registration required) https://transitiontn.org/assessment-database/
		
		(Transition Tennessee, 2023)

Ansell-Casey Life Skills Assessment	• Communication • Daily living • Housing and money management • Self-care • Social relationships • Work and study skills	Ansell-Casey Life Skills Assessment (crisoregon.org) (Columbia Regional Inclusive Services, n.d.)
Your Child Health Care Independence worksheet	• Health care including financial needs for health care, functional living needs	https://pediatrics.med.jax.ufl.edu/jaxhats/docs/hct_workbook_15-17.pdf (Reiss & Gibson, 2005b)
Informal assessments for transition: independent living and community participation	• Recreation and leisure • Living priorities and values • Activities and occupations • Psychological well-being	https://www.proedinc.com/Products/12478/informal-assessments-for-transition-independent-living-and-community-participation.aspx (Synatschk et al., 2008)
Quality of life questionnaires	• Symptoms and outlook • Physical health • Alcohol and other drugs • Social relations/support • Money • Activities of daily living • Goal attainment	http://wqli.fmhi.usf.edu/_docs/wqli-instruments/QualityOfLifeAssessmentManual.pdf (Becker et al., n.d.)

The Scales of Independent Behavior–Revised (SIB-R)	• Adaptive Behavior Full Scale
	• Problem Behavior Scale, Cluster Scores:
	  ◦ Motor Skills
	  ◦ Personal Living Skills
	  ◦ Social Interaction and Communication Skills
	  ◦ Community Living Skills
		https://www.riversideinsights.com/p/scales-of-independent-behavior-revised-sib-r-complete-package/
		
		(Riverside Insights, 1996)

Assessment of Adaptive Behavior: Street Survival Skills Questionnaire	• Basic concepts • Functional signs • Tools • Domestic management • Health, safety, and first aid • Public services • Time • Money • Measurements	http://mccarrondial.com (Linkenhoker & McCarron, 1993)

family members. Teachers need to collaborate with the family to engage them in the transition process to build trust and establish shared and equal partnership. Differences in cultural values, beliefs, life priorities, primary language, and day-to-day basic survival needs, along with many other challenges faced by CLD families of youth with disabilities, make it more difficult for CLD families to play an active role in transition planning (Greene, 2011, p. 24; Wilt & Morningstar, 2018). One essential characteristic of effective collaboration with CLD families is including committed experiences for families to get involved to give them equal power in decision making and service implementation (Blue-Banning, et al., 2004). Teachers should collaborate with families to gather their perspective and input and learn about the community living preferences each family has for their child. This includes the following:

- The role they envision for their child in the community setting

- The role they envision having in their child's community living experience

- Cultural values and expectations families have for the student

Additional responsibilities in the transition process include engaging parents/guardians, siblings, and relatives as assessors of their child's community living skills, which they observe at home, in the community, and in social settings. Providing families with opportunities to present their observations, cultural values, and familial expectations at individualized education program (IEP) meetings and parent–teacher conferences reinforces the partnership in which parents are equal contributors to the transition planning process (Gothberg et al., 2019; Harry, 2008).

Step 3: Design and/or Select Transition Assessments

Knowing the student's community living aspirations and preferences, with the added family perspective, lays the foundation for designing and/or selecting quality, culturally appropriate transition assessments focused on assessing the student's community living skills, knowledge, and experience. Formal and informal assessments can pinpoint the student's specific strengths and needs relevant to community living, allowing the team to compare the student's desires with the required skills and knowledge. The Life Skills Inventory Independent Living Skills Assessment Tool (Transition Tennessee, 2023), developed by the Division of Children and Family in 2000, is one example of a life skills assessment that measures the student's level of experience and knowledge across 15 independent living categories. Assessments like this can inform the team of the student's knowledge or experience in order to establish a baseline of community living skills, with an end-goal of strengthening those targeted skills prior to exiting school.

Community living transition assessments should assess critical living skills connected to the following topics: personal finances, health, hygiene and self-care, obtaining and maintaining employment, housing, emergency and safety skills, pregnancy and child care, educational planning, transportation, recreation and leisure, and social relationships. Table 7.1 provides examples of available life skills assessments and specific areas each assessment covers. To determine whether the assessment is culturally appropriate for the student, teachers should evaluate qualities of the selected assessment tools, such as language, including pronouns; environmental descriptors; and racial and cultural inclusivity.

Beyond what is learned about a student's community living skills and knowledge through formal community living assessments, teachers using a UDT approach to transition assessment should look to the general education curriculum to further identify the student's skills and knowledge necessary for community living. Teachers can easily use the general education curriculum to gather information about skills like collaboration and leadership, reading comprehension, and mathematical computation, to name just a few. Gathering input from various assessment methods will only strengthen the student's foundation of skill sets and knowledge tied to community living. A strong foundation will allow the team to tailor a functional academic approach that can be incorporated inside and outside the general education curriculum to support the student (with their family's continual engagement) to learn about community living.

Figures 7.1 and 7.2 show two consecutive activities that combine the Self-Determined Learning Model of Instruction, introduced in Chapter 3 (SDLMI; Shogren et al., 2019), with two well-known instructional strategies for students with disabilities, PATH (Pearpoint et al., 1993) and WOOP (Oettingen, 2014). The first strategy that activity in Figure 7.1 applies to is known as Planning Alternative Tomorrows With Hope (PATH; Pearpoint et al., 1993), a creative person-centered planning tool designed to help students identify their long-term aspirations; it also helps individuals break down doable action steps toward desirable futures. Figure 7.1 follows this model by having students describe their ideal living environment and compare that future vision with their current living environment. Once students identify their living aspirations in comparison to the features of their current living environment, students move on to the activity shown in Figure 7.2, which applies the WOOP method, which stands for Wish, Outcome, Obstacle, and Plan (Oettingen, 2014), a popular goal-setting and problem-solving strategy designed to help students initiate and sustain effort to achieve their goals. (A reproducible copy of this form is provided with the other online resources for this book available at the Brookes Download Hub.) Research indicates that person-centered planning and student-focused goal setting, such as PATH, in combination with assistance to get unstuck, as with the WOOP strategy, are highly effective for students from CLD backgrounds, especially because they offer the opportunity for collaboration among all transition team members including the families.

UDT is demonstrated in this example through the student identifying their goals; learning how to identify potential barriers based on the internal and external obstacles they identified (self-determination skills); exploring community living options that fit their own preferences; exploring potential challenges with acquiring their ideal living environment; and using multiple resources to obtain information, express information, and communicate the information.

COMMUNITY LIVING OPTIONS

Students should consider the following questions when deciding about *where* to live:

- *Can I access and retain employment in this setting?* Students should consider both location-bound and non–location-bound employment options in the community. For employment opportunities that are not location bound—for example, remote employment—students should consider factors such as internet speed, technology hardware and skills required, and access to information technology support to sustain employment. Employment that requires someone in a physical location

Community Living Acquisition Action Plan

Name: _____ Grade: _____ Date: _____

PHASE I: Goal Setting

Directions: To clearly identify your community living goals and learn about the specific steps you can take to be successful in accomplishing those goals, it is important that you compare your current living environment to your ideal living environment. Using what you wrote in the Community Living Aspirations worksheet, complete the tables below.

1. In my ideal living environment, I want to **feel**. . .	Does my current living environment give me these feelings?
a.	☐ YES ☐ NO
b.	☐ YES ☐ NO
c.	☐ YES ☐ NO
d.	☐ YES ☐ NO

2. In my ideal living environment, I want **access** to. . .	Do I have access to this in my current living environment?
a.	☐ YES ☐ NO
b.	☐ YES ☐ NO
c.	☐ YES ☐ NO
d	☐ YES ☐ NO

(page 1 of 5)

(continued)

Figure 7.2. Community Living Acquisition Action Plan worksheet.

Figure 7.2. *(continued)*

RESOURCE 7.2: Community Living Acquisition Action Plan *(continued)*

3. In my ideal living environment, I want **features** including. . .	Does my current living environment have this feature?
a.	☐ YES ☐ NO
b.	☐ YES ☐ NO
c.	☐ YES ☐ NO
d.	☐ YES ☐ NO

4. In my ideal living environment, I want to live with the **following people and/or animals**. . .	Do I live with this individual in my current living environment?
a.	☐ YES ☐ NO
b.	☐ YES ☐ NO
c.	☐ YES ☐ NO
d	☐ YES ☐ NO

Directions: Select ONE thing you identified you want in your ideal living environment after high school that you do NOT have in your current living environment. Then respond to the prompts.

5.   In my **ideal living environment**, I have a goal to live. . .

6.   What **internal barrier(s)** are preventing me from having THIS in my current living environment now?

7.   What **external barrier(s)** are preventing me from having THIS in my current living environment now?

PHASE II: Making a Plan

Directions: Respond to the questions.

8.   In **sequential** order, what five steps can I take in a week to work toward learning about my ideal living environment?

     a.

     b.

     c.

     d.

     e.

(continued)

Figure 7.2. *(continued)*

RESOURCE 7.2: Community Living Acquisition Action Plan *(continued)*

9. **Who** in my network can help me achieve my goal to learn more about my ideal living environment? How can they help me?

WHO can help me?	How can they help me?
a.	
b.	
c.	

10. What **internal obstacle(s)** would prevent me from accomplishing my goal?

11. If I face the **internal obstacle(s)**, then I will take the following effective action steps to combat the obstacle(s). . .

12. What **external obstacle(s)** would prevent me from accomplishing my goal?

13. If I face the **external obstacle(s)**, then I will take the following effective steps to combat the obstacle(s). . .

RESOURCE 7.2: Community Living Acquisition Action Plan *(continued)*

PHASE III: Learning Growth

14. **What** actions have I taken?

15. What have I learned thus far?

16. After doing research, my ideal living goal(s) is to. . .

17. What are the next steps I can take in the next month or so toward meeting my postschool ideal living environment?

18. What do I want to learn about during this time?

19. The next step(s) I can commit to today toward reaching my living goal(s) are. . .

requires students to consider transportation options that meet their physical and financial preferences, along with other factors involved with commuting, such as car maintenance, insurance, gas prices, and their own skills and preferences.

- *Can I afford to live in the area?* If the student plans to receive training or education after exiting high school, they should consider living arrangements that are affordable and sustainable during their educational pursuits, with a long-term goal of living elsewhere after education and/or training is complete.

- *Can I access and sustain the necessary supports I need to live in this setting?* For example, is the student's ideal living environment accessible to the supports they require in that location, such as public transportation? Is that mode of transportation sustainable to meet a variety of their community living needs, such as access to grocery stores, entertainment, medical care, and so forth?

- *Do this community and the specific domicile align with my living preferences, needs, and recreational interests?* If the student enjoys in-person social gatherings tied to a specific cultural activity, does the community offer that network? Does it offer accessibility to interests such as dog-walking, yoga, restaurants, or shared food gardens? Does the apartment building offer reliable lifts and ramps? Is the neighborhood safe? Does the building allow pets? Are there additional policies or rules that tenants need to abide by or additional fees for living in the community?

- *Does the area provide access to my health care needs?* The student should consider factors such as proximity to health care providers and medical professionals, whether local health care providers and other medical professionals take the student's preferred insurance, accessibility to medical care professionals, and frequency of medical care visits.

We caution transition teams not to overlook health care access when supporting students in navigating the process of community living decision making, especially for students who may not present themselves as having high medical needs. According to the 2018–2019 National Survey of Children with Special Needs, approximately 13.6 million children in the U.S. (18.8%) had a special health care need, which translates to approximately one in four households (24.8%) in the U.S (Data Resource Center for Children and Adolescent Health, 2020). Of the 13.6 million children with special health care needs, 16.9% of those children were African American/Black, 21.6% were Hispanic/Latine, 52.2% were White, and 9.3% were "other." Helpful starting points exist to engage students, families, and educators in understanding the student's health and wellness needs. Examples include the Your Child Health Care Independence Worksheet (University of Florida Health, 2023) and tools such as Health Care Transition Planning Guide for Youth and Families" developed by the Institute for Child Health Policy at the University of Florida (Reiss & Gibson, 2005a, 2005b), among others. More information about these resources can be found at the end of this chapter as well as in Table 7.1.

MULTIPLE MEANS OF REPRESENTATION, ENGAGEMENT, AND EXPRESSION

The transition team and special education teachers are not the only educators who can help prepare students for community living. General education teachers can do so as well. Applying a UDT style to academic instruction can allow for teaching functional skills in the general education classroom. For example, suppose a secondary math teacher is teaching a lesson on comparing the fuel efficiency of public transportation systems with that of other local transportation options. To create multiple opportunities for engagement, the teacher can allow students to choose transportation modes of interest to them or to compare other measurable features of transportation options, such as cost, safety, regulations, and so forth. Students can express their learning through options such as mini-video productions, moving portrait projects, or digital posters. With a UDL planning mindset, general education teachers can support students in preparing for the transition to community living by incorporating functional, practical experiences in their academic instruction. Concepts related to culture and diversity should be prioritized early in the lesson so students can personally connect to the material, further motivating them to engage and accept educational challenges presented.

General education teachers can incorporate other learning experiences for students that strengthen their community living knowledge and skills, as well as self-determination skills, in the following ways:

- Build in problem-solving experiences, where students gain experience using a variety of resources to find plausible solutions, that connect to community living skills.

- To vary means of representation, learn about cultural examples and current events that connect to lesson standards. Select reading materials written and produced by authors from diverse backgrounds; use visuals that mirror the racial and cultural profiles of your students, including skin tone, dress, hair styles, and so forth; and select instructional materials that address subjects related to differences with cultural and language groups that connect to your student population.

- To bridge the gap between the home and school cultures, recruit families in planning lessons that connect to cultural and family values.

- Embed opportunities for students to code-switch in the classroom, allowing students to express their learning through varying modes of communication that align with their social or family culture.

MULTIPLE PERSPECTIVES AND RESOURCES

Not all vital independent living skills can be easily embedded in the general education curriculum without significant interruptions. Preparing youth to live independently must go beyond teaching students daily living skills such as budgeting, laundering clothes, and basic home repair in a marking period elective or infrequent field trips to the district's mock apartment. A common theme among all critical independent living skills is the ability to identify a problem or barrier, learn about available resources, and implement a plan to address and solve the problem. This approach can be applied to nearly all community living experiences.

Community living skills such as those assessed on the Life Skills Inventory assessment tool—addressing topics including legal issues, housing management, and health and wellness—may not fit cleanly within the general education curriculum. Electives such as Family Consumer Science, for example, may provide an easy-to-see connection between course content and community living skills (e.g., following a recipe, laundry sorting), but experiences in the classroom with adult supervision and peer support make it difficult for our students to have an authentic real-world experience.

Additional learning experiences can be offered through special education services such as occupational therapy, extended school year services, or push-in/pull-out support. Special education teachers and transition specialists can apply a UDT approach when designing services implemented in the student's special education plan. These professionals can apply a UDT approach in the following ways:

- Facilitate community experiences (virtual or in-person) that increase a student's exposure to community living options. Consider recruiting leaders from minoritized groups from varying community living options, such as landlords, rental agents, and building superintendents, as a resource for unique field trips or as part of a housing hop day.

- Coach students on various ways they can express their community living preferences, as well as their learning growth, at their upcoming IEP meeting. Challenge the student to recruit professionals they would like to invite to their IEP meeting to learn more about community living resources.

- Involve community agency representatives in planning enriching experiences at school or in the local community. Allow students to engage with agencies about their questions, preferences, options, and client qualifications.

- Build a repertoire of easy-to-navigate resources that simplifies the topic of health care coverage, including how to qualify, cost, and policies.

- Plan community experiences that allow students to get firsthand experience using local transportation, applying budgeting practices, and expanding on their navigation skills.

- Engage students in the learning process by having them self-track their own progress toward learning new community living skills. Students can select a preferred method to track their progress over the course of a set time. Families can support the student in accountability when applying learned skills outside of the school environment.

- Utilize recent legislation, current events, and political movements to engage students in meaningful discussions. It is particularly beneficial to create learning experiences where students can strengthen self-determination skills, such as internal locus of control and self-advocacy and leadership.

SUPPORTS TO CONNECT TO THE COMMUNITY/NEIGHBORHOOD

During the transition process, students (with their families) need support navigating the journey from being a student of a public education agency to an adult who receives adult services from community, state, and federal resources. Far too often, schools fail to effectively link families to those resources to ease the responsibilities from school and family to self and service providers. Organizations can play a unique and vital role in this process. Community resource mapping (Crane & Mooney, 2005), introduced in Chapter 2, involves activities where students learn about various organizations and resources in their online or local community and assess the services and supports they provide through a four-step process including "pre-mapping, mapping, taking action, and Maintaining, Sustaining, and Evaluating Mapping Efforts" (Leake & Black, 2005, p. 2). Learning experiences such as community resource mapping require recruiting support from family members, agency providers, and social networks for students to leave the experience with a comprehensive list of organizations and services they provide.

Following is a lesson plan that connects both problem-solving skills and community resource mapping. Previous lessons taught within this unit involved students identifying their community living preferences, learning about the geographic area of interest, reviewing reliable data sources that inform readers about an organization or community program, deciding whom to enroll and recruit to help with the project, and determining best practices and methods to communicate with professional and organization leaders. This lesson builds on those concepts by allowing students to seek out new information applicable to their community living preferences and create an accessible resource they can use and build on as they make community living decisions. This lesson also gives students opportunities to strengthen their relationships with outside resources, including family members, organization leaders, and agency providers. UDT principles are demonstrated throughout the lesson, which addresses both academic and functional goals, as well as self-determination skills including problem solving and self-advocacy, choice making, and decision making. Additional self-determination skills strengthened in this lesson include self-knowledge, self-awareness, goal setting and attainment, and problem solving. The lesson includes multiple resources for students to utilize to learn about community organizations and opportunities.

▶ LESSON PLAN

COMMUNITY RESOURCE MAPPING

Purpose: The lesson will reinforce the skills needed to research community organizations and businesses through internet-based resources. Students will strengthen their understanding of connections between 1) their community living aspirations and 2) local resources that can support them in various aspects of acquiring and sustaining a suitable domicile.

They will understand the purpose and function of community organizations and the services these organizations provide. Finally, they will strengthen their familiarity with adult service providers in their community.

Objective: Students will investigate neighborhood and community resources available in person and on the web local to the area of their desired living aspirations and preferences. Given access to the document titled "Community Resource Mapping Findings" (see Figure 7.3), and access to printed and/or digital resources, the student(s) will identify in writing at least one community organization or business that aligns with their ideal living community environment to learn about . . .

A. Name and location of the community resource, organization, and/or business

B. Service the community resource, organization, and/or business provides

C. The qualifications to access and/or qualify for the community resource, organization, and/or business

D. The cost to access the community resource, organization, and/or business

E. Transportation methods to access the community resource, organization, and/or business (e.g., transportation modes required, online)

F. The point of contact for the community resource, organization, and/or business

G. The social media platforms the resource, organization, and/or business uses

(A reproducible copy of the document shown in Figure 7.3 is provided with the other online resources for this book available on the Brookes Download Hub.)

Universal Design for Learning Principles

1. **Multiple means of engagement**

   a. Activity: Revisit community living aspirations and identify one feature and/or accessibility the student desires in their future ideal living community environment.

   b. Activity: Use the internet to locate a resource, businesses, and/or organization in the students' desirable community, organizing what they find in their notes using Figure 7.3 or building an informational tool that addresses all of their findings to cover the topics listed in Figure 7.3.

   c. Activity: Identify a community resource of high interest, and then identify personal challenges that might impact their ability to utilize the resource to increase students' motivation to expand their learning about the community resource and prevent potential barriers.

   d. **Culturally responsive teaching principles:** Using experiences from students' lives

2. **Multiple means of representation**

   a. Students can gain information about community resources through the following:

      • Resource websites and other social media platforms

      • Recommended online videos

      • Printed resources

      • Interviews

      • PowerPoint presentations

   b. **Culturally responsive teaching principles:** Reduce barriers to print and support multiple literacies.

3. **Multiple means of action and expression:**

   a. Expression and communication—oral/visual: Students can present their findings to the class as well as compare and contrast their findings with those of other students in the classroom. They have the option to develop a printed poster-board presentation.

b. Expression and communication—digital/visual: Students can express and report their findings through organizing their findings using a shared digital file (such as Google Docs, or the website Portaportal (http://www. portaportal.com). They can develop a digital visual display using free flyer-building websites like Canva, possibly using digital pictures of the community resources).

c. **Culturally responsive teaching principles:** Honoring different methods of communication

Transition Principles

1. **Multiple life domains**

   a. Students seek out potentially helpful community resources across multiple life domains: employment, transportation, recreation and leisure, postsecondary education, and others.

   b. **Culturally responsive teaching principles:** Incorporating home and community cultures in instruction

2. **Self-determination**

   a. Students use self-determination skills to identify the most important community resource that will help them achieve their goals for adult life.

   b. Students will also consider their own needs and goals across multiple transition domains (e.g., employment, postsecondary education, health care/independent living, leisure and recreation) as they conduct research and determine which community resources are valuable to them.

   c. **Culturally responsive teaching principles** Having students determine what resource is most meaningful to them; fostering self-awareness, and self-advocacy and leadership

3. **Multiple resources and perspectives**

   a. Opportunities for family involvement: Students can interview a local community member to learn about a resource in the community that they personally use to learn about firsthand experience with using the community resource.

   b. Opportunities for community members' involvement: Students can conduct a virtual or in-person interview with an individual employed at the community resource to learn more about the organization, business, or agency.

   c. **Culturally responsive teaching principles:** Providing opportunities for bridging home, school, and community; opportunities to recruit support from families

4. **Multiple means of assessment:**

   a. Using the internet and poster assignment, students will be assessed on their ability to conclude with resources they may use for learning about what makes up a community. They may also use their findings for transition planning in the future. Students will increase their knowledge of connections they have in their own community.

b. **Culturally responsive teaching principles:** Assessments are designed to help students construct meaning from their world.

Resources: *Student*—computer with internet access; smartphone or digital camera; community resource mapping findings (digital or web based). *Teacher*—knowledge of student's reading levels; knowledge of student's cultural and ethnic backgrounds; printed and digital resources that provide information about community resources; list of community services

Accommodations and modifications: For students who struggle with writing, edit open-ended questions shown in Figures 7.1–7.3 to closed-ended questions that more closely mirror a questionnaire with dichotomous or multiple-choice options. Also consider the following:

- Using nonprint-based worksheets and instead having students share their responses to the questions shown in Figures 7.1–7.3 on an electronic device to minimize frustration, assist with spelling, and ease the writing experience

- Chunking the material into smaller components followed by a reward to reduce any anxiety about planning for their futures, make the learning more attainable, and maintain interest

- Pairing students with similar interests to interview one another and record their responses through an audio recording app to completely remove writing

- Researching available resources that are of interest to the student ahead of time to provide them a list of options that align with their interests to make the unit more approachable

- Providing alternative means of representation other than writing their responses on Figures 7.1–7.3, such as making a digital poster, presentation, Infogram, and so forth

Evaluation: Students' knowledge of their own community and neighborhood should evolve. Students should be able to express their knowledge in at least one of the final products listed previously (oral presentation, printed poster-board presentation, shared digital file, and/or digital visual display). In addition, students will be evaluated through the teacher's informal observations about whether they were involved in the project and can use the activity for transition planning.

Reflection

Think about strategies for supporting a student's transition into community living as described in this chapter. Consider how you might use these strategies with the students with whom you work. What concrete steps can you take to assist them in 1) determining the type of life they want to live in their community and 2) locating the resources that will assist them in doing so? What kind of assistance might your students require to prepare for community living? When planning instruction, how will you need to consider cultural, linguistic, and racial diversity?

RESOURCE 7.3

Community Resource Mapping Findings

Name: _____ Grade: _____ Date: _____

PHASE I: Identifying ideal community living features and access to resources

Directions: Revisit the features of your ideal community living that you identified in your community living action plan. Restate the features in the table below. Add additional table rows for any features beyond your top four.

1. In my ideal living environment, I want **features** including…	Does my current living environment have this feature?
a.	☐ YES ☐ NO
b.	☐ YES ☐ NO
c.	☐ YES ☐ NO
d.	☐ YES ☐ NO

2. In my ideal living environment, I want **access** to…	Do I have access to this in my current living environment?
a.	☐ YES ☐ NO
b.	☐ YES ☐ NO
c.	☐ YES ☐ NO
d	☐ YES ☐ NO

(page 1 of 4)

(continued)

Figure 7.3. Community Resource Mapping Findings worksheet.

Figure 7.3.   *(continued)*

RESOURCE 7.3: Community Resource Mapping Findings *(continued)*

PHASE II: Identifying one area you want to research

Directions: Select **ONE** ideal community feature you listed above that you currently do not access, that you would like to research to learn more about that feature. Write that ideal community feature and or access below.

3. In my ideal living environment, **one** feature and/or resource I want to access that I currently do not use and want to learn more about is…

4. I'm curious to learn more about this, specifically to learn more about…

PHASE III: Researching community resources aligned to your ideal community features

5. In researching community resources, organizations, and/or business, I learned about the following options that align with the **ONE** ideal community features and/or access areas. These include… (list all resources, organizations, and/or businesses that came up in your search)

6. The **name** of the community resource, organization, and/or business I want to learn more about and research further is…

7. The **specific location** of this resource is (e.g., web address, mailing address)…

8. Regarding this particular resource, organization, and/or business, I'm particularly curious about…

RESOURCE 7.3: Community Resource Mapping Findings *(continued)*

9. In reading about this resource, organization, and/or business, I learned the following information relevant to the following topics...

Topic	Findings
A. **Name and location** of the resource, organization, and/or business	
B. **The service(s) offered** at this resource, organization, and/or business	
C. To participate, access, and/or qualify for the resource, organization, and/or business I need to... (consider required age, application process, enrollment dates, documentation needed, etc.)	
D. To access the resource(s), I would need to pay... (consider how much it costs, how often payment is required, acceptable payment methods, etc.)	
E. **The transportation** I need to access the resource(s) would be... (include options for public and private transportation methods or technology needed to access resource online, etc.)	
F. To learn more about the resource(s), organization, and/or business, **I could contact the following person to learn more...** (include their full name, job title, email address, and phone number)	
G. To stay updated on the resource(s), organization, and/or business **I can follow them on the following social media platforms...**	

(continued)

Figure 7.3. *(continued)*

RESOURCE 7.3: Community Resource Mapping Findings *(continued)*

PHASE IV: Reflection and recruiting support to access the resources available at the organization and/or business

10. After reading about the resource, business, and/or organization I feel…

11. To learn more about the resource, business, and/or organization, I could…

12. My **parent(s)/guardian(s)** can help me utilize the resources offered by the organization or business by…

13. My **teacher(s)** can help me utilize the resources offered by the organization or business by…

WRAP-UP: PREPARING FOR COMMUNITY LIVING

Students with disabilities from CLD backgrounds face barriers and challenges to acquiring a fulfilled and independent adult life. Yet, if they work together in a shared partnership with families, educators, and community leaders, transition to community living is an attainable goal. Professionals can use a UDT approach grounded in culturally sustaining practices that makes the connections between functional and academic demands, provides students and their families with tools to seek and acquire the services and opportunities to become involved in their community, and provides students with ways to understand their own support needs in the community and connect with others in the community.

Here are some final tips that will help you to apply the principles of UDT to your students' transition to community living:

> ▶ **Tips for Preparing Students for Community Living**
>
> 1. **Support students in strengthening their self-awareness.** This includes two skills: self-knowledge and self-awareness. Students should learn to communicate personal attributes, including their abilities, preferences, and challenges, with others. Advocating for oneself is o nly possible when the individual has knowledge about their skills, challenges, and supports that aid them in being successful.
>
> 2. **Make sure students understand their rights, reinforcing their internal locus of control, self-advocacy skills, and leadership skills.** Once students leave the local education agency (public schools), they no longer have rights under the Individuals with Disabilities Education Improvement Act (2004). Students need to understand their rights in the public setting and how to navigate advocating and obtaining services within their rights under federal mandates such as the Americans With Disabilities Act (1990), the Fair Housing Amendments Act (1988), the Developmental Disabilities Assistance and Bill of Rights Act Amendments (2000), and the Rehabilitation Act (1973).
>
> 3. **Help students strengthen their problem-solving skills and self-instruction skills.** This is especially important when students are presented with unforeseen challenges or barriers in fulfilling a task in the initial phase of community living without the previously relied-upon adult and caregiver support.
>
> 4. **Support students in understanding goal setting and attainment.** This is particularly important in understanding the difference between internal and external community living goals, how to identify internal and external goals, understanding the difference short-term and distant future goals, and identifying their short-term and distance future goals. Research indicates that knowledge in these areas enhance minority students' motivation and learning in combination with an attitude that schoolwork is internally regulated by future goals (Andre et al., 2018).

REFERENCES

Americans With Disabilities Act of 1990, 42 U.S.C. § 12101 *et seq.* (1990). https://www.ada.gov/pubs/adastatute08.htm

Andre, L., van Vianen, A. E. M., Peetsma, T. T. D., & Oort, F. J. (2018). Motivational power of future time perspective: Meta-analyses in education, work, and health. *PLoS ONE, 13*(1), Article e0190492. https://doi.org/10.1371/journal.pone.0190492

Becker, M. A., Shaw, B. R., & Reib, L. M. (n.d.). *Quality of Life Assessment manual.* Quality of Life Assessment Project. http://wqli.fmhi.usf.edu/_docs/wqli-instruments/QualityOfLife-AssessmentManual.pdf

Blue-Banning, M., Summers, J. A., Frankland, H. C., Nelson, L. L., & Beegle, G. (2004). Dimensions of family and professional partnerships: Constructive guidelines for collaboration. *Exceptional Children, 70*(2), 167–184. https://doi.org/10.1177/001440290407000203

Cimera, R. E., Thoma, C. A., Whittenburg, H. N., & Ruhl, A. N. (2018). Is getting a postsecondary education a good investment for supported employees with intellectual disability and taxpayers? *Inclusion, 6*(2), 97–109. https://doi.org/10.1352/2326-6988-6.2.97

Columbia Regional Inclusive Services. (n.d.). *Ansell-Casey Life Skills Assessment, Youth Level III — Version 4.0.* https://www.crisoregon.org/cms/lib/OR01928264/Centricity/Domain/45/Documents/Ansell%20Casey%20Life%20Skills%20Assessment%20Y3_Version%204.0.pdf

Crane, K., & Mooney, M. (2005). *Essential tools: Community resource mapping.* http://www.ncset.org/publications/essentialtools/mapping/default.asp

Data Resource Center for Child and Adolescent Health. (2020). *2018–2019 National Survey of Children's Health data query: Percent of children with special health care needs (CSHCN), ages 0 through 17.* Child and Adolescent Health Measurement Initiative & U.S. Department of Health and Human Services. https://www.childhealthdata.org/browse/survey/results?q=7713&r=6&r2=1

Developmental Disabilities Assistance and Bill of Rights Act Amendments of 2000, Pub. L. No. 106-402, 42 U.S.C. §§ 6000 *et seq.* (2000).

Eilenberg, J. S., Paff, M., Harrison, A. J., & Long, K. A. (2019). Disparities based on race, ethnicity, and socioeconomic status over the transition to adulthood among adolescents and young adults on the autism spectrum: A systematic review. *Current Psychiatry Reports, 21*(5), 32. https://doi.org/10.1007/s11920-019-1016-1Fair Housing Amendments Act of 1988, Pub. L. No. 100-403, 42 U.S.C. §§ 3601 *et seq.* (1988).

Gothberg, J. E., Greene, G., & Kohler, P. D. (2019). District implementation of research-based practices for transition planning with culturally and linguistically diverse youth with disabilities and their families. *Career Development and Transition for Exceptional Individuals, 42*(2), 77–86. https://doi.org/10.1177/2165143418762794

Greene, G. (2011). *Transition planning for culturally and linguistically diverse youth.* Paul H. Brookes Publishing Co.

Harry, B. H. (2008). Collaboration with culturally and linguistically diverse families: Ideal versus reality. *Exceptional Children, 74,* 327–377.

Leake, D., & Black, R. (2005). *Essential tools: Improving secondary education and transition for youth with disabilities: Cultural and linguistic diversity: Implications for transition personnel.* National Center on Secondary Education and Transition.

Linkenhoker, D., & McCarron, L. (1993). *Street Survival Skills Questionnaire.* McCarron-Dial Systems, Inc. http://mccarrondial.com

National Longitudinal Transition Study-2. (2005). *Changes over time in postschool outcomes of youth with disabilities.* http://nlts2.org/pdfs/str6_completereport.pdf

Oettingen, G. (2014). *Rethinking positive thinking: Inside the new science of motivation.* Penguin Random House.

Pearpoint, J., O'Brien, J., & Forest, M. (1993). *MAPS and PATH: Differences & similarities.* http://www.northstarsls.org/sites/default/files/Maps%20vs.%20Path.pdf

Rehabilitation Act of 1973, Pub. L. No. 93-112, 29 U.S.C. §§ 701 *et seq.* (1973).

Reiss, J. G., & Gibson, R. W. (2005a). *Health care transition planning guide for youth and families: Ages 18 and older.* Institute for Child Health Policy. https://pediatrics.med.jax.ufl.edu/jaxhats/docs/hct_workbook_18up.pdf

Reiss, J. G., & Gibson, R. W. (2005b). *Health care transition planning guide for youth and families: Ages 15-17.* Institute for Child Health Policy. https://www.floridahats.org/wp-content/uploads/2016/03/HCT_Workbook_15-17.pdf

Riverside Insights. (1996). *Scales of Independent Behavior–Revised* (SIB-R). https://www.riversideinsights.com/p/scales-of-independent-behavior-revised-sib-r-complete-package/

Shogren, K. A., Raley, S. K., Burke, K. M., & Wehmeyer, M. L. (2019). *The Self-Determined Learning Model of Instruction teacher's guide.* Kansas University Center on Developmental Disabilities.

Synatschk, K. O., Clark, G. M., & Patton, J. R. (2008). *Informal assessments for transition: Independent living and community participation.* PRO-ED.

Transition Tennessee. (2023). *The Life Skills Inventory Independent Living Skills Assessment Tool.* Division of Children and Family. http://www.sped.sbcsc.k12.in.us/PDF%20Files/tassessments/Independent%20Living/Life%20Skills%20Inventory_Independent%20Living.pdf

University of Florida Health. (2023). *Your Child Health Care Independence Worksheet.* https://pediatrics.med.jax.ufl.edu/jaxhats/docs/hct_workbook_15-17.pdf

Whittenburg, H. N., Cimera, R. E., & Thoma, C. A. (2019). Comparing employment outcomes of young adults with autism: Does postsecondary educational experience matter? *Journal of Postsecondary Education and Disability, 32*(2), 159–172.

Wilt, C. L., & Morningstar, M. E. (2018). Parent engagement in the transition from school to adult life through culturally sustaining practices: A scoping review. *Intellectual and Developmental Disabilities, 56*(5), 307–320.

8

Social Inclusion and Engagement

Joshua Taylor, Sarah K. Howorth, Melissa J. Cuba,
Yetta Myrick, Roger Ideishi, and Deborah L. Rooks-Ellis

DIGGING DEEPER: What Teachers Have to Say

As an author team, we represent multiple identities and roles that we draw from in informing our discussion of the social inclusion of people with disabilities within their communities. Collectively, we are researchers, educators, parents of individuals with disabilities, and disability advocates; our team includes an occupational therapist, a behavior analyst, and a multilingual educator. We each have many roles that support social and community inclusion in schools and within the broader community. Some of us met through joint efforts to support museums and cultural arts institutions to provide inclusive engagement opportunities for individuals with intellectual and developmental disabilities, but our experiences extend to include how these issues impact schools, families, and community institutions. Others of us have been parent outreach ambassadors, provided social skills instruction to transition-age youth, and supported multilingual students with disabilities. We have also seen how ableism and racism intersect along with other systemic biases to disenfranchise culturally and linguistically diverse (CLD) individuals with disabilities and their family members. Although the case studies in this chapter are fictitious, they are drawn from lived experiences related to how these systemic biases have an impact on students.

Our experiences as advocates of CLD students and families have taught us to center their voices and experiences in addressing inequitable practices and processes to living a meaningful life. Creating space for these community voices led many of us to partner with others to advocate for immigrant families of children with disabilities. These families struggled to navigate their health care, education, and social systems as they tried to provide every opportunity for their child to become healthy and successful. It is through this work that we seek to reframe how we discuss social and community inclusion by prioritizing the multidimensional identities and needs of CLD individuals with disabilities and their families.

Essential Questions

▶ What person-centered approaches can educators use to promote community inclusion?

▶ What barriers to social inclusion exist for culturally and linguistically diverse (CLD) youth and their families?

▶ What strategies can facilitators use to engage CLD youth and their families in social inclusion?

▶ How can educators promote social inclusion through multiple life domains, multiple means of assessment, multiple resources and perspectives, and student self-determination?

Our exploration of the previous questions is informed by our varied experiences working with CLD youth with disabilities and their families. To begin this exploration, we turn now to the cases of four students preparing for the transition to adulthood, each of whom has a connection to cultures outside the dominant mainstream of the United States: Kenyon, Amira, Miguel, and Jonathon.

CASE STUDY: Kenyon

Missing Out on Social and Academic Opportunities

Kenyon is a rising 11th grader who is interested in politics and reading historical biographies, and he enjoys playing video games in his free time. A few years ago, he came out on the LGBTQ+ spectrum to his parents and a few close family members. Kenyon's parents are supportive, but they aren't sure how to talk about sex and relationships, and his self-contained class was left out of the school's general sexual education training. Kenyon's mother and father met at a prestigious Historically Black College and University, and both come from strong family traditions valuing education. Kenyon's father works for the state department, and his job demands that he spend substantial time overseas, often in unexpected periods of time from a few weeks to multiple years. Kenyon's mom earned her Juris Doctorate but did not pursue practice in law because she moved abroad with the family to her husband's first few international posts where she had Kenyon. Kenyon was educated in private schools overseas through elementary school, most recently in central Europe. Kenyon and his mom moved back to the U.S. to be closer to extended family when Kenyon was in middle school. This major transition was difficult for Kenyon, and he experienced conflicts with peers and teachers in his first year back in U.S. schools. After challenging his English teacher over the accuracy of his textbook, he was referred for special education services and found eligible under the category of emotional disturbance (ED). Currently, Kenyon lives in a suburban community and attends his local high school where his schedule is a mix of inclusive and self-contained classes. Among his family members, it has always been assumed that Kenyon would attend college after graduating from high school, but his family has grown increasingly frustrated with the services offered by the school.

CASE STUDY: Amira

Missing Out on Social Opportunities and Creative Interests

Amira is a rising 10th grader who is interested in music, sports, and art. In her free time, she writes her own songs and plays them on her father's acoustic guitar for her immediate family. She and her family immigrated from Afghanistan when she was 8 years old, just as she was learning to read and write in Dari at school. At home, Amira speaks mainly Dari with her mother, father, and two younger siblings, although this has shifted over time to the point that the family speaks a mix of Dari and English. Amira attends a public high school in an urban, ethnically diverse community and receives special education services under the label of learning disability. She stopped receiving English as a second language (ESL) services in fifth grade because her teachers felt that she "spoke English fine." Despite the fact that she did not "test out" of the English language proficiency assessments, she was pulled out of ESL services completely from that point on. Amira is included in most regular academic courses throughout her school day, but she takes a reading class for students who have not yet passed the mandated reading assessments. Although this class helps support her reading development, it prevents her from taking any elective classes related to her interests in music and art.

CASE STUDY: Miguel

Missing Out on Connections With Peers

Miguel is a bilingual (Spanish and English) 12th grader in a community high school in a rural, predominantly White community who enjoys photography, excels in math, and loves animals. He lives with his father, aunt, and uncle on a small farmstead and spends much of his free time helping with chores and odd jobs for his dad and uncle. His mother died when he was younger. Miguel was born in the U.S. but moved back to El Salvador for 4 years to live with his family, at which point his studies were interrupted. At his most recent eligibility meeting, Miguel was identified as eligible under the label of autism spectrum disorder (ASD). Previously, he received services under the developmental disability (DD) label as a child and later intellectual disability (ID) after his return to the U.S. in seventh grade. Miguel is on course to graduate in a few months with a special education certificate. He spends all of his school day in a self-contained autism classroom embedded in his community high school, but he does not spend time with any of his classmates after school. He has an individualized education program (IEP) goal for keeping his phone away during class time because he frequently takes it out to take photos. His teachers have asked his father to keep the phone at home so it is not a distraction, but Miguel's father and uncle work erratic hours and need to be in contact with him during the school day via his phone.

CASE STUDY: Jonathon

Missing Out on Peer Connections and Transition Planning Opportunities

Jonathon is a 12-year-old boy who enjoys video games, sports, and music. He is currently in seventh grade in middle school. Jonathon is fluent in English and Mandarin. His parents are primary Mandarin speakers with some understanding and use of English. He lives at home with his parents and an older 16-year-old brother. Jonathon is on the autism spectrum and receives special instruction, occupational and speech therapy, and behavioral services in an integrated classroom. Academically, he performs at grade level but requires one-to-one support for task completion for more than 50% of formal and informal classroom activities. He is often a bystander for social activities and is often alone in the classroom or lunchroom. Jonathon shows greater attention to activities that are presented in terms of a competition. He enjoys watching and going to sporting events. His current IEP includes some transition elements written by his school team but without input from him or his family members.

As we can see from the descriptions of Kenyon, Amira, Miguel, and Jonathon, CLD youth come from highly varied backgrounds whose perspectives, interests, and values affect what successful transition to adulthood looks like for each individual student. For every student, however, a successful transition means being engaged and included in multiple domains of social inclusion and community participation. Employment and education rightly receive a great deal of focus as important outcomes in transition planning. However, other aspects of community inclusion. including social engagement and friendship, recreation and leisure, and membership in social groups, are all vital parts of a full and meaningful life. In transition planning for students with disabilities, these elements are often included under the broad domain of independent living, but they clearly extend far beyond those skills and experiences related specifically to residence, home living, and other functional life skills. These aspects of community inclusion are central to achieving and maintaining several key indicators related to quality of life for youth and young adults with disabilities (e.g., Amado et al., 2013). If community inclusion is not considered at the forefront of transition planning, we are not fully preparing our students for success in adulthood. Although employment and postsecondary education (PSE) justifiably receive much of the focus of transition planning, there are multiple benefits to planning for and supporting social skills, relationships, and community inclusion in these domains as well. Sometimes, these connections are direct, as indicated by research showing that many young adults with ASD have difficulty maintaining employment related to social and behavioral expectations in the workplace (Whittenburg et al., 2020). However, social and community inclusion also lead to other benefits for transition-age youth, from networking and building relationships to developing critical soft skills needed for career development and advancement.

What do we mean by social and community inclusion? As with many parts of transition planning, the details of social and community inclusion depend largely on the individual but refer to a broad range of areas of membership in activities, institutions, and groups within a particular community. These include formal roles and interactions such as work experiences, membership in clubs, social groups, or faith organizations, and perhaps participation in volunteer and advocacy work (Hall, 2017). However, community inclusion also encompasses more informal activities such as engaging in self-directed recreation and leisure activities and maintaining meaningful friendships with peers (Hall, 2017). If our efforts to include our students in meaningful transition activities are limited only to planning for employment and college and engaging them during the school day, we are missing a huge piece of what is needed to ensure a successful transition to adulthood. As special educators and transition practitioners, we must also take responsibility for ensuring that community inclusion is an area of focus for students and families (Agran et al., 2017). To ensure that students are fully engaged in their communities as adults, it is necessary to reflect on the communities in which we reside, the resources and connections available there, and our own practices as school and transition professionals. Most important, however, we must first and foremost consider the strengths, interests, and preferences of our students and use person-centered approaches to planning for community inclusion.

As with other aspects of transition planning addressed in this book, social and community inclusion is also an area where persistent patterns of disconnection between practitioners and CLD youth and families have led to unsatisfactory transition outcomes (Achola & Greene, 2016). As a result, it is especially important for practitioners to select and implement culturally responsive practices for promoting social and community inclusion. Because this area of transition planning is dependent on an individual and family's social and cultural values, preferences, interests, language background, and personal networks, it is imperative that school and transition practitioners engage with CLD youth and families in person-centered planning (PCP), culturally responsive approaches, and multicultural pedagogies. Universal design for transition (UDT) offers a framework for reflecting on how practitioners can embed culturally sustaining practices into the four tiers of UDT: multiple life domains, multiple means of assessment, student self-determination, and multiple resources and perspectives. This chapter provides practitioners with the following:

- Practical strategies and person-centered approaches to promote community inclusion for CLD youth and families through the UDT framework across several key domains

- Opportunities for self-reflection

- Ideas for engaging more broadly in expanding inclusive opportunities for CLD youth and families with disabilities in our distinct and individual communities

BARRIERS TO SOCIAL AND COMMUNITY INCLUSION FOR CULTURALLY AND LINGUISTICALLY DIVERSE YOUTH AND FAMILIES

CLD youth and families face several barriers to social and community inclusion in the transition process. Research has revealed several glaring disparities in their transition outcomes and experiences. In a recent review, findings indicated that racial disparities were noted in social engagement after graduation and in independently accessing transportation within the community (Eilenberg et al., 2019). There is also evidence from multiple studies pointing to specific barriers related to school practices, adult service practices, and family perceptions and characteristics. Schools often demonstrate disregard for student and family values, reinforce inequitable and biased practices, and do not provide accessible materials to families. In turn, adult service agencies seldom use individualized, strength-based approaches that value the engagement of families to an individual's success (Hirano et al., 2018).

Many of these barriers highlight the endemically low expectations of many school and service providers toward students with disabilities, who are more often segregated from their peers, as well as teachers' intrinsic racial biases that manifests in key instructional decisions regarding students with disabilities (Fish, 2017). These biases may manifest in a variety of ways. For example, not providing a CLD parent with translated and culturally verified documents in their primary language with adequate time to process and understand may serve as a substantial barrier to engagement. Often, a literal translation or translation that is not contextually derived does not convey the appropriate meaning. This can lead to misunderstanding or potential lack of involvement or apprehension of the educational team, if the cultural interpretation conveys a judgment or diminishing of the student or family's engagement (Gonzales & Gabel, 2017). These low expectations are particularly harmful because they often lead to assumptions that CLD family members do not want to be engaged in transition planning for social and community inclusion. Despite the presence of several systemic barriers for CLD students and their families, school and transition practitioners can engage with students and families to provide culturally sustaining and evidence-based interventions while building capacity within communities to promote inclusion of diverse students with disabilities.

CASE STUDY: Kenyon, *continued*

Feeling Underestimated and Frustrated

Since she and Kenyon returned to the U.S., his mother has advocated for inclusive education but agreed to some self-contained programming with other students with ED at the encouragement of school staff. Overall, Kenyon is on course to graduate with a standard diploma and has had no problem passing his end-of-course exams, although his grade point average (GPA) is low given some inconsistency in homework and assignments, which school staff attribute to what they assume is a single-parent household. As he approaches his 11th-grade year, Kenyon's mother has been increasingly concerned about his educational plan, particularly his isolation from other students and lack of academic support. She was even more alarmed when presented with a draft IEP that did not include college enrollment in Kenyon's PSE goal. After reaching out for clarification, Kenyon's case manager explained that a vocational training program would be more appropriate for Kenyon based on his academic difficulties and low GPA. Kenyon and his parents are frustrated with the transition plan offered by the school and his increasing isolation from his peers.

CASE STUDY: Amira, *continued*

Feeling Left Behind and Worried

Amira's transition planning has not yet started despite her being older than the required age of transition in her state. In her high school coursework so far, Amira has passed all but one of her general education classes but has a low GPA and has not yet passed any of the state-mandated assessments needed to graduate with a standard diploma. Because she has not met this graduation benchmark, in her most recent IEP meeting, the team proposed to change her anticipated diploma and related education program to a special education certificate instead of a standard diploma. As a rising 10th grader without a formal transition plan, Amira has yet to articulate her goals for the future to her IEP team, but she knows that she would like to go on to college. However, her case manager has told Amira and her family that with her GPA and lack of passing scores on standardized content assessments, her options for PSE will be limited. At school, she is outgoing and social and has a small group of friends that she hangs out with at lunch and between classes. Outside of school, she usually spends most of her time with her family and with her mosque community. Amira used to play soccer in a recreational league in the community until a few years ago when she was discouraged from playing so that she could concentrate on her studies. Even though she enjoys spending time with her family and her mosque community, she feels increasingly isolated and worried that she will lose many of her friends who are already planning to go away to college.

CASE STUDY: Miguel, *continued*

Feeling Left Out and Unsupported

Miguel's transition plan has been fairly minimal up until this point—mainly focused on him continuing to live at home and work on the farm with his family. In order to limit the personnel involved in meetings, Miguel's Spanish teacher has served as both the general education teacher and the translator for his father in meetings. However, she speaks Castilian Spanish, so his father does not understand much of the discussion in meetings but does not protest in order to show appropriate respect and appreciation for the school staff. Because Miguel was not diagnosed with autism until he was already in high school, his previous labels of ID and DD affected the expectations of his teachers and the support they provided. Most importantly, his previous ID label led to teachers consistently overlooking his abilities in math. Although he received little rigorous academic instruction in math, Miguel is able to calculate large sums in his head and quickly grasp new concepts. Miguel spends most of his free time working on the farmstead or on other jobs, hanging out with his dad and uncle, and going to a Spanish-language service at a church in a nearby town. Around his peers and teachers, Miguel is extremely shy and withdrawn, which limits his opportunity for friendships and negatively impacts his access to support in the classroom.

CASE STUDY: JONATHON, *continued*

Feeling Ignored and Patronized

During Jonathon's transition planning meeting with the IEP team, his parents invited a family advocate as well as a translator. The school team presented an IEP that did not recommend continued special education services for high school because Jonathon was performing at grade level. The family advocate was a primary English-speaking, American-born advocate but of Asian heritage. Although the family's advocate was an expert on disability and education, the school team spoke to the advocate in a slower and louder manner using simplistic language to convey ideas based on the assumption that the advocate lacked English language proficiency. The parent and family advocate expressed strong disagreement with dismissal of special education services, and they provided additional context that Jonathon is currently performing at grade level because of the one-to-one support he receives for task completion. Another set of concerns brought forward were his social skills and interactions with peers, especially during lunch, and Jonathon's community interests and engagement in games and sports.

As we see from the experiences of Kenyon, Amira, Miguel, and Jonathon, CLD youth face many barriers to not only community inclusion but also in transition planning and programming as a whole. Many of these barriers are rooted in low expectations and misunderstandings from school staff about students' abilities as well as the social and cultural capital of individuals and families. Too often, these systemic issues and barriers bring about the poor outcomes discussed previously. However, special educators and transition practitioners can use certain strategies and approaches to positively impact students' lives and their community inclusion.

ENGAGING CULTURALLY AND LINGUISTICALLY DIVERSE YOUTH AND THEIR FAMILIES IN SOCIAL AND COMMUNITY INCLUSION

Until this point in the chapter, we have highlighted the importance of community inclusion for transition-age youth and the barriers faced by CLD individuals and families. However, after engaging students and families to identify priorities for transition, it is necessary then to match those goals with approaches that will empower students and their families to achieve meaningful outcomes; it is also necessary to provide instruction and opportunities for students to increase social engagement and strengthen networks within the community. Figure 8.1 provides a visual of these strategies for promoting social and community inclusion: PCP, family engagement, assessment and instruction, and building capacity within community organizations.

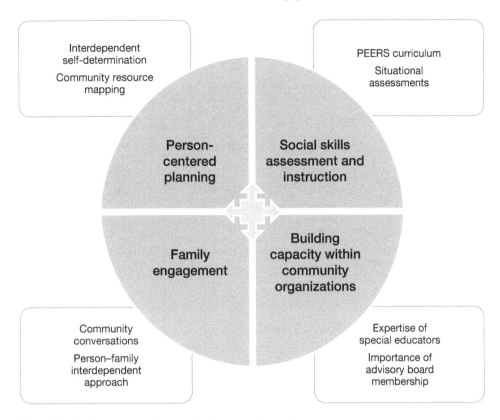

Figure 8.1. Strategies for promoting social and community inclusion.

Person-Centered Approaches

PCP involves active engagement of the youth themselves as the lead in planning their future. PCP is conducted interdependently with family and other key members of their self-identified support team and has been identified as a research-based practice for improving employment outcomes of transition-age youth with disabilities (Rowe et al., 2021). Although PCP emphasizes self-determination by focusing on student strengths, preferences, interests, needs, and dreams for the future, it also places importance on linking the individual to resources and opportunities that can support them in achieving these aspirations (O'Brien & O'Brien, 2002). PCP approaches often take place through structured processes by which an individual and their support team create action plans to achieve the individual's future dream by identifying roles for members of their network of support. Trainor (2007) examined the cultural relevance of PCP for CLD youth from two different backgrounds using facilitators called "cultural connectors" and found it to be a tool that increased both family participation and self-determination. Haines and colleagues (2018) found similar results using a specific PCP process with refugee families who recently immigrated to the U.S. Findings of this study also underscored the importance of staff educating themselves about the individual and family's culture and values by connecting with local experts and reading resources to challenge deficit thinking and mitigate microaggressions (Haines et al., 2018).

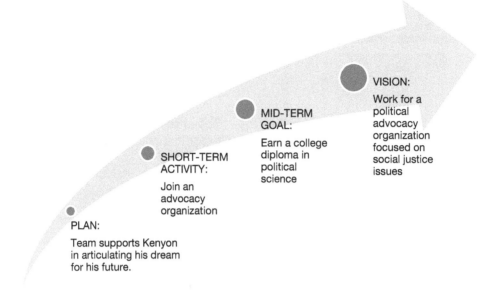

Figure 8.2. Person-centered planning example: Kenyon.

When considering planning for the community inclusion of CLD youth with disabilities, PCP offers a useful framework by providing a structured approach for facilitating flexible yet adaptive conversations that lead to meaningful, actionable steps. At its core, PCP ensures that the planning process is an individualized, strengths-based process that values the role of the family in the success of the student. For PCP to be successful, school and transition practitioners must be responsive to student and family values around individualism itself and how that may impact self-determination, agency, and family involvement in planning and implementation. From a practical standpoint, this can often be accomplished by simply asking the CLD youth and their family what they want, need, or are interested in, and then using these interests to build networks across the individual, families and social units, community, and organizational partners. Although our goal for our students is for them to have agency, it is also important to consider other social and cultural conceptualizations of the individual as more or less interdependent with the family and other members of their community.

Figure 8.2 shows an example of the PCP process as it was used with Kenyon, whose story will be revisited throughout this chapter. For more information about PCP, check out the Administration for Community Living's web site: https://acl.gov/programs/consumer-control/person-centered-planning

Community Resource Mapping

PCP provides a strength-based foundation for transition planning and goal setting, but we then need to provide structure and resources to achieve the goals identified through the PCP process. Community resource mapping is one strategy for identifying, organizing, and sharing resources available in the community that can promote positive outcomes for transition-age youth with disabilities. Mapping community resources and creating a plan with individuals and families is a vital part of the PCP process and should be connected directly with the vision of the future formulated by the individual. Community resource mapping is discussed in further detail in other chapters of this text; for more information and sample resource mapping activities, see Chapters 2 and 7.

Family Engagement

Along with centering the strengths of our students in transition planning through PCP, families have a critical impact on the successful transition from school to adult life, and family involvement is particularly important for youth with disabilities. Family involvement has been associated with positive outcomes for youth with disabilities, including higher levels of academic achievement and improved postschool outcomes (e.g., Papay & Bambara, 2014). Opportunities for parental involvement in planning educational programs have been mandated since 1975 (Education for All Handicapped Children Act, 1975). Similarly, the intent of the transition requirements of the Individuals with Disabilities Education Improvement Act (IDEA, 2004) was to increase family participation in the transition planning process. Parental participation may be particularly important for CLD youth, as a strong partnership between parents and school personnel can promote cultural understanding and responsiveness in transition planning, including language translation and supports. For example, CLD groups may emphasize different norm-related behaviors (e.g., removing shoes indoors for some cultures) and define adult roles differently. Overall, parents can be an indispensable resource in helping educators understand, identify, and support transition outcomes that are valued within a family's culture (Achola & Greene, 2016).

Research about involvement for families of transition age youth with disabilities highlights barriers to school–family partnerships that create inequities and contribute to differential postschool outcomes (Hirano et al., 2018). When examining the systemic barriers to family involvement in transition planning for youth with disabilities, researchers identified three broad categories: family, school, and adult service barriers (Hirano et al., 2018). Family barriers include family stress, limited resources, and low self-efficacy. School barriers include many related to racism and discrimination, as well preventing families from becoming empowered and lack of adequate transition programming. Finally, adult service barriers include low expectations and deficit-based view of students, as well as lack of adult services and postschool options (Hirano et al., 2018).

It is critically important for special education leaders from across the age span to collaborate in the development of family–student–school partnership models to help families feel valued and how best to contribute. From the earliest ages, these models need to incorporate opportunities that support CLD families. Family roles need to be conceptualized to ensure that parents and extended family have opportunities to be collaborators with their child in collective decision making.

Social and Cultural Capital   Social and cultural capital are important concepts in involving families and underscore the need to approach CLD families from an additive perspective. Too often, there is a breakdown in communication and partnership, which stems from low teacher expectations about the engagement of CLD families. Not only does this undermine potential partnerships, but it also dismisses the immense potential of engaging the social and cultural capital that CLD students, families, and communities bring to transition planning. In this context, *social capital* is defined as social connections and networks CLD students have in the community that could help them succeed (Yosso, 2005). On the other hand, *cultural capital* encompasses the aspirations (hopes and dreams) these students possess, linguistic abilities that are often overlooked and undervalued, familial and community networks, abilities to navigate different spaces, and resistance to injustice and inequities (Yosso, 2005). Social and cultural capital can be effective means of challenging school and transition practitioners to reframe how CLD students and families are viewed, so the partners can support the empowerment of these families as advocating partners and supporters of their child's education and future goals.

Community Conversations   Community conversations are another approach that builds from community resource mapping to not only identify and share resources but also engage individuals, families, and other stakeholders in systems change efforts to overcome barriers to preferred outcomes for youth (Carter & Bumble, 2018; Schutz et al., 2021). Engaging CLD individuals and families in community conversations and systems change efforts may be especially effective at addressing transition disparities by identifying and dismantling systemic bias and other barriers to success for CLD youth. This process capitalizes upon a specific community's unique culture, priorities, and available resources and brings together a diverse group of local stakeholders to address the transition needs of students with disabilities (Carter & Bumble, 2018). Stakeholders may include families, educators, disability agencies, prospective and current employers, community leaders, civic groups, and faith communities. Attendees participate in three small group conversations, with each round focusing on a single question prompting participants to identify resources, ideas, and personal connections to support transition programming for the students with disabilities who reside in that community. The concluding whole group discussion is then used to share actionable strategies heard during the small group conversations. This community-inclusive process ensures that the families and the school district are exposed to new perspectives, discuss creative ways to address persistent transition challenges, and explore connections with local partners. Figure 8.3 shows the implementation procedures needed for conducting a community conversation (Schutz et al., 2021).

Person–Family Interdependent Approach   Another promising practice is the person-family interdependent approach, which considers the close relationship between the quality of life of a CLD family and the future adult life of their child with a disability (Achola & Greene, 2016). This approach considers the family as a whole and requires transition professionals to reflect on the student's current and future roles in supporting their family, as well as their expected roles within the broader cultural community. Transition goals should be aligned with these cultural and family interdependent expectations. Next, the relationships between proposed transition activities for the student with a disability and their family's needs should be identified with consideration for the important roles that typically extend into adulthood that youth from certain cultures play within their families and cultural communities (e.g., child care, caring for relatives, providing financial support). Finally, the gender, birth order, and disability are influential family expectations of children in other cultures and nonjudgmental consideration should be provided to a family's beliefs and expectations about their young adults' future responsibilities.

Prepare a Team

Begin 2 mo before event

- Assemble a planning team of school personnel and others in the community
- Identify needs and goals for the event
- Assign team roles for the event planning process

Plan the Community Conversation Event

Begin 1.5 mo before event

- Choose a venue and date
- Recruit attendees and gather responses
- Develop conversation questions
- Prepare personnel and materials for the event
- Develop materials (e.g., placemats, note templates, registration sheets, decorations)
- Arrange for refreshments

Implement the Community Conversation Event

Day of event

- Set up the event and implement procedures
- Provide introduction to event
- Facilitate three rounds of small group conversation
- Facilitate one round of "harvest" whole group conversation
- Administer end-of-event survey
- Provide closing remarks and time for networking

Gather and Disseminate Ideas

Begin after event; occurs for 1–2 mo

- Gather ideas from event notes
- Prioritize promising ideas from notes
- Develop community conversation brief and distribute to community members

Implement Next Steps

Occurs for 6–12 mo

- Collect additional data if necessary
- Set goals for improvement
- Design action steps, assign responsibilities, and develop follow-up measures
- Implement follow-up measures
- Evaluate and adjust if necessary

Figure 8.3. Community conversation implementation procedures. (Used with permission of SAGE Publications from Schutz, M. A., Carter, E. W., Gajjar, S. A., & Maves, E. A. [2021]. Strengthening transition partnerships through community conversation events. TEACHING Exceptional Children, 53[5], 359–368; permission conveyed through Copyright Clearance Center, Inc.)

Assessment and Community Inclusion

Selecting and using meaningful assessment is a critical aspect of promoting community inclusion for students with disabilities. However, due to the diversity of our students as well as the complexity of assessing meaningful skills in real-life community settings, it is important to select tools that fit our students and the community contexts in which they will use these skills.

Assessment Tools for Community Inclusion   One widely used assessment tool measuring community participation overall is the Temple University Community Participation Measure (Salzer & Burns-Lynch, 2016), which is a self-directed tool that allows a person to explore their participation in their community and then engage in follow-up activities to further expand that participation. For students with ASD, the Community Based Functional Skills Assessment for Transition-Age Youth with Autism Spectrum Disorder (Schall et al., 2014) provides a structured means of assessing students' level of independence in the following domains of community life: career path and employment, self-determination/advocacy, health and safety, peer relationships, socialization and social communication, community participation and personal finance, transportation, leisure/recreation, and home living skills. For assessing an individual's level of independence and related support needs in personal, work-related, and social activities, the Supports Intensity Scale is a widely used and validated tool that examines support needed across several life domains (Thompson et al., 2021). Finally, given the importance of student self-determination to community inclusion and social participation, the Self-Determination Inventory is widely used in both research and in schools and community settings as a valid and reliable means of measuring levels of self-determination in youth and adults with and without disabilities (Shogren et al., 2021).

In addition, community participation involves a reciprocal dynamic between the person and the community environment to maximize engagement. For example, given many individuals with ASD have a sensory processing disorder, so attention to environmental features and the creation of naturally supportive community environments can be a useful strategy. The Participation and Sensory Environment Questionnaire: Community Scales is a tool to help assess the community environment's sensory qualities impacting participation (Pfeiffer et al., 2019).

The Participation and Sensory Environment Questionnaire is a useful assessment for helping educators and parents understand the impact of the sensory environment on a child's ability to participate in everyday activities. Resources can be found at: https://participationandsensoryenvironment.weebly.com/

Social Validity and Bias Considerations   All measurements should have social validity—reflecting beliefs of the culture, community, and environments where students will live, work, and play. For example, before choosing an assessment it will be important to obtain a list of culturally relevant goals from both the individual student and the family. What are their hopes and dreams for the future? What types of recreational activities bring them joy? What support may they need to be able to participate and enjoy these activities?

Educators should examine their own cultural biases when it comes to recreational and peer activities. For example, the recreational activities teachers expect students to enjoy and those they *actually* enjoy are not always the same. Current and future living environments should be based on student and family preferences, requiring very specific assessment to gain information that addresses how students function in those settings. For example, one family may put a heavy cultural emphasis on participation in sports such as soccer and cricket. Another family may find cooking and recreation with elders as more important. Identifying these interests, finding peers who share these interests, and then joining social groups to participate in these interests are important for quality of life.

Assessment of Relationship Skills   Relationship skills should be assessed to determine where the individual has areas of strength, and areas of weakness. Specific instruction can then be used to target the areas of weakness. Due to cultural differences, it is important to use social skill assessments that have been validated for use across many cultures and languages. The measures used, for example, as part of the UCLA PEERS curricula (University of California, Los Angeles Program for the Education and Enrichment of Relationship Skills) have been validated for use with speakers of multiple languages such as Spanish, Korean, Japanese, Chinese, English and include the Test of Adolescent Social Skills Knowledge (TASSK; Laugeson & Frankel, 2010), and the Test of Young Adult Social Skills Knowledge (TYASSK; Laugeson et al., 2015). These assessments are available in at least four languages and measure an individual's conversation skills, friendship skills, ability to host and participate in successful get-togethers, and dating etiquette.

It may also be important to use resources such as the Skillstreaming Checklist or the Adapted Skillstreaming Checklist to target skill strengths and weaknesses related to alternatives to aggression, dealing with stress, and negotiating and planning skills—all relevant for arranging recreational activities with friends. Results of these assessments can demonstrate opportunities to further provide instruction and support.

Situational Assessments   Situational or environmental assessments are most often used in supported employment and customized employment processes to collect information about a job seeker's strengths, preferences, interests, and needs (SPINs) that help to inform the job development process (Wehman et al., 2018). In customized employment, situational assessment is part of a person-centered process called Discovery that explores how these SPINs can be aligned with employer needs. However, situational assessment may also be used to collect important information to inform community inclusion goals and instruction by observing the individual in different types of community settings and environments. This type of naturalistic assessment can provide valuable information about the nuances of how the individual interacts with actual aspects of community and social life. For example, conducting a situational assessment in a museum setting could provide insight not only into a student's interests in the museum itself but also in asking for help and directions from staff, using maps to navigate, and perhaps even using public transportation.

Social Skills Instruction and Opportunities

Community inclusion is highly social. Social activities are also inherently bound by cultural norms and expectations for behavior (Banks & Obiakor, 2015). Being part of a group of peers is essential to a sense of community belonging. Considering social engagement and social skills is a critical component of transition planning for community inclusion. However, it should be noted that social skills and expectations vary widely based on culture. There are certain core social skills, such as sustaining a

Table 8.1.   Social skills and their community impact

Social skill	Community impact
Having conversations	Peer development
Self-identifying interests	Leisure activity choices and inclusion
Electronic communication etiquette	Peer development
Planning get-togethers	Leisure activity choices and peer development

conversation, finding common interests with potential peers, and asking for help in the community. Other social skills are much more culturally and contextually dependent, underscoring the importance of creating an open dialogue with CLD individuals and families in selecting social skills that are culturally relevant. Language is also a critical component of cultural relevance in social skills instruction and should incorporate students' dominant language when possible (Gersten & Baker, 2000). Table 8.1 lists several social skills and the impact they have on a person's ability to participate in their community.

As children become teens, their social demands become intensified by puberty and teenage social norms and expectations. Cultural dynamics between family and school professional expectations may also come into play. For example, it is a well-documented phenomenon that CLD students with disabilities are more likely to be bullied by their peers and to receive exclusionary discipline, such as suspension and expulsion, from their teachers (Santiago-Rosario et al., 2021). Direct instruction in prosocial and interpersonal skills for developing friendships is essential. Programs such as the UCLA PEERS curriculum (Laugeson et al., 2015) and Skillstreaming (Goldstein & McGinnis, 1997) are evidence-based, manualized programs. The PEERS program has been validated cross-culturally in North American, European, South American, and Asian populations (Laugeson et al., 2015).

Social communication demands associated with many disabilities may result in rejection and social isolation having a profound impact on their social and academic success. Those who support the transition planning of individuals with disabilities should pay close attention to their own cultural biases for what qualifies as a social skill required for successful friendships and employment. For example, results of a comparison of national outcomes indicated that those perceived by their teachers as having "lower functioning" behavioral skills received fewer supports during transition planning, particularly in interpersonal skill development (Kim & Morningstar, 2005).

Real and perceived social communication deficits can also impact postsecondary and job-related outcomes for individuals with disabilities. Particularly for individuals with ASD, difficulties with social skills can serve as barriers to getting and keeping a job (Whittenburg et al., 2020). The relative lack of social skills instruction may partly explain why only about 15% of young adults with ASD are engaged in competitive integrated employment, as compared to 54% of young adults overall (Schall et al., 2020).

Helping teens with disabilities identify their interests and locate relevant peer groups is crucial to creating supportive, lifelong friendships. Basing social skills practice, and social group participation, on the interests of teens with disabilities is crucial. Finding a group that centers its activities on these interests will provide important opportunities to practice social skills in settings that emphasize individual strengths, preferences, and interests. In this sense, promoting community inclusion through social skills instruction and engagement is closely related to self-determination. Although self-determination is discussed in greater detail in Chapter 4, effective application of UDT principles to promote community inclusion of CLD students necessitates that a focus on self-determination and student choice and agency be infused throughout transition planning.

The Family Voice United Toolkit is a useful tool for educators and allies to build cultural awareness, facilitate conversations, and improve partnerships with CLD families. Resources can be found at https://familyvoices.org/famu/tools/

Building Capacity Within Community Organizations

As mentioned previously, the focus of transition planning as a whole and in terms of community inclusion should be individualized and use PCP approaches. However, educators and transition practitioners also have unique skills that are highly useful to community organizations and can be impactful in creating systemic improvements for including youth with disabilities. Organizations within the community, such as museums, cultural arts centers, places of worship, professional sports organizations, recreation centers, and a wide assortment of clubs and interest groups, can provide unique opportunities to engage youth in their communities. Many of these institutions and organizations may lack experience or capacity in ensuring the accessibility of individuals with more significant support needs. Educators can provide key expertise in providing training, adapting programming and services, and serving on advisory boards to give insight into issues of equity and inclusion for CLD youth with disabilities. Not only do these activities promote systemic improvements in making communities more inclusive, but they also provide educators with relationships and networks of their own to facilitate opportunities for specific students whose interests may be well aligned with these organizations. Those participating on advisory boards should also be mindful of the representation of planning groups to ensure that family members and stakeholders from diverse groups are given a place at the table in making decisions about programming. Providing compensation for family participants through stipends, transportation costs, and meals should be considered in engaging families in this capacity.

CASE STUDY: Kenyon, *continued*

Supporting Self-Advocacy and Relationships

Kenyon's case manager responded to his parents' frustration and reached out to a mentor who suggested conducting a PCP session using the PATH (Planning Alternative Tomorrows With Hope) model to help articulate Kenyon's and his family's vision for the future. With support from his mother and case manager, Kenyon invited key members of his support team—including his father, joining by video teleconference, and a cousin about his age who shared similar interests. After a long meeting and support from everyone present, Kenyon was able to articulate that he wanted to work for a political advocacy organization focused on social justice issues. Using community resource mapping based on his vision, the team identified a LGBTQ+ advocacy organization in a nearby city that had a school club chapter he could join for weekly meetings and community outings.

The team also identified a summer program for developing self-determination leadership skills for youth with disabilities Kenyon could take part in that culminated in going to the state capital to meet with policymakers to discuss key issues. Through his participation in this disability advocacy group, Kenyon learned about disproportionality and the overrepresentation of Black male students for the ED label and underrepresentation in ASD, and he brought these topics up with his family. He and his family advocated for him, and after a reassessment eligibility process, his label was changed from ED to ASD. Finally, the conversation about the lack of sexual education for Kenyon led to a broader conversation about the need to differentiate the curriculum for all students. As a result, explicit instruction in sexual education and healthy relationships is individualized for all students in Kenyon's district.

CASE STUDY: Amira, *continued*

Supporting Artistic and Social Pursuits

Knowing how overwhelming high school cafeterias can be, Amira's special education teacher always made their classroom available for students to eat in when they had the period free. One day, Amira was having lunch with a few of her friends, and she sang part of a recent song she had written. Her special education teacher (a musician themselves) immediately commented on how impressive it was and asked about Amira's musical interest and ability. After realizing her musical talent, Amira's case manager approached the gifted education teacher about having her evaluated and identified as gifted (and twice exceptional or 2e). Following her identification as 2e, Amira's transition planning took a new path, and her strengths and interests were centered at the forefront of her educational planning and programming.

Amira's case manager also advocated for a more thorough assessment of her English language development, which found that whereas her social language in English was more advanced, her academic use of English was less developed and likely contributed to her poor testing results. Based on the knowledge of her giftedness in music and the new assessment data on her English language development, her IEP and transition goals were substantially revised, and Amira's school day looks very different now. Amira receives strategic support from an ESL specialist who provides some direct instruction but mainly collaborates with her general and special education teachers in adapting instruction. This has led to Amira passing all but one of her most recent end-of-course assessments, putting her on course to graduate with a standard diploma.

More dramatically, Amira has completely come out of her shell in both school and the community. With the support she receives from the ESL specialist, she no longer requires the reading remediation class and has her electives free to engage in her interests at school. She now plays cello in the school orchestra and sings in the school chorus. Her case manager has been working with her gifted education teacher to identify music scholarship opportunities at universities around the country, and she and her family are excitedly reviewing brochures and planning school visits.

CASE STUDY: Miguel, *continued*

Supporting Academics, Social Connections, and Family Engagement

A member of their church and former school principal recently informed Miguel and his dad about their rights related to the age of eligibility for special education services until age 22 and offered to attend the next meeting as an advocate. At that meeting, this family friend advocated for interpretation services being provided by a trained professional rather than the Spanish teacher. As a result, Miguel's father was more engaged in the process. He shared how impressed he was at Miguel's ability to analyze calculations related to farm operations and was interested in training programs to further develop those skills. Miguel's father also expressed concern that Miguel spent all of his time with adults related to work. As a result, Miguel and his team identified his interest in photography as a means of building his social connection in the community. Miguel was connected with the art teacher at his school, who organized a social media group focused on photography in the area. The transition team agreed to revise Miguel's IEP to shift toward more of a focus on academics needed for an associate degree in farming management and husbandry, along with opportunities to participate in a local apprenticeship program. Miguel will also be included in a newly formed social skills group using the PEERS curriculum, which will help him develop friendships and help him advocate for himself in his current and future academic courses.

CASE STUDY: Jonathon, *continued*

Supporting Family Communication and Social Inclusion

Jonathon's school transition planning required multiple meetings, allowing for adequate language translation, processing, and understanding for both the parent and the education team. These multiple meeting sessions allowed time to process and understand the perspective and needs of the parent and student, which included academic as well as community and socially engaged preparation activities. Ground rules were established for when the parent would receive translated documents and when an IEP meeting would be called, allowing adequate time for the parent to process the documents. The IEP team created an expectation of earlier time frames and increased frequency for meetings to ensure mutual understanding.

In addition, a fading program for one-to-one support was established to assess Jonathon's ability to stay on task without support prior to his transition to high school. A social skills plan was established for lunch, with the parent identifying opportunities in the community to reinforce these social skills. The IEP team used community resource mapping to identify and then partner with community organizations with supportive inclusive programs to help transition Jonathon within a family context for engaging in community activities. As a result, Jonathon is significantly more engaged in community activities and networks related to his interests.

BRINGING IT ALL TOGETHER:
UDT AND PROMOTING COMMUNITY INCLUSION

Now that we have looked at several different dimensions of community inclusion and their importance to CLD transition-age youth with disabilities, this last section further highlights how this area of planning and programming aligns with the four key pillars of UDT: multiple life domains, multiple means of assessment, student self-determination, and multiple resources and perspectives.

Multiple Life Domains

The first key component of UDT is that transition planning should be holistic in addressing the preparation of transition age youth for adulthood and address multiple areas, including PSE, vocational education, employment, independent living, and community participation. Given that community inclusion and social engagement are often overlooked areas of transition planning for youth, this consideration should not only remind practitioners of the importance of this area but also draw attention to the overlap between domains. As mentioned previously in this chapter, community inclusion is highly connected with, and mutually dependent on, all other transition planning domains discussed in this textbook, from independent living and self-determination to employment and PSE. If youth lack social skills and networks, they will likely face substantial barriers in other aspects of their transition outcomes. Conversely, youth who exit school with a solid foundation of skills, opportunities, and networks within the community will have the opportunity to leverage each of these to accomplish major career and educational goals.

Multiple Means of Assessment

Independent recreation and living goals will vary depending on each person's SPINs. Person-centered planning should be at the heart of this process. For example, it is critical to use multiple means of assessment to determine a strength-based approach to develop leisure skills that are relevant to each individual. Informal assessments may include conversations with the individual to determine their recreational interests. Skills assessments needed for social interactions and leisure—including those skills in the areas pertaining to quality of life such as dating, sexuality, sexual vulnerability, ending relationships, and communication—should also be considered. Ensuring that students have the skills and opportunities necessary to make and maintain social relationships and engage in recreational activities with peers is critical, given the strong correlation between community and social inclusion and quality of life (Amado et al., 2013).

It is also important that we provide opportunities for individual choice, based on preferences, strengths, interests, and needs. To determine individual preferences, it is essential to use multiple means of assessment. Assessment areas may include 1) community travel and transportation skills, 2) shopping, 3) cooking, 4) housecleaning, 5) money management, and 6) arranging get-togethers with friends.

Student Self-Determination

As with other domains of transition planning, community inclusion has a two-way relationship with self-determination, meaning that opportunities for community inclusion are likely to positively impact students' self-determination, and conversely, increased self-determination will lead to youth participating more actively and intentionally in their communities. Youth who are self-determined are better able to select and engage in personally meaningful activities in their communities.

For example, the process of identifying one's strengths, interests, and network of support through a PCP approach will likely pinpoint opportunities to engage directly in leisure, recreational, and social activities contributing to a greater sense of community inclusion. On the other hand, the engagement of youth in organizations and groups aligned with their strengths and interests presents an ideal opportunity to further develop self-determination. For example, a young adult may join a social club in the area related to a specific area of interest and through that engagement develop relationships as well as skills related to self-determination.

Multiple Resources and Perspectives

Finally, the importance of multiple perspectives and multiple resources cannot be overstated in ensuring that CLD transition-age youth achieve successful community inclusion outcomes. First and foremost, individuals and families must be engaged as partners in shaping transition planning, and leading discussions about what meaningful community inclusion means for them. Community inclusion is a unique experience for each individual, molded by cultural, familial, and individual values that influence every aspect of community inclusion planning from determining what a successful outcome is to identifying meaningful connections and activities in the community. By emphasizing the social and cultural capital of individuals and families in the transition process through PCP approaches, transition teams can engage multiple perspectives in planning. Likewise, the use of strategies such as community resource mapping can identify key strategic means of promoting opportunities to increase community inclusion for youth with disabilities.

Reflection

Think about the challenges that Kenyon, Amira, Miguel, and Jonathon experienced in preparing for adult lives in which they would be able to participate in their community and enjoy social connections and relationships. What strengths did the students and families have that initially went unnoticed? What other factors did their transition teams have to consider and address to help make these goals possible?

Now consider these questions in relation to one of your own students. What interests beyond schooling and employment might they want to pursue in adulthood? What barriers (including communication barriers) might be interfering with planning for this transition domain? What actions can you take to address any barriers and to learn about and capitalize on your students' strengths?

WRAP-UP: PREPARING FOR SOCIAL INCLUSION AND ENGAGEMENT

Social and community inclusion is a critical part of transition planning to ensure quality of life of individuals with disabilities. CLD youth and families face many barriers to social and community inclusion, but there are culturally sustaining practices and strategies that can help mitigate those barriers. Through person-centered planning, family engagement, social skills assessment and instruction, and building capacity within community organizations, educators can help ensure that transition-age youth, including those from CLD backgrounds, achieve success in social and community inclusion. The UDT framework provides a useful structure for planning and implementing strategies to promote the inclusion of individuals with disabilities within the social fabric of their communities.

▶ **Tips for Promoting Social Inclusion and Engagement**

1. **Focus on student strengths and interests.** As students leave school and enter adulthood, their engagement in their communities will be increasingly based around their strengths, preferences, interests, and needs. By centering students' strengths and interests, educators can better prepare students to sustain meaningful social and community activities.

2. **Engage families from an "additive perspective."** Families provide support to students with disabilities in multiple and diverse ways. Educators should challenge "deficit-oriented" views of families and instead emphasize families' social and cultural capital and its role in promoting improved transition outcomes.

3. **Assess and provide direct instruction in social skills.** For many students with disabilities, particularly those with autism and intellectual and developmental disabilities, social skills are a key area that should be evaluated in terms of a student's transition goals. Direct instruction using evidence-based practices is recommended.

4. **Partner with community organizations.** Ensuring successful social and community inclusion outcomes cannot be accomplished by educators in isolation. Partnership is key. Likewise, many community organizations have a need for the input and engagement of special educators in terms of including and engaging individuals with disabilities.

KEY RESOURCES: SOCIAL INCLUSION AND ENGAGEMENT

Online Resources

Person-centered planning
https://acl.gov/programs/consumer-control/person-centered-planning

Participation and Sensory Environment Questionnaire
https://participationandsensoryenvironment.weebly.com/

Family Voices Tools to Get You Started
https://familyvoices.org/famu/tools/

Engage All Abilities
https://depts.washington.edu/particip/

Virginia Commonwealth University: Community Based Functional Skills Assessment for Transition-Age Youth With Autism Spectrum Disorder
http://www.vcuautismcenter.org/documents/FinalCommunityAssessment711141.pdf

REFERENCES

Achola, E. O., & Greene, G. (2016). Person-family centered transition planning: Improving post-school outcomes to culturally diverse youth and families. *Journal of Vocational Rehabilitation, 45*(2), 173–183. https://doi.org/10.3233/JVR-160821

Agran, M., Wojcik, A., Cain, I., Thoma, C., Achola, E., Austin, K. M., Nixon, C. A., & Tamura, R. B. (2017). Participation of students with intellectual and developmental disabilities in extracurricular activities: Does inclusion end at 3:00? *Education and Training in Autism and Developmental Disabilities, 52*(1), 3–12.

Amado, A. N., Stancliffe, R. J., McCarron, M., & McCallion, P. (2013). Social inclusion and community participation for individuals with intellectual/developmental disabilities. *Intellectual and Developmental Disabilities, 51*(5), 360–375.

Banks, T., & Obiakor, F. E. (2015). Culturally responsive positive behavior supports: Considerations for practice. *Journal of Education and Training Studies, 3*(2), 83–90.

Carter, E. W., & Bumble, J. L. (2018). The promise and possibilities of community conversations: Expanding opportunities for people with disabilities. *Journal of Disability Policy Studies, 28*(4), 195–202. https://doi.org/10.1177/1044207317739408

Education for All Handicapped Children Act of 1975, Pub. L. No. 94-142, 20 U.S.C. §§ 1400 *et seq.* (1975).

Eilenberg, J. S., Paff, M., Harrison, A. J., & Long, K. A. (2019). Disparities based on race, ethnicity, and socioeconomic status over the transition to adulthood among adolescents and young adults on the autism spectrum: A systematic review. *Current Psychiatry Reports, 21*(5), 32. https://doi.org/10.1007/s11920-019-1016-1

Fish, R. E. (2017). The racialized construction of exceptionality: Experimental evidence of race/ethnicity effects on teachers' interventions. *Social Science Research, 62,* 317–334. https://doi.org/10.1016/j.ssresearch.2016.08.007

Gersten, R., & Baker, S. (2000). What we know about effective instructional practices for English-language learners. *Exceptional Children, 66*(4), 454–470.

Goldstein, A. P., & McGinnis, E. (1997). *Skillstreaming the adolescent: New strategies and perspectives for teaching prosocial skills.* Research Press.

Gonzales, S. M., & Gabel, S. L. (2017). Exploring involvement expectations for cultural and linguistically diverse parents. *International Journal of Multicultural Education, 19*(2), 61–81.

Haines, S. J., Francis, G. L., Shepherd, K. G., Ziegler, M., & Mabika, G. (2018). Partnership bound: Using MAPS with transitioning students and families from all backgrounds. *Career Development and Transition for Exceptional Individuals, 41*(2), 122–126. https://doi.org/10.1177/2165143417698123

Hall, S. A. (2017). Community involvement of young adults with intellectual disabilities: Their experiences and perspectives on inclusion. *Journal of Applied Research in Intellectual Disabilities, 30*(5), 859–871.

Hirano, K. A., Rowe, D., Lindstrom, L., & Chan, P. (2018). Systemic barriers to family involvement in transition planning for youth with disabilities: A qualitative metasynthesis. *Journal of Child and Family Studies, 27*(11), 3440–3456. https://doi.org/10.1007/s10826-018-1189-y

Individuals with Disabilities Education Improvement Act (IDEA) of 2004, Pub. L. No. 108-446, 20 U.S.C. §§ 1400 *et seq.* (2004).

Kim, K. H., & Morningstar, M. E. (2005). Transition planning involving culturally and linguistically diverse families. *Career Development for Exceptional Individuals, 28*(2), 92–103.

Laugeson, E. A., & Frankel, F. (2010). *Social skills for teenagers with developmental and autism spectrum disorders: The PEERS treatment manual.* Routledge.

Laugeson, E. A., Gantman, A., Kapp, S. K., Orenski, K., & Ellingsen, R. (2015). A randomized controlled trial to improve social skills in young adults with autism spectrum disorder: The UCLA PEERS® program. *Journal of Autism and Developmental Disorders, 45*(12), 3978–3989. https://doi.org/10.1007/s10803-015-2504-8

O'Brien, C. L., & O'Brien, J. (2002). The origins of person-centered planning: A community of practice perspective. In S. Holburn & V. M. Vietze (Eds.), *Person-centered planning: Research, practice, and future directions* (pp. 3–27). Paul H. Brookes Publishing Co.

Papay, C. K., & Bambara, L. M. (2014). Best practices in transition to adult life for youth with intellectual disabilities. *Career Development and Transition for Exceptional Individuals, 37*(3), 136–148. https://doi.org/10.1177/2165143413486693

Pfeiffer, B., Pillar, A., Bevans, K., & Shiu, C. (2019). Reliability of the Participation and Sensory Environment Questionnaire: Community Scales. *Research in Autism Spectrum Disorder, 64*, 84–93.

Rowe, D. A., Mazzotti, V. L., Fowler, C. H., Test, D. W., Mitchell, V. J., Clark, K. A., Holzberg, D., Owens, T. L., Rusher, D., Seaman-Tullis, R. L., Gushanas, C. M., Castle, H., Chang, W.-H., Voggt, A., Kwiatek, S., & Dean, C. (2021). Updating the secondary transition research base: Evidence- and research-based practices in functional skills. *Career Development and Transition for Exceptional Individuals, 44*(1), 28–46. https://doi.org/10.1177/2165143420958674

Salzer, M. S., & Burns-Lynch, B. (2016). *Peer Facilitated Community Inclusion Toolkit.* Temple University Collaborative on Community Inclusion for Individuals with Psychiatric Disabilities. www.tucollaborative.org

Santiago-Rosario, M. R., Whitcomb, S. A., Pearlman, J., & McIntosh, K. (2021). Associations between teacher expectations and racial disproportionality in discipline referrals. *Journal of School Psychology, 85*, 80–93.

Schall, C., Brooke, V., Wehman, P., Palko, S., Brooke, A., Ham, W., Carr, S., & Gerhardt, P. (2014). *Virginia Commonwealth University and Autism Speaks Community Based Functional Skills Assessment for transition aged youth with autism spectrum disorder* [Scholarly project]. Virginia Commonwealth University Autism Center for Excellence. http://www.vcuautismcenter.org/documents/FinalCommunityAssessment711141.pdf

Schall, C., Wehman, P., Avellone, L., & Taylor, J. P. (2020). Competitive integrated employment for youth and adults with autism. *Child and Adolescent Psychiatric Clinics of North America, 29*(2), 373–397. https://doi.org/10.1016/j.chc.2019.12.001

Schutz, M. A., Carter, E. W., Gajjar, S. A., & Maves, E. A. (2021). Strengthening transition partnerships through community conversation events. *TEACHING Exceptional Children, 53*(5), 359–368. https://doi.org/10.1177/0040059920987877

Shogren, K. A., Rifenbark, G. G., & Hagiwara, M. (2021). Self-determination assessment in adults with and without intellectual disability. *Intellectual and Developmental Disabilities, 59*(1), 55–69.

Thompson, J. R., Anderson, M. H., & Shogren, K. A. (2021). Measuring the support needs of people with intellectual disability and autism spectrum disorder with the Supports Intensity Scale–Adult Version. *Education and Training in Autism and Developmental Disabilities, 56*(1), 18–26.

Trainor, A. A. (2007). Person-centered planning in two culturally distinct communities: Responding to divergent needs and preferences. *Career Development for Exceptional Individuals, 30*(2), 92–103. https://doi.org/10.1177/08857288070300020601

Wehman, P., Taylor, J., Brooke, V., Avellone, L., Whittenburg, H., Ham, W., Brooke, A. M., & Carr, S. (2018). Toward competitive employment for persons with intellectual and developmental disabilities: What progress have we made and where do we need to go? *Research and Practice for Persons with Severe Disabilities, 43*(3), 131–144. https://doi.org/10.1177/1540796918777730

Whittenburg, H. N., Taylor, J. P., Thoma, C. A., Pickover, G. S., & Vitullo, V. E. (2020). A systematic literature review of interventions to improve work-related social skills of individuals with autism spectrum disorder. *Inclusion, 8*(4).

Yosso, T. J. (2005). Whose culture has capital? A critical race theory discussion of community cultural wealth. *Race, Ethnicity and Education, 8*(1), 69–91. https://doi.org/10.1080/1361332052000341006

III

Culturally Sustaining UDT Planning: Implementation

9

Individualized Education Planning

Leena Jo Landmark and Rebekka J. Jez

DIGGING DEEPER: What Teachers Have to Say

Leena

On my first day as a special education teacher of record, I quickly realized that the training I had received from the alternative certification program had not fully prepared me to meet the needs of all the students in my classes and on my caseload. I had assumptions about learning, behavior, and family involvement that were, I realize now, based on hegemonic and individualistic ideas. I was not prepared for the cultural mismatch between me and my students and their families, and I certainly had never been asked to reflect on my own identity and how it impacted my work as an educator. The alternative certification program taught me the technicalities of special education, but the relational and cultural aspects of education were missing.

I wanted to be the best teacher I could be so my students could have the futures they and their families wanted. This desire led to my attending professional development, engaging in self-study through texts, and eventually enrolling in graduate school. When I came across the writings of scholars and educators such as Geneva Gay, Gloria Ladson-Billings, Beth Harry, Maya Kalyanpur, and James Banks, I realized that cultural responsiveness was vital to my work as a special educator. The more I learned, the better I was able to meet the needs of my students.

I began my journey toward becoming a culturally responsive educator by focusing on my individualized education program (IEP) practices because the IEP was the foundation of everything I did with and for my students and their families. I reflected on my beliefs about education, family involvement, race/ethnicity, and culture. I started meeting with families prior to the IEP meeting to learn more about what they wanted for their children. I listened more and sought to empower families by sharing the hidden curriculum of special education and the IEP process. Instead of viewing differences through a deficit lens, I worked to understand how differences can be sources of strength. I had high expectations for my students and their futures. Over the years, I have learned more about myself and how to be a culturally responsive special educator. I am still growing to this day.

Rebekka

My teaching career began with me working as a mild/moderate special education high school teacher on an emergency credential (meaning that I was not enrolled in a teacher preparation program the first year) in a large urban district. I taught in one of the four portable classrooms set up in a parking lot with a chain-linked fence around the perimeter. Based on the transcripts, the administration asked me to teach 10 classes in seven periods. When I asked about curriculum, I was told, "Just keep everyone safe." Because I came from a family of educators, this did not sit well with me. I called on my family members for help, and we put together my first term curriculum.

I remember asking myself at the time, "What are we doing here?" I thought deeply about my role in my students' futures. We started with weekly class meetings to build a community by learning about each other. It was during this time that my students began to share their goals and dreams. Students shared about wanting to become artists, barbers, entrepreneurs, social workers, and lawyers. They talked about wanting to live in apartments with friends or buy a house for their mom. Many shared stories about friends and family members who attended community college, 4-year universities, or training programs. As I began to work on their IEPs and on meeting their families, I quickly realized that what was written about them in their paperwork did not seem to align with the goals the students were sharing with me. I learned two important lessons in that first term: 1) a compliant IEP may not address the student's needs and goals, and 2) to really get to know my students and their families, I needed to learn more about the community and myself. The more I got to know my students, their families, and my own unconscious bias, the more I realized that effective IEPs require students to be supported in multiple areas as they grow toward becoming the adults they want to be. Eventually, this led to my work in culturally sustaining transition practices (Gay, 2013; Jez, 2014, Jez et al., 2022; Ladson-Billings, 2014; Paris, 2012).

Essential Questions

▶ What roles should students and families have in the IEP process and transition to adulthood? Why are these roles important?

▶ What steps are involved in a transition-driven IEP process? What are some ways educators can incorporate universal design for transition (UDT) and culturally sustaining practices into their IEP and transition planning, meetings, and implementation?

▶ What can educators do to meet the needs of culturally and linguistically diverse (CLD) students during the IEP process? Give examples that use evidence-based practices.

The IEP is the educational blueprint for the child with a disability who receives special education and related services. The purpose of the IEP is to provide the student with a free appropriate public education that prepares them for future education, employment, and independent living in their community (Individuals with Disabilities Education Improvement Act [IDEA], 2004). Table 9.1 presents the critical components of the IEP, according to IDEA regulations, for transition-age students and provides an overview of UDT and culturally sustaining considerations for educators. The IEP document details the student's academic achievement and functional performance in relation to the general education curriculum and specifies the specially designed instruction, related services, and accommodations that students need to make progress toward their academic and functional annual goals. IEPs are reviewed and updated annually, and a team of stakeholders, importantly including the student and their family, collaborate in the development and implementation of the IEP. The IEP is individualized based on the student's strengths and needs.

IDEA requires postsecondary goals and transition services in the IEP for each student no later than age 16 years, although state education agencies and IEP teams can choose to begin transition planning earlier. The knowledge and skills required to live, learn, and work in adult environments take years to develop, but because formal transition planning is not required until the student is 16 years old, educators may believe that the transition portions of the IEP are additions or supplements to the IEP. However, recalling the purpose of the IEP, it is evident that transition should be the driving force of the entire IEP process (Kohler, 1998, Kohler & Field, 2003). It is vital for the IEP team to have the student's transition from compulsory education to their chosen postschool environments at the forefront when developing and implementing the IEP. Although younger children with disabilities may not have postsecondary goals and transition services in their IEPs yet, it is still necessary for their educators to consider their long-term outcomes when developing annual IEPs and planning daily instruction. An effective IEP, developed using a UDT framework for blending academic and transition goals, includes ambitious annual goals that are supportive of the child and family's postschool wishes for the child.

Table 9.1.   UDT and culturally sustaining practices educator considerations for developing the critical components of the IEP for transition-age students

Components of the IEP*		UDT and CSP considerations
As used in this part, the term **individualized education program** or **IEP** means a written statement for each child with a disability that is developed, reviewed, and revised in a meeting in accordance with §§300.320 through 300.324, and that must include the following:		
Present levels	A statement of the child's present levels of academic achievement and functional performance, including how the child's disability affects the child's involvement and progress in the general education curriculum (i.e., the same curriculum as for nondisabled children)	• Explore funds of identity when learning about child (Esteban-Guitart & Moll, 2014). • Learn about and consider the student and family's culture (Gay, 2013). • Make decisions based on information from all parties. • Identify ways the school's culture differs from the family's culture and the possible inequities impacting culturally and linguistically diverse students based on intersectionality (Suk et al., 2020). • Identify positive behavior supports to address social, emotional, and behavior goals (e.g., social emotional learning, restorative justice, trauma-informed approaches). • Identify unbiased and linguistically appropriate assessments for data collection. • Collect data from multiple sources (e.g., different teachers, employers, school personnel).
Annual goals	A statement of measurable annual goals, including academic and functional goals designed to meet the child's needs that result from the child's disability to enable the child to be involved in and make progress in the general education curriculum; and meet each of the child's other educational needs that result from the child's disability. For children with disabilities who take alternate assessments aligned to alternate academic achievement standards, a description of benchmarks or short-term objectives	• Identify and communicate goals and supports necessary for the student to achieve high expectations. • Make connections with the child's culture within the context you are teaching. • Build on the child and family's assets when making choices about pedagogy (Paris & Alim, 2014). • Critique the goals to ensure they support the family's values rather than promote Eurocentric values. • Explicitly teach independent transition skills such as financial literacy, self-determination, etc. • Communicate high expectations within the goals set for the child and provide supports to meet expectations.

Components of the IEP*		UDT and CSP considerations
Measurement of progress	A description of how the child's progress toward meeting the annual goals . . . will be measured; and when periodic reports on the progress the child is making toward meeting the annual goals (e.g., through the use of quarterly or other periodic reports, concurrent with the issuance of report cards) will be provided	• Identify a method for collection, monitoring, and sharing progress data in a way the child's family will understand. • Include the child in the progress monitoring process and problem solving based on helpful strategies, interventions, and support people. • Collect data from multiple sources (e.g., different teachers, employers, school personnel). • Use family and youth-friendly language as opposed to educational jargon. • Effectively communicate using a method the family can access. • Replace deficit perspectives of students and communities utilizing the cultural capital of the community (Gay, 2013; Yosso, 2005).
Related services and supplementary aids	A statement of the special education and related services and supplementary aids and services, based on peer-reviewed research to the extent practicable, to be provided to the child, or on behalf of the child, and a statement of the program modifications or supports for school personnel that will be provided to enable the child to advance appropriately toward attaining the annual goals; to be involved in and make progress in the general education curriculum . . ., and to participate in extracurricular and other nonacademic activities; and to be educated and participate with other children with disabilities and nondisabled children in the activities described in this section	• Design emancipatory and liberating instruction from oppressive educational practices (Gay, 2010). • Use specially designed instruction that is backed by empirical evidence (e.g., high-leverage practices and evidence-based practices). • Use multi-tiered systems of support strategies to teach restorative justice, high-leverage practices, and social-emotional learning to combat ableism, racism, biases, genderism, and socioeconomic challenges.
Participation in general education	An explanation of the extent, if any, to which the child will not participate with nondisabled children in the regular class and in the activities described . . .	• Identify and provide access to supports and/or materials to empower the child/family to meet their social, academic, and transition goals (Gay, 2013). • Examine disciplinary policies for discriminatory practices (Wood et al., 2018).

(continued)

Table 9.1. *(continued)*

Components of the IEP*		UDT and CSP considerations
Accommodations, modifications, and assessment	A statement of any individual appropriate accommodations that are necessary to measure the academic achievement and functional performance of the child on state and districtwide assessments . . . and if the IEP team determines that the child must take an alternate assessment instead of a particular regular state or districtwide assessment of student achievement, a statement of why the child cannot participate in the regular assessment; and the particular alternate assessment selected is appropriate for the child	• Provide the accommodations available on the assessments during daily instruction so the child can access learning and subsequent assessment. • Regularly evaluate the rationale for alternative assessments. • Ensure that assessments are linguistically appropriate. • Have the student and family identify helpful accommodations and modifications necessary for achievement. • Have high expectations for the child and only suggest alternate assessment if the child is unable to be instructed in the general education curriculum without modifications. • Explain to the family the potential ramifications of the child not participating in statewide or districtwide assessments.

Transition services. Beginning not later than the first IEP to be in effect when the child turns 16, or younger if determined appropriate by the IEP team, and updated annually, thereafter, the IEP must include the following:

| Postsecondary goals based on transition assessment | Appropriate measurable postsecondary goals based on age-appropriate transition assessments related to training, education, employment, and, where appropriate, independent living skills; and | • Replace deficit perspectives of students and communities (Gay, 2013).
• Understand how and why culture and difference are essential ideologies (Gay, 2013).
• Learn about and consider the student and family's culture (Gay, 2013).
• Make decisions based on information from all parties.
• Identify a method for collection, monitoring, and sharing progress data in a way the child's family will understand.
• Include the student in the progress monitoring process and problem solving based on helpful strategies, interventions, and support people.
• Collect data from multiple sources (e.g., different teachers, employers, school personnel). |

Components of the IEP*		UDT and CSP considerations
Transition services	The transition services (including courses of study) needed to assist the child in reaching those goals.	• Work collaboratively with the student and their family in developing self-awareness. • Create opportunities for self-advocacy. • Promote social and academic empowerment (Gay, 2010). • Review opportunities to support postsecondary educational pathways, such as AP courses or SAT/ACT accommodations. • Connect with services and networks. • Include students in meetings and value their input when discussing transition services. • Educate families about transition rights and options.
Age of majority rights	Beginning not later than 1 year before the child reaches the age of majority under state law, the IEP must include a statement that the child has been informed of the child's rights under Part B of the Act, if any, that will transfer to the child on reaching the age of majority . . .	• Learn about and consider the student and family's culture (Gay, 2013). • Include the student in the progress monitoring process and problem solving based on helpful strategies, interventions, and support people.

*Edited for ease of reading from the Individuals with Disabilities Education Improvement Act of 2004 regulations.
Key: AP, Advanced Placement; CSP, culturally sustaining pedagogy; IEP, individualized education program; UDT, universal design for transition.

Despite the time and effort that goes into planning and implementing the IEP, young adults with disabilities continue to have poorer postschool outcomes when compared with their nondisabled peers (Newman et al., 2011; Sanford et al., 2011). Many students with disabilities from marginalized diverse cultural, racial, ethnic, linguistic, and socioeconomic groups are disproportionately represented in special education and related services (Artiles et al., 2010; Whiting, 2006). In addition, these students tend to have the most disappointing postschool outcomes among all the students with disabilities (Newman et al., 2011). Therefore, not only do their IEPs need to be compliant and of quality in development and implementation to help them achieve their postsecondary goals, but they also need to acknowledge and address the myriad disparities while building on these students' strengths. Using UDT and culturally sustaining practices, teachers can address the unique experiences impacting CLD students and families leading up to and during the transition process (Jez et al., 2022; Scott & Bruno, 2018).

This chapter describes what this approach to IEP planning entails, beginning with discussion of how educators can honor students' and families' perspectives and goals. This is followed by discussion of the steps in the transition-driven IEP process, considerations for the IEP meeting, and IEP implementation. We turn now to descriptions of the students we discuss as examples in the chapter: Priscilla, Huy, and Derrick.

CASE STUDY: Priscilla

Preparing for a Nursing Career and Learning Self-Advocacy

Priscilla is a 17-year-old Latine student in an urban school. She lives with her parents, her three siblings, and her grandmother. She has always dreamed of going to college to study nursing but has not chosen a school. Priscilla has an after-school job that helps her family out financially. She is involved in the choir at her family church and volunteers at the Red Cross on the weekends. She is very close with her family and often translates for her grandmother when they are watching television or at a doctor's appointment. Priscilla qualified for special education services under the category of specific learning disability due to her auditory processing challenges since the fourth grade. Currently, she is working on learning self-advocacy skills (sharing her strengths and needs with others) with the resource teacher at the school.

CASE STUDY: Huy

Preparing to Become a Barber and Start a Family

Huy's parents and older sister moved to the Little Saigon area of Houston 5 years before Huy was born. Huy's parents work at a nail salon owned by a family member. When Huy was a child, his mother and father would work different shifts so one of them was always home with him. Once Huy was old enough to accompany his parents to work, he would hang out in the break room, watching TV and folding towels. Huy is now 19 years old and continues to receive special education services for transition. He enjoys fashion and would like to be a barber. Huy's parents expect him to live with them or his sister before hopefully finding a partner and starting a family. Huy's parents are optimistic he will be able to work despite the support needs he requires due to his autism.

CASE STUDY: Derrick

Preparing for College—But Facing Uncertainties

Derrick participates in the golf club at his high school and works seasonally as a grounds crew laborer at a golf course. He lives with his great aunt who works full-time at an Amazon warehouse. Derrick was born 10 weeks premature and had a lengthy stay in the neonatal intensive care unit. Derrick has not seen his mother since he was 3 years old, and his father is incarcerated. Although his great aunt encourages him to continue his education, she has made it clear that Derrick will need to finance college himself. Derrick receives special education services under the categories of other health impairment (due to spastic hemiparesis) and a specific learning disability in math. Derrick's case manager/teacher reports that it can be difficult to schedule time to talk with Derrick's great aunt, and IEP meetings have been rescheduled at the last minute. Derrick is a sports enthusiast, and he is not sure what he wants to do after high school.

THE STUDENT AND THEIR FAMILY

Sociopolitical consciousness is the awareness of, and desire to, dismantle current systems that disadvantage marginalized CLD groups (Jackson & Knight-Manuel, 2019; Ladson-Billings, 2014). As Wilt and Morningstar (2018) asserted, "culturally sustaining pedagogy during transition planning would take a stance of explicit resistance to systems perpetuating the dominant professionalized approach to transition" (p. 309). Thus, the student and their family should be involved and empowered in the IEP process. When educators are working with students from CLD backgrounds and their families during IEP and transition planning and implementation, they need to ask themselves several questions:

- How do my cultural beliefs impact how I work with students and their families?

- What information do students need to learn about transition to counter the historic inequities experienced by many historically marginalized youths?

- How does the student's culture intersect with the transition ideals of IDEA?

- Are CLD students being academically prepared for postsecondary education (PSE)?

- How can I use the strengths of the student, their family, and their community to prepare them for their future?

Educators who take the time to self-reflect and learn about their students and their families at a deeper than surface level are better able to support their students and partner with families during the IEP process. Educators can support CLD students by connecting transition to real-life experiences, empowering students' educational excellence, ensuring equitable access to resources, developing students' agency, and intentionally providing opportunities for networking within the community at large (Gay, 2013). Educators can build on students' assets while also purposefully facing the impact of privilege and oppression within their individual context in a manner that sustains the cultural pluralism of students and their families (Paris, 2012; Paris & Alim, 2014). Equally important, educators can empower students with self-determination skills that complement the values within their specific communities (Jez et al., 2022; Paris & Alim, 2014; Zhang et al., 2010).

CLD students, in particular, benefit from educators incorporating the UDT framework into transition planning. Transition planning traditionally focuses on adult outcomes centered around education/training, employment, and independent living from a Eurocentric, and often individualistic, perspective (Black et al., 2003; Leake et al., 2004; Reed et al., 2013). Yet, many families from culturally, ethnically, and linguistically diverse backgrounds value a more holistic and collective approach to planning (Leake et al., 2004). Developing postsecondary goals, transition services, and annual goals cannot be done in a manner consistent with UDT and culturally sustaining practices without the intentional collaboration of the student and their family. For one, the family continues to be involved in the youth's life long after the student exits from IEP services; therefore, the transition assessment process and transition decisions about a student's postschool goals regarding further education/training, employment, and community involvement need to be in line with the student and their family's culture.

Understanding the Values of the Student and Family

Working with students and families during transition requires educators to critically examine their personal assumptions, biases, and views as they support students' transition plans. Educators need to be cautious of the dominant (White/Eurocentric) culture inadvertently impacting their students in the planning process. By analyzing how their personal values complement and/or contradict their students and their families' ideals, teachers can challenge personal biases that can interfere with supporting CLD students with their transition. Namely, teachers should use a UDT culturally sustaining practices approach to unpack the nuances within transition while addressing federal laws such as the Every Student Succeeds Act (ESSA, 2015), which mandates college and career readiness for all learners in kindergarten through Grade 12. ESSA highlights the 4-year college path as the optimum goal, whereas students and families should collectively decide the trajectory for their child, whether that means attending a 4-year university, community college, or training program, or staying at home and helping the family. Contradictory values and goals can create a divide within the often-precarious family–school relationship. However, when educators understand these challenges, they can work collaboratively with the IEP team in addressing them.

To illustrate, this issue impacts Priscilla and her family. If the IEP team focuses on supporting her in attending a 4-year nursing program across the state, they have addressed the letter of the law for transition. Yet, by including her family in the discussion of her postsecondary goals, they may aid Priscilla in finding a nursing program at a local community college, which in turn may allow her to support her family while pursuing her career. In this way, the team can not only fulfill the legal requirements for transition planning but also do so in a manner that is culturally sustaining and consistent with UDT.

As Priscilla's story illustrates, the assumption that all families have the same ideals regarding adulthood is flawed, and educators need to use the multiple resources and perspectives of the family when engaging in transition planning and implementation. The IEP must be individualized for each student, and the student cannot be fully understood without understanding how their family's culture impacts the student's education and eventual transition from compulsory school.

Honoring Cultural Values and Hopes

Educators can learn about their students' and their families' cultural values and hopes for the child through interviews and conversations. Using this information, the teacher can then identify how their own cultural beliefs and postsecondary experiences differ from their students'. Another way the IEP team can ensure that the student's and family's culture are being honored throughout the process is by intentionally including them throughout the transition assessment process, consistent with the UDT principle of multiple means of assessment. By recognizing the knowledge, resources, and strengths (i.e., funds of knowledge) that students, their families, and their communities possess, teachers can dismantle the deficit perceptions frequently held about CLD youth. Furthermore, fruitful discussion about pathway options, even if these options differ from traditional Western ideals, can occur. Educators need to navigate different perspectives and acknowledge cultural capital in conversations about adulthood. When one uses funds of knowledge to define oneself, the cultural factors become funds of identity. The youth recognize the intersection of their own identity plus their "cultural experience" (Esteban-Guitart & Moll, 2014, p. 32). In Derrick's case, the IEP team could honor Derrick and his great aunt's assets, such as her encouragement of his extracurricular activities and PSE, by connecting them with links to educational scholarships and federal loan programs. Intersectionality

(Crenshaw, 1989) gives students and educators a schema with which to examine how different identities disadvantage or privilege their experiences. For example, a Black female student with a learning disability from a family with inconsistent housing may encounter racism, sexism, ableism, and financial insecurity yet have a strong community network of support, whereas a White male student with a learning disability from a family who owns their own house may have more access to financial, academic, and institutional resources when planning to attend a 4-year college. If IEP teams explored elements of intersectionality and used UDT, they may be better able to equitably prepare both students and families for postschool success. This is a necessary shift based on the national data reports that show students receiving special education services from historically marginalized groups have less-positive postsecondary outcomes than their White peers with disabilities (OSEP, 2021).

A TRANSITION-DRIVEN IEP PROCESS

The annual transition-driven IEP process is shown in Figure 9.1. First, age-appropriate transition assessment is conducted to determine the student's strengths, preferences, interests, and needs (SPINs) in relation to adult outcomes in the areas of education/training, employment, and independent living. The student's SPINs are part of their present levels of academic achievement and

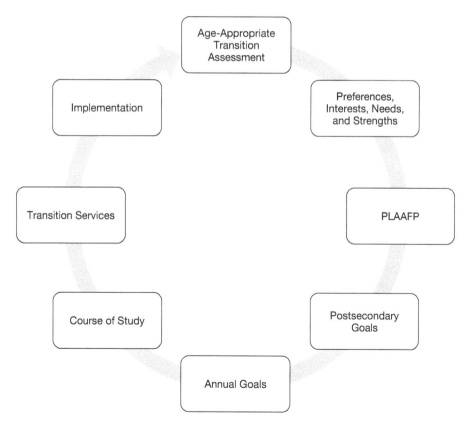

Figure 9.1. Transition-driven individualized education program process. (*Key:* PLAAFP, present levels of academic achievement and functional performance.)

functional performance (PLAAFP). The PLAAFP is a statement in the IEP where the educator shows how the student's disability affects how the student is progressing in the general curriculum as compared to a typically developing peer.

Next, postsecondary goals for education/training and employment are developed based on the information the IEP team has from the age-appropriate transition assessment, SPINs, and PLAAFP. For some students, a postsecondary goal for independent living is developed based on the student's needs. After the postsecondary goals are developed, the IEP team constructs the student's annual goals that support the student's achievement of their postsecondary goals. Then, the course of study is determined. The course of study includes the courses and credits required by the district and state for graduation, as well as courses that help the student gain the knowledge and skills they need to ultimately achieve their postsecondary goals. Finally, transition services that support the achievement of the postsecondary goals are specified, and the IEP is implemented. The sections that follow discuss each of these steps in greater depth.

Conduct Age-Appropriate Transition Assessment

Age-appropriate transition assessment is the foundation of the transition-driven IEP process (see Chapter 2 for in-depth information on age-appropriate transition assessment). Educators have a legal and ethical responsibility to learn about students and families through age-appropriate transition assessment. The age-appropriate transition assessment process seeks to answer questions the IEP team has about the student's future education/training, employment, and independent living. By identifying specific questions that need answering so transition planning can proceed, the team can individualize age-appropriate transition assessment for each student. At a minimum, questions educators should ask when planning for age-appropriate transition assessment include the following:

- What are the student's and family's preferences, interests, needs, and strengths in relation to the student's adult education/training, employment, and independent living?

- How does the student's academic and functional performance compare with that of their typically developing peers?

- What are the student's postsecondary goals for further education/training, employment, and community living?

- How are the student's culture and the family's wishes honored within the student's postsecondary goals?

- What knowledge, skills, and community connections do the student and family have that will help the student achieve their postsecondary goals?

- What knowledge and skills does the student need to achieve their postsecondary goals?

By using the UDT tenets of multiple means of assessment, multiple resources, and multiple perspectives, the IEP team can discover many things about learners. Yet, even when educators use multiple transition assessments, students are not always assessed in a culturally or linguistically appropriate manner. The information may not necessarily reflect the student's and their family's hopes for the future, or educators may not address the current realities that the student may face as an adult. This can be especially true for CLD youth from historically marginalized communities. Many transition assessments focus on establishing self-reliance or identifying college and career paths. These do not factor in how transition planning is different for a student who is responsible for taking care of their siblings or grandparents, working a job to help their family put food on the table, or taking on the role of translator for their family members. Rarely, if ever, do teachers assess the impact of racism, ableism, and genderism that the student may encounter in adulthood, let alone their own cultural competence. Moreover, conversations about budgeting for housing, transportation, food, and bills may assume access to banking, credit, or loans, for which some students may not qualify due to the family's financial challenges or citizenship status. Assessing family responsibilities from the family's perspective is an important step in the assessment process when working with communities that value collective decision making.

After the age-appropriate transition assessment data have been collected, the data need to be synthesized and summarized for the IEP team. Although many educators believe that this task should be assigned solely to them, it is important to share the educator's initial synthesis of the data with the student and family prior to the actual IEP meeting. By doing so, the educator is able to prepare the family for a more in-depth exchange of ideas and therefore bring in the multiple perspectives of the student and the family. In addition, this initial sharing of the findings from the data serves to verify that what the educator is gleaning from the data is indeed what the student and the family believe is accurate. Including the student in this task is another way of increasing the student's self-determination because the student can see for themselves how they are performing, which increases their self-knowledge. Furthermore, by sharing the assessment synthesis part of the transition assessment process with the student's family, the educator can check in with the family to ensure that they feel their culture is respected in the assessment results. For example, a family's cultural practices may dictate that men do not prepare meals. However, the educator believes that every teenager should be able to prepare a meal and has determined that the student is unable to prepare a sandwich for himself, so the educator wants to include meal preparation as a goal for the student. By working with the family and discussing assessment findings, the educator may decide not to include that type of annual goal because it is not congruent with the family's cultural practices.

Determine Strengths, Preferences, Interests, and Needs

One result of the age-appropriate transition assessment should be a summary of the student's SPINs as they relate to the student's future education/training, employment, and independent living. For example, knowing a student and their family's preferences for types of work settings can ensure that the student is not being trained for a job in a setting where the family will not allow the student to work once school is finished. Understanding a student's interests can help an educator motivate the student with instruction in that area and assist the student in pinpointing a career cluster for future employment opportunities. As opposed to typical assessment practices that are deficit focused, age-appropriate transition assessment should find the student's and family's strengths that can be used to assist the student in meeting their postschool goals. For example, some of the strengths of Huy and his family include Huy having a desire to work in a specific industry (fashion), strong family and community supports, and high expectations for Huy's future. By using the student's and family's preferences, interests, and strengths, the educator can then focus on the needs the student has to be successful in environments that are congruent with their preferences, interests, and strengths. In Huy's case, his educators need to collaborate with his family to find work settings in the Vietnamese community where Huy can practice work skills and make connections for paid employment. In addition, including Huy in the human services track of career and technical education (CTE) at the high school would provide Huy with skills in the area in which he is interested in working as an adult.

Describe Present Levels of Academic Achievement and Functional Performance

Typically, the first step in the IEP process is to review the student's IEP from the previous year to note their progress and to assess the student in order to develop their present levels of academic achievement and functional performance. Students are assessed to determine how they are functioning in relation to typically developing students and the general curriculum; the educator is seeking to determine the gap in functioning and the impact the disability has on the student's functioning in academic and functional areas. For transition-age students, present levels of academic achievement and functional performance as related to postschool education or training, employment, and independent living are assessed through age-appropriate transition assessment and can be included in the present levels section of the IEP. In addition to writing the summary of the age-appropriate transition assessment results in the PLAAFP section of the IEP, the educator can include this information in the student's full individual evaluation report. Regardless of where the summary is written in the IEP document, the important thing is that it is recorded in the document and not kept in a separate folder to which only the transition specialist for the district has easy access. The summary should include the names of the assessments given, the dates they were given, who administered the assessments, and the findings that explicitly state the student's preferences, interests, needs, and strengths related to living, learning, and working.

Articulate Postsecondary Goals

Postsecondary goals are goals that the student hopes to achieve after finishing or exiting high school; they are not goals that will be met during high school. A student's postsecondary goals should be reflective of the student's SPINs and compatible with the family's cultural beliefs and practices. The legal requirements of transition are Eurocentric in that all transition-age students with an IEP must have a PSE/training goal, a postsecondary employment goal, and a postsecondary independent living goal if deemed appropriate by the IEP team, which assumes that everyone wants to engage in further education/training, be employed, and live independently. Culturally appropriate postsecondary goals are those that the student's family supports. For example, Priscilla may want to go to college, but her family does not want her to live away from home until she is married. The educator can work with Priscilla and her family to develop a PSE goal that meets both of their needs: "After graduating from high school, Priscilla will attend Blinn College to receive an Associate of Applied Science Degree in vocational nursing."

Postsecondary goals should be specific and measurable. It is not uncommon for younger students with fewer life experiences to have more general postsecondary goals; however, as the student progresses closer to finishing high school, their goals should become more specific. It can be helpful to think about the student's desired postsecondary employment goal before drafting the student's other postsecondary goals because the employment goal dictates the type of education or training the student will need to achieve their desired employment. For example, Derrick enjoys yard work and sports. This was Derrick's first postsecondary employment goal: "After high school, Derrick will work for a landscape company." This was his first PSE/training goal: "After high school, Derrick will receive on-the-job training." As Derrick got closer to finishing high school, his postsecondary employment goal became more specific: "After high school, Derrick will work full time as a greenskeeper at the Rivers Edge Golf Club." Derrick's PSE/training goal became the following: "After high school, Derrick will obtain the Level 1 Certificate for turfgrass and golf course management at Palo Alto College."

Just like students, families may not be aware of the different options when it comes to PSE/training, employment, and community living (Landmark & Zhang, 2019). For instance, families may not know that some postsecondary institutions of higher education are for profit and that students at those schools assume higher debt than if they attended a nonprofit school that offers the same programming or degrees (Belfield, 2013). They may not know that there are postsecondary programs for adults with intellectual and developmental disabilities at many colleges and universities (Institute for Community Inclusion, 2022). Families may inaccurately believe the only employment option for their child with high support needs is a sheltered workshop or a day habilitation program. The transition planning process not only helps the educator identify the student's postsecondary goals and needed transition services but it also serves as an opportunity to educate the family and help them get the supports in place they need to make their child's postschool future a success.

Write Annual Goals

After the student's postsecondary goals are drafted, annual goals that support the achievement of the postsecondary goals need to be drafted. Many educators draft annual goals prior to drafting the student's postsecondary goals. However, drafting the postsecondary goals prior to the annual goals is a more effective way of ensuring that the annual goals support the achievement of the postsecondary goals. As specified in Indicator 13 (IDEA, 2004), each postsecondary goal should have at least one annual goal that supports the achievement of the student's postsecondary goals. Annual goals can be academic (e.g., achieving a specific proficiency level in mathematics) or functional (e.g., increasing self-determination or organizational skills).

The annual goals need to be ambitious enough so that the student makes "progress appropriate in light of the child's circumstances" (*Endrew F. v. Douglas County School District RE-1,* 2017, p. 999). No longer is minimal educational progress the standard for a free appropriate public education. Well-written annual goals are SMART goals: specific, measurable, action-oriented, realistic and relevant, and with a time limit for accomplishment (Peterson et al., 2013; see Figure 9.2). Annual goals address the gaps between the student's current performance and the expected performance of typically developing peers in those environments. In addition, annual goals should help the student obtain the knowledge and skills necessary for them to be able to achieve their postsecondary goals.

Peterson et al. (2013) suggested that educators draft triangulated annual goals to support the achievement of a student's postsecondary goals. Triangulated annual goals link postsecondary goals with state education standards (e.g., Common Core) and industry standards. The industry standards are the knowledge and skills one needs to enter the three general transition domains: education/training, employment, and independent living. To determine the standards for PSE, educators can consult

Specific	Measurable	Action-oriented	Realistic and relevant	Time limit for accomplishment
Priscilla will address functional language skills as outlined in the ELA/ELD standards and frameworks	using a rubric that addresses speaking, listening, and writing domains	by interviewing (asking questions, listening to the responses, and writing key ideas)	4 out of 5 people in the community with 90% accuracy	by May 2023.
When provided with a task or situation in which a solution is not readily apparent,	Derrick will identify the problem and generate at least two possible solutions	using "if-then" statements (either written or verbal)	that identify the benefits and consequences of each decision based on collective family values with 90% accuracy	over the 6-week instructional term.

Figure 9.2. Examples of culturally sustaining annual SMART goals. (*Key:* ELA, English language arts; ELD, English language development.)

with school counselors, the district transition specialist, and admissions offices at institutions of higher education. Employment industry standards can be found on the O*NET website (U.S. Department of Labor, 2021). Independent living industry standards can be obtained from adult disability service providers or a local center for independent living.

Determine the Student's Course of Study

After the annual goals are written, the IEP team determines the courses the student requires to meet the state and local graduation requirements and to learn the knowledge and skills needed for advancement toward their postsecondary goals. Much of the course of study is prescribed by the state and local education agencies. However, there should be room in it to learn skills that directly apply to the student's postsecondary goal needs. Rather than having students take a variety of CTE courses, planning a sequence of CTE courses in one career cluster allows the student to gain more skills in a specific industry. Students who have IEPs can take CTE courses with accommodations and even modifications. Contrary to what many educators may believe, it is not a requirement that a student be able to pass the industry certification test for the student to take a CTE course. If the student needs modifications, additional support in the classroom in the form of a paraprofessional can be provided using Perkins V (Strengthening Career and Technical Education for the 21st Century Act, 2018) funds.

Another important consideration regarding a student's course of study is to make sure it contains the courses needed for admission to a college or university if that is one of the student's postsecondary goals. Many postsecondary institutions require students to take a certain number of mathematics or foreign language courses during secondary school. If the student's course of study does not include those courses, the student may not be able to gain admittance to their desired postsecondary institution. For Priscilla to obtain a nursing degree, she will need to take the required courses in science and mathematics needed for admittance into a nursing program before finishing high school.

Plan Transition Services

Transition services are a coordinated set of activities that may include instruction, related services, community experiences, employment objectives, adult living objectives, and functional vocational evaluation. Aligned with the UDT framework, the transition services section of the IEP brings together the multiple resources available from the school and the community so the student will be able to live, learn, and work in their community. Putting together the activities that make up transition services requires a team effort. We recommend considering each area of transition services and including a statement explaining why the service is not required at the time if that is the case. However, the IEP team should not be quick to dismiss the need for specific transition services. For example, a functional vocational evaluation may be useful in Huy's situation because the IEP team will need to know if he has the fine motor skills, endurance, and social skills needed for a career as a barber. Transition services can be mapped for the student's high school career or for one year at a time. Assigning the transition service activity to an individual or agency makes them accountable for completing the activity (see Figure 9.3 for an example). Generally, the student and family should not be the ones indicated as solely responsible for completing the transition service activity; however, this practice varies by state and local education agency. Because the IEP document is a legal document, if the person or agency responsible for the transition service activity does not complete the activity, then the IEP team needs to reconvene and adjust.

Write a Summary of Performance

Prior to exiting from special education services, a Summary of Performance (SOP) is required (Madaus et al., 2006). Exiting may occur due to graduation, aging out, or dropping out of school. The SOP includes the youth's background information, a summary of academic and functional levels including accommodations and modifications, postsecondary goals, recommendations for meeting postsecondary goals, and student input. This truncated version of the IEP may be provided to PSE/training/vocational institutions, employers, and/or employment support offices. The SOP is designed to provide enough information so that the youth could get services and supports without the extraneous information included in the traditional IEP. The development of the SOP should be completed jointly with the educator and student. The SOP is another opportunity for the student to practice their self-determination skills.

Transition service activity	Person/agency responsible
Instruction: *Instruction and practice in goal setting and problem solving in different class settings* *Identity-mapping activities to examine potential challenges that Huy might encounter (e.g., racism) and self-advocacy skills to address them*	*Special education case manager*
Related services: *Explore community transportation options (transit, ridesharing).* *Attend department of rehabilitation's job skills workshops.*	*Special education case manager & family* *Department of rehabilitation*
Community experiences: *Investigate community recreational activities for adults (e.g., Soaring Phoenix Dragon & Lion Dance Association).* *Participate in organized community groups (e.g., church) to increase network.*	*Special education case manager, Huy, & family*
Functional vocational evaluation: *A functional vocational evaluation was considered, but because Huy is participating in community-based vocational instruction currently, we have data to make decisions about his employment needs at this time.*	*N/A*
Employment objectives: *Huy will participate in the summer work experience (pre-employment transition services).*	*Special education case manager & vocational rehabilitation transition specialist*
Adult living objectives: *Learn about upcoming health care transition and supported decision making.*	*Special education case manager, Huy, & family*
Linkages with adult services: *Get Huy on Medicaid waiver lists.*	*Family & special education case manager*

Figure 9.3.   Example of the transition services section of the individualized education program.

THE IEP MEETING

During the IEP meeting, the IEP team reviews the progress the student made during the prior year and then discusses drafted results of any assessments, postsecondary goals, annual goals, course of study, transition services, and other parts of the IEP. The IEP team consists of the student, the family, various educators (general education and special education), an administrator, and any invited agency representatives. Although the student and their family provide important input and are decision makers regarding the IEP, many times the student and family's participation during the IEP meeting is passive (Landmark & Zhang, 2019; Martin et al., 2006). There are several reasons families have provided for their passive participation in IEP meetings, including not having a translator available to help when English is not their first language, having had previous negative experiences themselves with teachers and schools, not being knowledgeable about special education and its jargon, and not feeling as though their input is valued (Ju et al., 2018; Landmark et al., 2007, 2013). For some families, participation in the IEP meeting is limited because they are unable to take off work to attend the meeting during the day or they do not have child care or transportation that would allow them to attend the meeting (Ju et al., 2018; Landmark et al., 2013). These barriers do not indicate a lack of interest on the part of the family. Rather, these barriers indicate systemic issues within the school that educators need to address, and one way of doing so is to meet frequently with the student and family during the transition planning process and drafting of the IEP document before the actual IEP meeting (Landmark et al., 2022). This issue affects Derrick because his great aunt works 12-hour shifts and is unable to leave her post to take phone calls during work. She also picks up extra shifts at the last minute for overtime pay. Educators who do not understand how the great aunt's work responsibilities impact her ability to attend or participate in Derrick's IEP meetings may believe his great aunt does not have an interest in his education, which is inaccurate. Flexibility in scheduling is key.

In addition, the power dynamics of the IEP meeting may make it difficult for the family to contribute equally. Even the way the room is set up for the meeting can be unwelcoming. Having all the educators on one side of the table and the family and student on the other side of the table creates an unintentional "us-versus-them" situation. Furthermore, it is not uncommon for family members to walk into the meeting room and find the educators already in the room, chatting with each other and enjoying a coffee or soft drink. Educators in this situation can be more welcoming by ceasing their personal conversations, greeting the family, and offering them a beverage. During the IEP meeting, the family members may be intimidated and reluctant to ask the meaning of a phrase or word. The astute educator will have had an informal meeting prior to the actual IEP meeting to go over the drafted IEP document (Landmark et al., 2022). Having an informal meeting with the family and the student before the formal IEP meeting helps the family have time to think about the instruction and services proposed in the IEP and ask questions without feeling ignorant in front of a group of educational professionals—some of whom the family may not have met until that day. When meeting with the family, the educator should intentionally explain educational jargon using nontechnical language. Figure 9.4 provides examples of typical types of statements educators make that have been translated into language that is easier to understand. In addition, during the IEP meeting, the educator can sit next to the family members, observe their body language, and ask questions on behalf of the family based on the body language of the family members and the complexity of the jargon. For example, when a school psychologist is reviewing the eligibility assessment

Educational jargon	Nontechnical language
"Huy's postsecondary goals are based on transition assessment."	"Huy's goals for after graduation from high school are based on student and family interviews, the O*Net Interest Profiler, and the Enderle-Severson Transition Rating Scale."
"The transition services include Priscilla applying for the FAFSA and Blinn College."	"The transition services include applying for the Free Application for Federal Student Aid (financial aid for education after high school) and for admittance to Blinn College (personal essay, application information, transcripts, letter of recommendation)."
"An FVE is needed for Derrick."	"Derrick needs a functional vocational evaluation to determine how his spastic hemiparesis impacts his ability to work in various work environments. A functional vocational evaluation is an assessment process that identifies the student's abilities and needs in work settings."

Figure 9.4.   Educational jargon translated into nontechnical language for families. (*Key:* FAFSA, Free Application for Federal Student Aid; FVE, functional vocational evaluation.)

results, some of the language may be unfamiliar to the family. An astute educator who has a relationship with the family will notice their confusion and will ask for clarification from the school psychologist in a way that appears as though the educator is seeking clarification for themselves when, in reality, they are helping the family members preserve their dignity while also increasing their understanding.

Another way of equalizing power during an IEP meeting is to prepare the student to take a greater role in it. This may be as simple as having the student introduce everyone at the meeting; answer questions about their strengths, preferences, interests, and needs in relation to their postsecondary goals; and state their postsecondary goals. Alternatively, the student can be prepped to serve as the facilitator or lead of the IEP meeting. Doing so allows the student to increase their self-determination skills and understanding of transition (Seong et al., 2015). There are curricula (e.g., Whose Future Is It, Anyway? Wehmeyer, 2004; Self-Directed IEP, Martin et al., 1997; Culturally Responsive Student Transition Portfolio, Jez, 2014) available to teach students to lead their IEP meetings, but educators can create their own lessons on the IEP transition process. Students can use a graphic organizer with the sections of the IEP listed with notes so that the student can use the organizer as a guide for leading the meeting. Alternatively, a slide show can be created by the student and educator that the student can present during the meeting.

IMPLEMENTATION OF THE IEP

After the annual IEP has been approved by the IEP team, the educators begin implementing it and monitoring the student's progress. Educators should use evidence-based practices when implementing their students' IEPs. The National Technical Assistance Center on Transition: The Collaborative (NTACT:C, 2016) reviews the research literature annually and updates the evidence-based practices for transition. For example, some evidence-based practices for teaching academic skills include using mnemonics, peer-assisted instruction, self-management instruction, technology integration, and visual displays (Morningstar & Mazzotti, 2014). Video modeling is an evidence-based practice for teaching independent living skills and for teaching children with emotional and/or behavior problems or autism (NTACT, 2016; Seok et al., 2018). Video modeling has great promise and utility for being effective in teaching students in the employment and independent living domains. Pairing video modeling with a task analysis is another way for the educator to document the student's progress. Educators may lament not having time to create a video model and task analysis, but including students in the process is a good learning experience for students, too. A student can record another student completing the task. Then, the student can state every step that the model in the video does while someone else writes down each step. Those steps can then be used to create a task analysis data collection chart. The target student can use the video model as a prompt and the task analysis to self-monitor. The family can use the video model at home, too, increasing generalization.

Regarding progress monitoring, including the student in monitoring their progress toward their goals increases the student's self-determination; teaches them valuable skills regarding goal setting, goal attainment, and problem solving; and increases the motivation of the student. Progress toward IEP annual goals is reported to the family multiple times during the school year, and the student should have a role in collecting and reporting the data toward their goals. For example, one of Derrick's annual goals is "In 36 instructional weeks, when provided a weekly work schedule, Derrick will set alerts on his smartphone's calendar, accounting for time to prepare for work and transportation time to the work setting, with 100% accuracy over 4 consecutive weeks." With his teacher's assistance, Derrick can be involved in the weekly charting of his progress on this goal. Then, when it is time for a progress report on his IEP goals, Derrick can discuss his progress with his teacher and later explain his progress to his aunt.

Reflection

Think about the recommendations made in this chapter for meeting the needs of CLD students during the IEP process. Consider how you might apply these recommendations in working with one of your own students. How can you involve the student and their family in planning that reflects their values, hopes, and goals? What steps can you take to incorporate a culturally sustaining UDT approach to transition into this student's IEP?

WRAP-UP: CULTURALLY SUSTAINING UDT APPROACHES TO THE IEP

Using a culturally sustaining UDT approach to IEPs is a promising practice for students, families, and educators. This work requires educators to continually evaluate their beliefs and biases and in turn learn about the students, their families, and the community around their school. As educators work toward cultural competence, youth and their families, especially CLD families, may begin to build stronger, more positive relationships with schools. By beginning the transition process earlier (e.g., elementary school), youth, families, and communities can create additional opportunities for career awareness and exploration along with building essential self-determination skills for adulthood (Landmark et al., 2022). This collective approach to preparing youth for life after secondary school has the potential to increase student engagement in the IEP process through self-awareness, self-advocacy, and self-regulation within and beyond the school walls. Although it is clear that the UDT approach to transition requires careful selection of unbiased, linguistically appropriate, and age-appropriate assessments from multiple sources, the results can lead to clear goal development, a larger community network, and equitable resources for our learners. By honoring the complexities of CLD students and families, we are supporting the development of a more pluralistic and affirming society.

▶ **Tips for Creating IEPs**

1. **Reflect on your own biases and assumptions that may affect your IEP planning.** Be aware of ways in which your experiences and values inform your perspectives about educational programming and planning for adulthood. Consider how your students and their families may have perspectives that differ from yours. In addition, be mindful of how federal law and typical approaches to transition planning in the U.S. reflect the values of the dominant culture, which may not align with the values of every student and family.

2. **Keep transition planning at the forefront throughout every step of the IEP process.** Collect data from multiple sources and communicate with team members throughout the process. This may include identifying curriculum to address transition skills development or providing access to supports and/or materials that empower the student to meet their social, academic, and transition goals. Focus on the long-term goals of the student and family as opposed to only thinking about the current year.

3. **Prioritize student and family participation in the IEP meeting and be aware of potential barriers to their participation.** Learn about the student's and family's culture and identify how the school's culture differs from the family's culture so you can be the bridge between the two cultures. Use family- and youth-friendly language, as opposed to educational jargon, when communicating with the student and family. Be flexible with IEP meeting times so families can participate. Critique the IEP and postsecondary goals to ensure that they support the family's values rather than promote Eurocentric values.

KEY RESOURCES: CULTURALLY SUSTAINING PRACTICES FOR THE IEP

Print Resources

Greene, G. (2011). *Transition planning for culturally and linguistically diverse youth.* Paul H. Brookes Publishing Co.

Ruppar, A., & Kurth, J. (2023). *Equitable and inclusive IEPs for students with complex support needs: A roadmap.* Paul H. Brookes Publishing Co.

Online Resources

Cage, C. (2019, September). *Culturally responsive transition planning.* VCU Center on Transition Innovations. https://centerontransition.org/publications/download.cfm?id=90

Center for Self-Determination Theory. (2022). *Motivation and self-determination across cultures.* https://selfdeterminationtheory.org/research/motivation-and-self-determination-across-cultures

Gadd, S., & Butler, B. R. (2018). *Culturally responsive (sustaining) practices for students with and at risk for disabilities annotated bibliography.* National Technical Assistance Center on Transition. https://files.eric.ed.gov/fulltext/ED601043.pdf

IRIS Center. (2021). *IEPs: Developing high-quality individualized education programs.* https://iris.peabody.vanderbilt.edu/module/iep01/

IRIS Center. (2021). *What do you see? Perceptions of disability.* https://iris.peabody.vanderbilt.edu/module/da/

Leading Equity. (2022). *How to design culturally responsive and relevant IEPs with Dr. Brenda Barrio* [Podcast]. https://www.leadingequitycenter.com/87

Parker, C. E., & Christensen, L. L. (2018, Sept.). *Individualized education programs for English learners with significant cognitive disabilities* (ALTELLA Brief No. 4). University of Wisconsin–Madison, Wisconsin Center for Education Research, Alternate English Language Learning Assessment project. https://altella.wceruw.org/pubs/ALTELLA_Brief-04_IEPs.pdf

Vermont Agency of Education. (2019). *Family engagement toolkit and self-assessment.* https://education.vermont.gov/sites/aoe/files/documents/edu-vermont-family-engagement-toolkit-and-self-assessment.pdf

Zarrow Institute on Transition & Self-Determination. (2023). *Curriculum.* https://www.ou.edu/education/zarrow/resources/curriculum

REFERENCES

Artiles, A. J., Kozleski, E. B., Trent, S. C., Osher, D., & Ortiz, A. (2010). Justifying and explaining disproportionality, 1968–2008: A critique of underlying views of culture. *Exceptional Children, 76*(3), 279–299.

Belfield, C. R. (2013). Student loans and repayment rates: The role of for-profit colleges. *Research in Higher Education, 54*(1), 1–29.

Black, R. S., Mrasek, K. D., & Ballinger, R. (2003). Individualist and collectivist values in transition planning for culturally diverse students with special needs. *The Journal for Vocational Special Needs Education, 25*(2/3), 20–29.

Crenshaw, K. (1989). Demarginalizing the intersection of race and sex: A black feminist critique of antidiscrimination doctrine, feminist theory and antiracist politics. *University of Chicago Legal Forum, 1989*(1), 139–167.

Endrew F. v. Douglas County School District RE-1, 137 S. Ct. 988 (2017).

Esteban-Guitart, M., & Moll, L. C. (2014). Funds of identity: A new concept based on the funds of knowledge approach. *Culture & Psychology, 20*(1), 31–48.

Every Student Succeeds Act, 20 U. S. C. § 6301 (2015). https://www.congress.gov/114/plaws/pubi95/PLAW-114publ95.pdf

Gay, G. (2010). Acting on beliefs in teacher education for cultural diversity. *Journal of Teacher Education, 61*(1–2), 143–152.

Gay, G. (2013). Teaching to and through cultural diversity. *Curriculum Inquiry, 43*(1), 48–70.

Individuals with Disabilities Education Improvement Act, Pub. L. No. 108-446, 20 U.S.C. § 1400 *et seq.* (2004).

Institute for Community Inclusion. (2022). *College search.* University of Massachusetts Boston. https://thinkcollege.net/college-search

Jackson, I., & Knight-Manuel, M. (2019). "Color does not equal consciousness": Educators of color learning to enact a sociopolitical consciousness. *Journal of Teacher Education, 70*(1), 65–78.

Jez, R. J. (2014). Postsecondary transition planning for families and teachers with CLD students with disabilities. In D. Michael & L. Lo (Eds.), *Promising practices to empower culturally and linguistically diverse families of children with disabilities* (pp. 33–48). Information Age Publishing.

Jez, R. J., Osborne, K. M., & Hauth, C. M. (2022). Educators coming together to empower learners, families, and teachers to develop culturally sustainable transition planning tool during COVID-19. In L. Meda & J. Chitiyo (Eds.), *Inclusive pedagogical practices amidst a global pandemic: Issues and perspectives around the globe* (pp. 241–262). Springer.

Ju, S., Landmark, L. J., & Zhang, D. (2018). Culturally and linguistically diverse family involvement in transition planning: A research synthesis. *Journal of Special Education Leadership, 31*(1), 16–26.

Kohler, P. D. (1998). Implementing a transition perspective of education: A comprehensive approach to planning and delivering secondary education and transition services. In F. R. Rusch & J. Chadsey (Eds.), *High school and beyond: Transition from school to work* (pp. 179–205). Wadsworth.

Kohler, P. D., & Field, S. (2003). Transition-focused education: Foundation for the future. *Journal of Special Education, 37*(3), 174–183.

Ladson-Billings, G. (2014). Culturally relevant pedagogy 2.0: Aka the remix. *Harvard Educational Review, 84*(1), 74–84.

Landmark, L. J., Roberts, E. L., & Zhang, D. (2013). Educators' beliefs and practices about parent involvement in transition planning. *Career Development and Transition for Exceptional Individuals, 36*, 114–123.

Landmark, L. J., Stockall, N., Cole, C. V., Mitchell, V. J., Duran, J. B., & Gushanas, C. M. (2022). Using vertical transitions from early childhood to postsecondary environments to improve transition outcomes. *TEACHING Exceptional Children, 55*(2). https://doi.org/10.1177/00400599211073141

Landmark, L. J., & Zhang, D. (2019). Self-determination at a career and technical school: Observations of IEP meetings. *Advances in Neurodevelopmental Disorders, 3*, 152–160. https://doi.org/10.1007/s41252-019-0096-6

Landmark, L. J., Zhang, D. D., & Montoya, L. (2007). Culturally diverse parents' experiences in their children's transition: Knowledge and involvement. *Career Development for Exceptional Individuals, 30*(2), 68–79.

Leake, D. W., Black, R. S., & Roberts, K. (2004). Assumptions in transition planning: Are they culturally sensitive? *Impact: Feature Issue on Achieving Secondary Education and Transition Results for Students With Disabilities, 16*(3), 1.

Madaus, J. W., Bigaj, S., Chafouleas, S. M., & Simonsen, B. M. (2006). What key information can be included in a comprehensive Summary of Performance? *Career Development for Exceptional Individuals, 29*(2), 90–99.

Martin, J. E., Van Dycke, J. L., Greene, B. A., Gardner, J. E., Christensen, W. R., Woods, L. L., & Lovett, D. L. (2006). Direct observation of teacher-directed IEP meetings: Establishing the need for student IEP meeting instruction. *Exceptional Children, 72*(2), 187–200. http://doi.org/10.1177/001440290607200204

Morningstar, M. E., & Mazzotti, V. L. (2014). *Teacher preparation to deliver evidence-based transition planning and services to youth with disabilities* (Document No. IC-1). https://ceedar.education.ufl.edu/wp-content/uploads/2014/08/transition-planning.pdf

National Technical Assistance Center on Transition. (2016). *Evidence-based practices and predictors in secondary transition: What we know and what we still need to know.* https://transitionta.org/wp-content/uploads/docs/EBPP_Exec_Summary_2016_12-13.pdf

Newman, L., Wagner, M., Knokey, A. M., Marder, C., Nagle, K., Shaver, D., & Wei, X. (2011). *The post-high school outcomes of young adults with disabilities up to 8 years after high school. A report from the National Longitudinal Transition Study-2* (NCSER 2011-3005). SRI International.

O*NET. (2021). *O*NET online.* https://www.onetonline.org/

Paris, D. (2012). Culturally sustaining pedagogy: A needed change in stance, terminology, and practice. *Educational Researcher, 41*(3), 93–97. http://doi.org/10.3102/0013189X12441244

Paris, D., & Alim, H. S. (2014). What are we seeking to sustain through culturally sustaining pedagogy? A loving critique forward. *Harvard Educational Review, 84*(1), 85–100. https://doi.org/10.17763/haer.84.1.982l873k2ht16m77

Peterson, L. Y., Burden, J. P., Sedaghat, J. M., Gothberg, J. E., Kohler, P. D., & Coyle, J. L. (2013). Triangulated IEP transition goals: Developing relevant and genuine annual goals. *TEACHING Exceptional Children, 45*(6), 46–57.

Reed, K., Hocking, C., & Smythe, L. (2013). The meaning of occupation: Historical and contemporary connections between health and occupation. *New Zealand Journal of Occupational Therapy, 60*(1), 38–44.

Sanford, C., Newman, L., Wagner, M., Cameto, R., Knokey, A., & Shaver, D. (2011). The post-high school outcomes of young adults with disabilities up to 6 years after high school. Key findings from the National Longitudinal Transition Study-2 (NLTS2) (NCSER 2011-3004). U.S. Department of Education. https://files.eric.ed.gov/fulltext/ED523539.pdf

Scott, L. A., & Bruno, L. (2018). Universal design for transition: A conceptual framework for blending academics and transition instruction. *The Journal of Special Education Apprenticeship, 7*(3), 1–16.

Seok, S., DaCosta, B., McHenry-Powell, M., Heitzman-Powell, L. S., & Ostmeyer, K. (2018). A systematic review of evidence-based video modeling for students with emotional and behavioral disorders. *Education Sciences, 8*(170), 1–17. https://doi.org/10.3390/educsci8040170

Seong, Y., Wehmeyer, M. L., Palmer, S. B., & Little, T. D. (2015). Effects of the self-directed individualized education program on self-determination and transition of adolescents with disabilities. *Career Development and Transition for Exceptional Individuals, 38,* 132–141. https://doi.org/10.1177/2165143414544359

Strengthening Career and Technical Education for the 21st Century Act, Pub. L. No. 115-224, 20 U.S.C. § 2301 *et seq.* (2018).

Suk, A. L., Sinclair, T. E., Osmani, K. J., & Williams-Diehm, K. (2020). Transition planning: Keeping cultural competence in mind. *Career Development and Transition for Exceptional Individuals, 43*(2), 122–127.

Wehmeyer, M. L. (2004). *Whose future is it, anyway?* (2nd ed.). University of Kansas.

Whiting, G. W. (2006). From at risk to at promise: Developing scholar identities among Black males. *Journal of Secondary Gifted Education, 17*(4), 222–229.

Wilt, C. L., & Morningstar, M. E. (2018). Parent engagement in the transition from school to adult life through culturally sustaining practices: A scoping review. *Intellectual and Developmental Disabilities, 56*(5), 307–320. https://doi.org/10.1352/1934-9556-56.5.307

Wood, J. L., Harris, F., III, & Howard, T. C. (2018). *Get out! Black male suspensions in California public schools.* Community College Equity Assessment Lab and the UCLA Black Male Institute.

Zhang, D., Landmark, L., Grenwelge, C., & Montoya, L. (2010). Culturally diverse parents' perspectives on self-determination. *Education and Training in Autism and Developmental Disabilities, 45*(2), 175–186.

10

Embedding Technology Using an Equity Literacy Framework

Kim W. Fisher, Scott Kupferman, Heather J. Williamson, and Jarrod Hobson

DIGGING DEEPER: What Teachers Have to Say

In our former roles as special educators, an assistive technology specialist, and an occupational therapist, we worked closely with students, families, and other team members to plan and implement technology in educational and community-based experiences. Often, the focus of this work supported student engagement in school, such as reading a textbook, taking notes, and communicating in written form. We also collaborated with families to discuss how best to support students' technology use in the home and community. For example, we provided instruction and support for students and their families on how to connect with friends and family online safely and securely, obtain and share news or information, or search for leisure information. We partnered with park district and library personnel to support students searching for events, classes, books, videos, and music. Vocational specialists worked closely with the team to implement lessons supporting students throughout the online job search and application process. The identified supports and goals depended on both the family's and other team members' technological perspectives and use. More recently, however, to be an engaged citizen means to utilize technology throughout many aspects of life.

Expanding our understanding of technology in many life domains is essential if we are to support students to be engaged citizens. We use technology for social, civic, and political participation. This includes obtaining and maintaining social relationships; engaging in our communities through volunteering, group activities, or voting to better our community; and communicating with key policy makers and legislators at the local, state, and national levels to improve policies that better our lives. In our work, using technology throughout all aspects of life was discussed, as was how students purchased computers or smartphones, purchased cellular and broadband plans for home use, and navigated device security and upkeep. Utilizing the universal design for transition (UDT) planning process assisted the team in supporting the student's technology access and use across many life domains.

A UDT perspective requires transition professionals and, in particular, special educators to fully understand the integration of technology throughout the multiple life domains. Furthermore, it requires special educators to understand the use of policy and practices, including individualized education program (IEP) and transition goals or UDT lesson planning, to address technology access related to motivation, physical, skills, and use. However, special educators should recognize the inequitable access and opportunities families and youth have related to technology and work to address inequities using an equity-focused perspective (Gorski, 2016). This requires special educators to prepare students and families to utilize technology for social, civic, and political activity while also considering technology inequities.

Essential Questions

▶ How can educators consider technology access through motivation, physical, skills, and use and the inequities experienced by people with disabilities from diverse and underserved backgrounds?

▶ What two theoretical frameworks can help special educators 1) imagine technology and its role in their students' lives, and 2) understand potential inequities experienced by students and what to do about them?

▶ What opportunities do teachers have to address technology through the multiple life domains, and from an equity-focused teaching perspective, within transition, IEP, and instruction planning?

This chapter begins with an overview of the inequities in access to technology that constitute the digital divide. This is followed by discussion of how educators can use UDT to reduce these inequities and improve technology access for all students. Equity is explained in relation to two theoretical frameworks: Resources and Appropriations Theory (van Dijk, 2017) and the Equity Literacy Framework (Gorski, 2016). We conclude by describing opportunities and solutions for supporting technology access and decreasing the digital divide across multiple domains.

TECHNOLOGY INEQUITIES

Despite how essential technology is to everyday life (McClain et al., 2021), a digital divide persists because not everyone has equivalent access to technology, including technology hardware or software and internet access in their home. The digital divide is important to consider when planning for technology use during transition planning, because not all students will have access to technology outside of school (Schaeffer, 2021). For instance, Black and Hispanic homes are less likely to have a computer or broadband access compared to White homes but have similar access to smartphones and tablets (Atske & Perrin, 2021). American Indian and Alaska Native homes are also less likely than White homes to have a computer or high-speed internet (Ujifusa, 2020). Those residing in rural areas are less likely to have home broadband access or own a home computer or a tablet compared to suburban residents (Vogels, 2021). Access to and use of technology for some students may end as soon as they leave the school property (Anderson & Kumar, 2019). Schools in low-income areas and rural areas may also have less access to technology, limiting opportunities for learning about and utilizing technology during transition planning.

USING UDT TO IMPROVE EQUITABLE TECHNOLOGY ACCESS

UDT emphasizes a more equitable and universally designed approach to teaching students in the transition stage as well as planning and supporting them as they transition from school to postschool life. Because of the integral nature of technology in our lives, it is imperative to think about the use of technology as part of everyday activities and about how technology can serve as a resource to address inequities experienced in students' daily lives as they transition to adulthood. In this section, we introduce two theories to guide technology planning and action: 1) Resources and Appropriations Theory (van Dijk, 2017) and 2) the Equity Literacy Framework (Gorski, 2016). Resources and Appropriations Theory outlines the different ways students access technology and allows for entry into the digital divide cycle at different points depending on students' needs. The Equity Literacy Framework provides a framework about considering and acting to redress inequities experienced at the individual level and the system level. It provides a series of steps toward becoming a more equitable teacher by recognizing, redressing, cultivating, and sustaining equitable changes in the digital divide. Using these theories when thinking about technology access and inequities experienced by the student will guide planning, support, and advocacy in a more equitable way.

The Digital Divide and Motivation, Physical, Skills, and Use Access

Resources and Appropriations Theory identifies the digital divide as motivation, physical, skills, and use access perpetuated by technological isolation or integration (van Dijk, 2017); each of these areas is discussed in the following sections. Society has an unequal distribution of resources, causing unequal access including financial, physical, and literacy inaccessibility of technology. Because technology is inaccessible, a digital divide occurs in the areas of motivation, physical, skills, and use access and, thus, perpetuates the unequal distribution of technological resources and expands the digital divide. This theoretical framework is particularly useful when thinking about how schools, and special educators specifically, can support technology motivation, physical, skills, and use access by students with disabilities, in particular marginalized or minoritized youth with disabilities, because it expands our understanding of the multiple ways technology can be addressed.

Motivation access explores the usefulness an individual perceives for technology to be in their lives across multiple life domains and influences whether a person sees the usefulness in having access to technology and learning the skill to use technology for a variety of purposes. For instance, educators can explore a student's motivation to use technology for social connection and inclusion or their desire to learn technological skills such as social media branding and marketing. Motivation and attitude toward technology are highly influenced by the social context in which one resides.

Physical access refers to access to devices, sustaining and maintaining devices, and access to digital spaces. Important considerations here include the cost of purchasing and maintaining physical devices such as smartphones, tablets, or computers, but also the cost in accessing the internet from a variety of locations through Wi-Fi services or broadband. Understanding the ways to purchase and maintain technology as well as obtain and maintain access to the internet within a budget is also important. Educators play a role in supporting students' knowledge of how to access and maintain technology into adulthood as well as providing technology access during school.

Skills access refers to the skills needed to use technology for a variety of purposes and in a variety of digital spaces. This includes digital literacy and digital citizenships skills, such as communicating and locating reliable information online, creating digital information online for a variety of purposes, or engaging online in safe and purposeful ways. Educators play a critical role in supporting the skills access of students with disabilities, including integrating digital literacy or citizenship skills within lesson planning, IEPs, and transition plans using grade-level standards.

Use access refers to how and how often one uses technology across all aspects of life. This includes using technology for educational purposes to participate in formal education (e.g., writing, researching, reading, learning) and informal education (e.g., community and political participation, being an informed citizen). Use access also refers to using technology for social connection by engaging in digital spaces where connections are obtained and maintained, such as social media or gaming platforms. Finally, use access considers technology use for professional activities such as obtaining, maintaining, or changing employment or leisure activities, such as gaming, podcasting, and visual arts.

Altogether, considering the digital divide across motivation, physical, skills, and use access is essential during the transition planning process and must be integral to the education experience of all students. In fact, educators can play a critical role in decreasing the digital divide for students with disabilities by incorporating technology across multiple access points and by examining the digital divide question from an equity literacy position. This includes examining lack of access from the individual and systemwide perspective and provides actionable steps teachers can take.

Planning to Address the Digital Divide Through an Equity Framework

Along with knowledge, physical skills, and use access, special educators should consider what specific inequities their students experience, or inequities perpetuated by the system and how to address them using the Equity Literacy Framework (Gorski, 2016). In his article, "Rethinking the Role of 'Culture' in Educational Equity:

From Cultural Competence to Equity Literacy," Gorski discusses the limitations of cultural, multiculturalism, or cultural responsivity work in education. This work is important to recognizing and integrating the multiple cultures students, families, and teachers bring to the classroom and education planning; however, when thinking about disparities and inequities in access, solely focusing on culture centers the conversation on the individual and not the system that created the inequities. Nor does this force the educator to address the systemic change needed that can bring more justice into people's lives. Gorski stated, "The implication of making culture the center of the conversation, comforting privilege rather than discomforting inequity, though, is that by doing so we mask racism, xenophobia, and other oppressions, undermining the goal of equity" (Gorski, 2016, p. 224). Special educators need to understand culture, including disability culture, as a central part of an adolescent's or young adult's life. However, by focusing solely on cultural responsiveness, we may not address the systemic policies that continue to oppress students both within the school and community. As a result, the onus of making changes, for example addressing the digital divide, lies solely with the individual and the family. However, this does not acknowledge the power inequities faced by people with disabilities in society and their families, and particularly those who live intersectional identities, as they navigate the world. When considering issues of equity, teachers can engage in the following step-by-step process:

1. Recognize inequity.

2. Respond to the inequity in the immediate term.

3. Redress biases with long-term change.

4. Cultivate equitable opportunity with systemic change.

5. Sustain change even in the face of resistance.

To illuminate how a teacher may engage in Equity Literacy Framework actions, consider the following case study.

CASE STUDY: Pine Creek High School

Addressing the Digital Divide in a Rural-Remote School

Pine Creek High School (PCHS) is considered to be a "rural-remote" school, which is a term used by the National Center for Education Statistics to classify census-defined rural territories that are more than 25 miles from an urbanized area and also more than 10 miles from an urban cluster (NCES, n.d.). In other words, Pine Creek residents often refer to their community as being "somewhere in the middle of nowhere."

Based on local and national data, as well as informal data collected during IEP meetings and parent–teacher conferences, PCHS special educators recognize that many students and their families do not own computers and even fewer have reliable internet. Furthermore, many families only have a single technology device, often a mobile device shared among family members, and they lack basic technology literacy and online safety skills. With this recognition in mind, PCHS special educators have responded by opening the PCHS computer lab for 1 hour after school to serve as a community computer hub, used by students and families alike, as they chat online with friends, apply for jobs, and further their education. PCHS educators also collaborated with the parent–teacher–student organization and the local library to provide technology and digital literacy training for families. Now, a team of special educators, other PCHS educators, family members, and community members develop and implement trainings several times per year.

PCHS special educators have also integrated lessons on basic technology skills and safe online behavior into transition planning activities. For example, they engaged students in an exploration of internet privacy laws and how to protect personal information online during a LinkedIn résumé development activity. As a second example, students also expressed their transition goals by learning how to use Google Apps to compile photos, videos, and other material for an electronic Summary of Performance/transition portfolio. Google Apps was selected for this activity based on the results of a PCHS student-led survey of local employers. The majority of local employers also used Google Apps; thus, the students' newly acquired technology skillset was a competitive advantage during subsequent job searches.

Even though increased federal funding has been allocated to help bridge the digital divide in rural communities like Pine Creek, PCHS students are at risk of being left behind in a technology-focused society where information sharing and a digital identity are becoming increasingly necessary to obtain gainful employment, pursue postsecondary education (PSE), and build social networks. Thus, PCHS special educators are partnering with families and community members, such as their local independent living center, to conduct systems change advocacy on a regional and statewide level. For example, they created a regional disability collaborative that advocates to legislators to fulfill the following aims:

- Expand bandwidth coverage in rural areas, including Pine Creek.

- Increase funding allocations for technology, such as an allowable benefit expense for purchasing and maintaining technology for independent living and community participation.

- Train direct support workers, including paraprofessionals, to support students and adults with disabilities in using technology.

Together, this collaborative cultivates a stronger voice in advocating for technology rights of rural residents with disabilities, particularly in times when budgets are stressed.

Special educators can use the digital divide and equity literacy frameworks to take concrete steps to decrease the digital divide and improve technology and digital space access for students with disabilities. As the case study highlights, integrating the UDT domains, your understanding of the digital divides individuals experien`ce, and an equity framework will allow you to leverage multiple perspectives, people, and systems to support your students. To support this work, we provide a planning tool for integrating both the digital divide and equity literacy frameworks and an example of how to use the tool when considering the digital divide (see Figure 10.1 and Figure 10.2, respectively).

Addressing the Digital Divide Planning Tool

Step 1: Identify the UDT domain and technology's role in the domain. Describe the UDT domain and technology's role:	Steps 2 & 3: Based on the UDT domain, what digital divide is my student experiencing? Describe the digital divide access issue below:
Step 4: Given the digital divide, how can I respond immediately? Who can I partner with? Brainstorm ways to respond and potential partners:	Step 4 Actional Steps: Identify what to do and with whom to partner. Brainstorm actionable steps and with whom you will partner:

(continued)

Figure 10.1. Addressing the Digital Divide Planning Tool. (*Key:* UDT, universal design for transition.)

217

Figure 10.1. *(continued)*

RESOURCE 10.1: Addressing the Digital Divide Planning Tool *(continued)*

Step 5: **Based on the digital divide, how can I make changes over the long-term?** Brainstorm long-term changes:	Step 5 Actionable Steps: **Identify what to do and with whom to partner.** Brainstorm actionable steps and with whom you will partner.
Step 6: **Based on the digital divide, how can I cultivate and sustain change within my school and community?** Brainstorm cultivating and sustaining change:	Step 6 Actionable Steps: **Identify what to do and with whom to partner.** Brainstorm actionable steps and with whom you will partner.

218

Addressing the Digital Divide Planning Tool

Step 1: **Identify the UDT domain and technology's role in the domain.** Describe the UDT domain and technology's role:	**Steps 2 & 3:** **Based on the UDT domain, what digital divide is my student experiencing?** Describe the digital divide access issue below:

Examples:
· *Social inclusion*
· *Independent living*
· *Community participation*
· *Postsecondary education*
· *Self-advocacy*
· *Employment*
	Potential digital divide areas to address:
	· *Motivation access*
	  · *Student and family do not see digital literacy or digital security as relevant.*
	· *Physical access*
	  · *Family provides student with smart phone but cannot afford reliable and consistent cellular service.*
	· *Skills access*
	  · *Student does not know how to discern misinformation or to verify online information; family does not have this experience as well.*
	· *Use access*
	  · *Student uses technology to interact with family members and friends; does not use it to advocate for their rights.*

Step 4 **Given the digital divide, how can I respond immediately? Who can I partner with?** Brainstorm ways to respond and potential partners:	**Step 4 Actional Steps:** **Identify what to do and with whom to partner.** Brainstorm actionable steps and with whom you will partner:
Examples: · *Student* · *Collaborate with general educators* · *Inclusion* · *Lesson planning*	*Potential actionable steps:* · *Talk to the student about strengths and areas of growth.* · *Identify grade-level standards and lesson plans to implement; adapt as needed.* · *Connect with school colleagues to address.* · *Identify experts with whom to collaborate.*

(continued)

Figure 10.2. Sample completed Addressing the Digital Divide Planning Tool. (*Key:* AEM, accessible education material; FCC, Federal Communications Commission; IEP, individualized education program; UDT, universal design for transition.)

Figure 10.2. *(continued)*

RESOURCE 10.1: Addressing the Digital Divide Planning Tool *(continued)*

Step 5: **Based on the digital divide, how can I make changes over the long-term?** Brainstorm long-term changes:	**Step 5 Actionable Steps:** **Identify what to do and with whom to partner.** Brainstorm actionable steps and with whom you will partner.
Potential areas to address change: • IEP planning • Transition planning • School policies • Partnering with community	*Potential actionable steps:* • Embed IEP goals and supports that address digital divide through grade-level standards. • Focus transition goals and planning on decreasing digital divide. • Address digital divide opportunities in scheduling, courses, and education. • Connect with transition professionals or with community partners to streamline digital divide actions. • Partner with cities, counties, and industry to support low-cost or free internet, such as the FCC Emergency Broadband Benefit Program.
Step 6: **Based on the digital divide, how can I cultivate and sustain change within my school and community?** Brainstorm cultivating and sustaining change:	**Step 6 Actionable Steps:** **Identify what to do and with whom to partner.** Brainstorm actionable steps and with whom you will partner.
Potential ways to cultivate or sustain change: • Staff and family training • Budgeting and purchasing • School policies • Partnering with community	*Potential actionable steps:* • Embed training to general and special education staff and families on UDT, technology, and digital divide. • Address access and accessibility in ed-tech conversations and purchases; technology partnerships with industry to address digital divide. • Build co-teaching opportunities in courses and clubs where technology prepares youth to engage and participate in society. • Advocate school use AEM principles. • Build transition collaboratives that involve businesses, school and transition staff, families, and community members to identify skills and needs for successful participation in adulthood.

OPPORTUNITIES AND SOLUTIONS

In the following section, we explore several opportunities and solutions to support technology access and decrease the digital divide. We begin with technology accessibility and legislative solutions. We then integrate the framework within the UDT domains by considering the transition, IEP, and lesson planning process while keeping an eye to the digital divide and equity-focused solutions to exact and sustain change.

Technology Access and Accessibility

Given what we know about the digital divide, we can think of technology accessibility as physical access to hardware and software, functionality, and affordability of obtaining and maintaining technology. Certainly, digital participation is central to fully engaging in American society. Since the pandemic, transition planning and services through technology has been essential, particularly for rural communities (Rowe et al., 2020). So, integrating technology supports and planning in the process is critical, as is partnering with county and regional governments in obtaining and maintaining rural broadband. Successful technology integration is also predicated upon the technology's physical accessibility. As defined by the Partnership on Employment and Accessible Technology (PEAT, 2021), "accessible technology is technology that can be used successfully by people with a wide range of functional abilities." When technology is accessible, students have the option to use technology via their preferred method. For example, PEAT describes how, when using a desktop computer, people have multiple ways to input information, including but not limited to the use of a mouse, keyboard, eye gaze, or speech-to-text software. If the operating system on the desktop computer is accessible, it will work with any input method. Conversely, PEAT describes several instances of inaccessible technology for transition-age youth, including online job applications with a "Submit Your Job Application" button that is inaccessible to students who use screen readers. For practical purposes, most technology companies summarize their level of accessibility in an openly available document called a Voluntary Product Accessibility Template (VPAT). VPAT offers special educators insight into accessibility compliance and potential barriers their students might encounter when using the hardware and software.

Legislative and Policy Solutions to Access

Several laws and policies related to inclusive education can be used as leverage in school-level and district-level meetings and policy making to address, in a more equitable way, technology access to address the digital divide and can be integrated into the planning processes. The Individuals with Disabilities Education Improvement Act (IDEA) of 2004 requires access to general education and educational opportunities that prepare students to enjoy "full participation, independent living, and economic self-sufficiency" (IDEA, 2004, p. §1400.c.1). In practice, this requires educators to develop IEPs and transition plans using grade-level standards and consider ways to accommodate or modify general education environments so that all students can participate. Furthermore, the Every Student Succeeds Act (ESSA) of 2015, the law governing public elementary and secondary education in the United States, requires that teachers use research-based practices in their instruction, including universal design for learning. It also requires all students have access to rigorous grade-level content taught using research-based practices. Because both IDEA and ESSA require general education access, educators can use these laws as leverage when identifying what should be taught in lesson plans, in IEPs, and planned for and supported in transition plans. For example, special educators can use grade-level standards within social sciences education (e.g., civics, economics), English/language arts education (e.g., writing, reading, communicating), fine arts, physical education or health learning, and social-emotional learning as the foundation for addressing technology within the IEP and transition plans.

In addition to education laws, civil rights laws can be used to leverage access and the focus of educational resources to address technology access and participation in digital spaces. Access to accessible digital information and accessibility in digital spaces is identified and supported in the Americans with Disabilities Act (ADA) of 1990. For example, public entities such as libraries, health departments, and city councils should create accessible digital and electronic communications and information including their websites. In particular, Sections 504 and 508 attend to the digital participation rights and accessibility of technology and digital spaces, respectively, for individuals with disabilities. Technology integration is also central to the Workforce Innovation and Opportunity Act (2014). This focus centers digital literacy as an allowable activity in Title II and recognizes digital information access, usage, and communication as key to participation (U.S. Department of Education, 2015). The Vocational Rehabilitation Act (VRA) of 1973 stated that individuals with disabilities have, among other rights, every right to "contribute to society" and "enjoy full inclusion and integration in the economic, political, social, cultural, and education mainstream of American society" (VRA, 1973, §701.a.3.A–F). Furthermore, Section 508 of the VRA requires that federally funded entities, including schools, ensure that their online and digital content meets specific accessibility standards, including, but not limited to, the use of video captions, alternative text that describes images, and so forth. These accessibility standards align with the Web Content Accessibility Guidelines 2.1. Together, these laws address digital access, opportunity and contribution, and support for individuals with disabilities. Furthermore, considering access to content through assistive technology is essential for providing access to general education. This can be addressed not only as a requirement for faculty and schools in creating inclusive classrooms, schools, and systems but also for students with disabilities in advocating and communicating their rights within the education system.

Opportunities and Solutions for the Multiple Life Domains

The UDT framework with integrated technology components can optimize, enrich, and expand opportunities within traditional transition planning. Technology integration can promote a variety of means for content representation, student engagement, and student expression. Multiple life domains are used from a comprehensive perspective to adequately prepare students for a variety of essential postsecondary outcomes, including social inclusion, community participation, independent living, PSE, employment, and self-determination (Scott & Bruno, 2018). In Figure 10.3, we provide examples of UDT domains, ways technology is integrated into these domains, and solutions with the transition, IEP, and lesson planning process.

Social Inclusion and Community Participation   Social inclusion refers to the relationships one has with others, often referred to as a social network. Educators can think of this as a youth's personal network or the people a student knows and to whom they are connected. We can consider both how a student's digital network is formed

Opportunities and Solutions

Opportunities			Solutions: Planning to get there		
UDT life domains	Technology access	Transition plans	Individual education programs (IEPs)	Lesson planning	Addressing the digital divide
Multiple transition domains: Social inclusion					
	Social activity	Ability to connect with family and friends through technology	Social and emotional learning standards used to make IEP goals for relationship and handling building using CASEL (2021)	American Library Association's DigitalLearn materials (Public Library Association, n.d.)	Rich and sustained discussions on leveraging grade-level standards and least restrictive environment to enhance technology instruction and integration within education planning documents, activities, and professional development:
	Building relationships and social interaction online; professional and personal	Identify and participate in online communities of interest in healthy way	IEP goals related to International Society for Technology in Education (ISTE; 2022) student standards for a digital citizen	Digital citizenship curriculum (lessons and materials), such as Common Sense Media (n.d.-a)	
	Building community online	Monitor technology mental health including time spent online or addressing online bullying or violence	IEP goals related to digital monitoring mental health, time management online, and evaluating online interactions and relationships using CASEL (2021) principles and grade-level standards	MacArthur Foundation Civic Engagement and Civic Action curriculum Digital Civics Toolkit (MacArthur Research Network on Youth and Participatory Politics, 2018a)	District and family training on CASEL framework (CASEL, n.d.) related to technology using the CASEL Guide to Schoolwide SEL Essentials (CASEL, 2021)
	Communicating ideas through technology and in digital spaces	Critical reviewer of news sources	Speaking and Listening English Language Arts (https://learning.ccsso.org/wp-content/uploads/2022/11/ADA-Compliant-ELA-Standards.pdf) grade-level goals (Grades 9–10; Grades 11–12) related to social inclusion (e.g., CC.ELA.Literacy.9-10). Make strategic use of digital media (e.g., textual, graphical, audio, visual, interactive elements) in presentations to enhance understanding of findings, reasoning, and evidence and to add interest, or for critical reasoning of online sources		ISTE (2022) student standards
	Obtaining and evaluating news	Discussion with family on the value of technology and social inclusion		Common Sense Media's (n.d.-b) Digital Well-Being	Children Online: Research and Evidence (CO:RE; European Schoolnet, n.d.) has several resources to help you learn to speak to administrators, policy makers, and community members on well-being and children's and adolescents' use of technology.
	Digital literacy	Manages digital information intake independently or with support	Social Sciences College, Career, and Civic Life (C3) Standards (Swan, n.d.) related to civic education and identifying misinformation	Stanford's Civic Online Reasoning Resource (Stanford History Education Group, n.d.)	
	Digital safety and privacy				
	Accessibility and functionality of websites and systems				

(continued)

Figure 10.3. Opportunities and solutions. (Key: AEM, accessible educational materials; AT, assistive technology; CTE, career and technical education; UDL, universal design for learning.)

Figure 10.3. *(continued)*

RESOURCE 10.2: Opportunities and solutions *(continued)*

		Extracurriculars to support technology-enhanced social inclusion (e.g., school newspaper, student council)		
		Accommodations and assistive technology (AT) for social inclusion (accessible hardware and software for social inclusion; check-ins on mental health and relationship building)		

Multiple transition domains: Community participation

Digital citizenship	Uses social media and the internet to identify politicians' positions on issues important to them; communicates needs and positions to politicians to influence policy decisions	Uses the internet to identify key institutions and responsibilities of institutions related to issues important to student (e.g., Swan, n.d.) related to civic education and identifying misinformation; D2.Civ.1.9–12. Distinguish the powers and responsibilities of local, state, tribal, national, and international civic and political institutions.	MacArthur Foundation Civic Engagement and Civic Action curriculum Digital Civics Toolkit (MacArthur Research Network on Youth and Participatory Politics, 2018a)	Partnering with social studies and civic educators to embed digital civic activities in curriculum and school activities
Civic participation			Stanford's Civic Online Reasoning Resource (Stanford History Education Group, n.d.)	Partnering with social service agencies doing advocacy work on digital advocacy and communication with legislators
City and county council meeting/public participation				
Voting and being an informed voter	Identifies and advocates for accessible voting information and procedures; understands and communicates voting rights to family, direct support personnel, and voting officials at the time of voting	Demonstrates knowledge of accessible meetings requirements in Section 508 (General Services Administration, n.d.); advocates for integration of AT and accessibility features in public meetings such as school presentations or school board meetings	CAST UDL Resources related to accessible education materials and principles of POUR (perceivable, operable, understandable, robust) (CAST, n.d.-b)	
Volunteering				
Communicating needs with elected officials		Identifies key components of voting rights; identifies polling places and candidate positions	Section 508 resources related to creating accessible documents and universal design and accessibility (General Services Administration, n.d.-a; n.d.-c)	
Accessibility and functionality of websites and systems	Understands policies related to accessibility or disability rights for public meetings and communication (Section 508 VOCA)		Self-Advocates Becoming Empowered (SABE, n.d.) Voter Education Toolkit	

224

RESOURCE 10.2: Opportunities and solutions *(continued)*

Multiple transition domains: Independent living

Transition domain				
Maintaining communication with disability services	Engages with case managers and other support providers using technology; advocates for services through technology	Demonstrates formal and informal online communication to identify and direct school services	American Library Association's DigitalLearn materials (Public Library Association, n.d.)	Partnering with accessible gaming organizations such as Able Gamers (n.d.; https://ablegamers.org/) for training and advocacy work; utilize resources such as National Library Service for the Blind and Print Disabled Video Gaming Accessibility (https://www.loc.gov/nls/resources/general-resources-on-disabilities/video-gaming-accessibility/)
Digital literacy		Selects a banking system that is aligned with student's support needs	Digital citizenship curriculum (lessons and materials) such as Common Sense Media (n.d.-a)	
Budgeting and online financial management	Independently or with support manages financials online	Engages in gaming for leisure in a healthy way	Understanding cybersecurity through CTE (Cybersecurity Guide, 2022)	
Purchasing and maintaining technology and skills	Monitors budget using multiple online tools	AT support to assist family in identifying accessible gaming equipment	National Disability Institute's (2021) financial wellness tools	Collaborating with families and community partners to improve technology funding access (e.g., ITEM Coalition, n.d.; https://itemcoalition.org/)
Finding and arranging housing	Engages in inclusive gaming opportunities		Disability advocacy initiatives through major disability organization (e.g., The Arc of Illinois' They Deserve More (n.d.) or Going Home Coalition (2023) advocates campaign (https://www.goinghomeillinois.org/)	
Health management (e.g., appointment sign-ups, medication monitoring, exercise and health monitoring)				
Leisure (park district activity; concert or sporting events registration)			Collaborate with AT department to explore accessible gaming resources and embed support in lesson plans as well as IEPs and transition plans	
Accessibility and functionality of websites and systems				

(continued)

Figure 10.3. *(continued)*

RESOURCE 10.2: Opportunities and solutions *(continued)*

Multiple transition domains: Postsecondary education

Course registration, financial monitoring, scholarship applications	Demonstrates ability to register for classes	Demonstrates ability to manage class materials and assignments using online learning management system	Integrating technology training through the ISTE (2022) standards	Using UDL principles to conduct curriculum mapping with general education teachers to embed technology and digital skills and use instruction using grade-level standards
Understanding and communicating content through digital means	Monitors course materials, assignments, and grades using learning management system	Utilizes AT tools to engage with reading material or in producing written communication or products	Using modules and information from industry as self-directed learning opportunities such as Innovation Center for Design Excellence's Design Garage (2022), AccessComputing (University of Washington, 2023a) or AccessCSforAll (University of Washington, 2023b)	Advocating for accessibility consideration throughout the technology procurement and support processes (AEM accessibility requirements; CAST, n.d.-a)
Accessible education materials	Communicates needs to instructors including accommodations and AT	Communicates accommodation needs with teachers		Supporting families' knowledge on knowledge, physical, skills, and use access
Disability rights and safety	Advocates for education rights and monitors support needs with accommodations; requests adjustments as needed	Demonstrates knowledge of accessibility and advocates for accessible education materials	American Academy of Pediatric Dentistry (n.d.) IT Security toolkit	
		Access to usable AT that student values		

Multiple transition domains: Employment

Digital literacy	Identifies and engages in technology skills and use related to career through digital skills	Knowledge, skills, and use related to digital literacy	American Library Association's DigitalLearn materials (Public Library Association, n.d.)	Using Partnership on Employment and Accessible Technology (PEAT) resources such as The Future of Work (https://www.peatworks.org/futureofwork/) and Disability Accessibility Toolkits (https://www.peatworks.org/digital-accessibility-toolkits/) to lead discussions on inclusive education opportunities and in school and interagency collaborations
Digital citizenship		Demonstrates knowledge of accessible web design		
Digital skills throughout the employment cycle	Utilizes social media platforms (e.g., LinkedIn, Twitter) to connect with potential employers and other professionals	Utilizes project management software to	Utilizing CTE standards and access to general curriculum (Illinois State Board of Education [ISBE], n.d.) as essential to educational experiences (e.g., ISBE CTE workplace skills unit on time management, https://www.isbe.net/CTEDocuments/BMCE-770046.pdf)	
Safety and privacy		Demonstrates successful time management techniques using digital applications through CTE courses)		
Disability rights	Creates and integrates accessible technology and web design where they work			

RESOURCE 10.2: Opportunities and solutions *(continued)*

	Utilizes multiple digital resources for project management process and for time management	Tech coaching centers through The Arc of United States to receive employment-related technology training (SABE, n.d.) Studies accessible web and technology design through training opportunities such as Teach Access (2022) tutorial or Teach Access (n.d.) Study Away	Partnering with CTE departments in school and the district for planning technology and workforce needs. Use College in High School Alliance's Unlocking Potential report (n.d.) in district and regional conversations about partnerships and training.

Multiple transition domains: Self-determination

Social participation using technology Using technology to advocate (health, rights, policy) Decision making or processing information through technology Data privacy and right to information	Actively uses a variety of social media tools to engage with friends and family Uses online resources to learn about advocacy issues and to advocate with key policy makers about issues of importance	Uses social media to engage with friends Uses technology to communicate with policy makers or to learn about key issues	Measure student technology usage through the Youth Participatory Politics Survey resources (MacArthur Research Network on Youth and Participatory Politics, 2018b) Digital Citizenship curriculum (lessons and materials) related to online safety, privacy, and rights through Common Sense Media (n.d.-a)

(e.g., who are they connected to or not and how) and the resources exchanged between the student and their network members across digital spaces (e.g., friendship advice across gaming systems). Special educators should focus on helping the student identify who they are connected to and supporting the expansion of digital networks or digital communication in ways the student identifies is needed. Furthermore, special educators can help support the student's ability to exchange resources (e.g., emotional, social) across their digital networks.

Community participation consists of full integration in social, civic, and political participation. Similar to social inclusion, participating in social activities involves creating and maintaining one's social connections or social networks for either one's social or emotional benefit or to exchange new opportunities and information. Civic activity participation is often referred to as civic engagement, and it involves a series of activities that promote civic and political life to better communities and it requires both individual actions and interactions with others to improve the quality of life of community members (Cho et al., 2020). In digital spaces, this includes participating in online community events or public meetings, voting and voting resources, as well as digital-based political activities such as protesting or contacting legislators.

Independent Living   Technology skills and supports related to independent living include using technology to manage self-care, health care and healthy living, financial management, organization and personal management, accessing and using services, and overall well-being. Educators will need to support students' and their families' motivation to use technology for these purposes and the skills needed to navigate multiple online resources, software, and hardware. Educators cannot provide physical access to technology for students or families beyond a school-issued system; therefore, educators will need to partner with industry to identify affordable funding mechanisms for technology purchasing as well as broadband access (FCC, 2021) so that students and families in need have options to obtain physical access. Working through the equity literacy framework may involve advocating to policy makers alongside families and people with disabilities for technology funding in disability benefits.

Postsecondary Education   Educators preparing students for the technology-related PSE needs should explore technology access to engage in education and accessibility. Students and families should have a clear understanding of their accommodation rights under their IEP program and understand the ways they will be able to obtain those rights once their disability rights are no longer guaranteed under IDEA (2004) and are under the Rehabilitation Act of 1973 or ADA (1990). This includes rights to accessible education material and assistive technology as well as accommodations such as notetaking. Students need opportunities to explore technological resources in advance to prepare for variations in accommodations between secondary and postsecondary institutions (Hamblet, 2014). Furthermore, utilizing inclusive general education opportunities will be critical to learning about acquiring and communicating information as well as being a critical reader of online resources by identifying misinformation. Finally, building interdepartmental collaborations with career and technical education departments at your school can build teaching teams and content resources related to career preparation and development. These collaborations will provide students with access to experts and inclusive opportunities as well as cultivate change.

Employment   Employment-related supports and services include exploring interests, identifying employment avenues and education needed, job development and acquisition process, and in-job supports such as coaching or employment advancement. The technology-related knowledge, physical skills, and use access related to employment is vast and should include preparation for employment in technology-based fields. Special educators should also work to prepare students for the digital skills related to applying for jobs (see above), including online interviews and disability disclosure considerations, as well as specific technology-related competencies related to their future career. Finally, youth will need to understand their rights relating to accessible work environments.

Self-Determination   Students who understand and advocate for their technological rights are an important component of the transition process. Educators can consider the right to accessible information and digital spaces in addition to using technology to communicate rights to friends, family, and support personnel. Furthermore, advocating for disability rights and policy changes in legislation is critical. Educators should prepare students to use technology to research legislators and their positions on digital policy and key components of policy that would make their lives better, as well as to advocate to policy makers through digital means.

> ### *Reflection*
> Consider the potential barriers to technology access that exist for your students. This may include general barriers within their community and/or barriers specific to individual students. Resources and Appropriations Theory (van Dijk, 2017) to think through and list motivation, physical, skills, and use barriers. In what ways are these barriers systemic?

WRAP-UP: UDT, THE DIGITAL DIVIDE, AND EQUITY

Experts, overall, agree that technology engagement promotes well-being, including increasing connection, access, and commerce. Furthermore, technology, and specifically internet usage, provides expanded citizenship opportunities for those who "engage in online (and offline) civic activities that were once beyond the scope of everyday life demands" (Cho et al., 2017, p. 100). However, there is also recognition that harm can occur, including digital deficits (i.e., cognitive abilities to manage technology), digital duress or information overload, and digital dangers such as bullying, threats, and violence (Anderson et al., 2018). Because of this, technology experts indicate that technological advances in training, including digital citizen behaviors, are needed to promote democracy worldwide. Utilizing a UDT for technology transition, IEP creation, and the lesson planning process can mitigate these harms. Experts agree that technology is here to stay, and whether the harms related to digital life can be mitigated depends on a multipronged approach to recreate digital tools and systems, regulate technology and technological experiences, and formulate digital citizenship across all ages and abilities (Anderson et al., 2018). By examining multiple factors of the digital divide, ways to address inequities for lasting change through an equity literacy framework, and ways to embed technology within the UDT planning process, you will be helping to support your students as they navigate their technological lives.

▶ **Tips for Addressing the Digital Divide**

1. **Consider multiple factors that may be barriers to technology access for your students and their families.** Keep in mind that some barriers may not be obvious. Consider motivation, physical, skills, and use barriers as described in Resources and Appropriations Theory (van Dijk, 2017).

2. **Use a step-by-step process to engage in Equity Literacy Framework actions (Gorski, 2016) to address the digital divide.** First, begin by having the ability to recognize technology inequities in the immediate circumstance, such as understanding how transition-age youth access technology in a variety of ways and use technology for a variety of purposes. Assess how your student is or is not accessing or using technology across multiple life domains. When inequities occur, address them immediately through education, advocacy, and coalition building. To address sustainable change, build coalitions with others in your school or community to embed accessible digital literacy and citizenship in instruction for all students and address inequities in obtaining and maintaining technology and internet services. Finally, sustain change over time and in the face of resistance.

3. **Understand the issues of technology access and equity as they relate to special education law.** The educational standards for a variety of subjects such as English language arts, social sciences, or career and technical education require transition-age youth to read and understand information in digital spaces including for obtaining information and identifying misinformation. The International Society for Technology in Education (2022) also provides digital literacy and digital citizenship standards. Read and understand these standards and use them to write your student's standards-based IEP goals. In addition, the Workforce Innovation and Opportunity Act (2014) supports activities that integrate technology instruction for workforce development and preparation. Understand resources in your community that utilize Workforce Innovation and Opportunity Act funding and how those resources can be applicable to your students. Use universal design for learning provisions in ESSA (2015) to demand accessible digital educational spaces for your students. Use resources from the CAST center on accessibility (CAST, n.d.) using POUR principles (perceivable, operational, understandable, robust) to assist you in identifying accessibility issues and to make resources accessible. Educate your students on their rights to accessible information including Title II of the ADA and Section 508 of the Rehabilitation Act Amendments of 1998, and anti-discrimination provisions in Section 504 of the Rehabilitation Act.

4. **Embed technology in instruction across multiple life domains.** Use the multiple life domains to assess access to and use of technology. Consider how your student uses technology for social inclusion such as building relationships online, communicating their ideas in digital spaces, and knowing their rights to accessible digital environments. Understand how your community uses technology for civic life and teach your students how to navigate and understand this so they can be fully integrated into society

through volunteering, being informed and participating in local and national politics, and voting. Address your students' technology support needs for independent living including financial literacy and health online, managing their disability services through digital means, findings and obtaining housing, transportation, leisure, and health services. Address digital access, use, and skills for obtaining and maintaining PSE and employment. Finally, integrate instruction and support so students can advocate for their rights and make choices to lead self-determined lives.

REFERENCES

American Academy of Pediatric Dentistry. (n.d.). *IT security toolkit.* https://www.aapd.org/resources/member/safety-toolkit/it-security/

Americans With Disabilities Act of 1990 (ADA), 42 U.S.C. § 12101 *et seq.* (1990). https://www.ada.gov/pubs/adastatute08.htm

Anderson, M., & Kumar, M. (2019, May 19). *Digital divide persists even as lower income Americans make gains in tech adoption.* Pew Research Center. https://pewrsr.ch/2vK1HIo

Anderson, M., Rainie, L., & Caiazza, T. (2018, April 17). *The future of well-being in a tech-saturated world.* Pew Research Center Internet & Technology Project. http://assets.pewresearch.org/wp-content/uploads/sites/14/2018/04/14154552/PI_2018.04.17_Future-of-Well-Being_FINAL.pdf

Arc of Illinois. (n.d.). *They Deserve More.* https://www.theydeservemore.com/

Atske, S., & Perrin, A. (2021, July 16). *Home broadband adoption, computer ownership vary by race, ethnicity in the U.S.* Pew Research Center. https://www.pewresearch.org/fact-tank/2021/07/16/home-broadband-adoption-computer-ownership-vary-by-race-ethnicity-in-the-u-s/

CASEL. (n.d.). *Interactive CASEL wheel.* https://casel.org/fundamentals-of-sel/what-is-the-casel-framework/#interactive-casel-wheel

CASEL. (2021). *The CASEL guide to schoolwide SEL essentials.* https://schoolguide.casel.org/resource/the-casel-guide-to-schoolwide-sel-essentials/

CAST. (n.d.-a). *Communicating digital accessibility requirements.* National Center on Accessible Educational Materials. https://aem.cast.org/acquire/communicating-accessibility-requirements

CAST. (n.d.-b). *Designing for accessibility.* National Center on Accessible Educational Materials. https://aem.cast.org/create/designing-accessibility-pour

Cho, A., Byrne, J., & Pelter, Z. (2020). *Digital civic engagement by young people.* UNICEF. https://www.unicef.org/globalinsight/reports/digital-civic-engagement-young-people

College in High School Alliance (CHSA). (n.d.). Unlocking potential report. https://collegeinhighschool.org/wp-content/uploads/2022/10/UNLOCKINGPOTENTIAL-AStatePolicy-RoadmapforEquityandQualityinCollegeinHighSchoolPrograms-4.pdf

Common Sense Media. (n.d.-a). *Digital citizenship curriculum.* https://www.commonsense.org/education/digital-citizenship/curriculum

Common Sense Media. (n.d.-b). *Digital well-being.* https://www.commonsensemedia.org/digital-well-being

Cybersecurity Guide. (2022). *Student guide to internet safety.* https://cybersecurityguide.org/resources/internet-safety/

European Schoolnet. (n.d.). *Children Online: Research and Evidence (CO:RE) education toolkit.* https://core-evidence.eu/education-toolkit

Every Student Succeeds Act (ESSA), 20 U.S.C. § 6301 (2015). https://www.congress.gov/bill/114th-congress/senate-bill/1177

Federal Communications Commission (FCC). (2021). *Emergency broadband benefit.* https://www.fcc.gov/broadbandbenefit

General Services Administration. (n.d.-a). *Create accessible digital products.* https://www.section508.gov/create/

General Services Administration. (n.d.-b). *Create accessible meetings.* https://www.section508.gov/create/accessible-meetings/

General Services Administration. (n.d.-c). *Universal design and accessibility.* https://www.section508.gov/develop/universal-design/

Gorski, P. (2016). Rethinking the role of "culture" in educational equity: From cultural competence to equity literacy. *Multicultural Perspectives, 18*(4), 221–226. https://doi.org/10.1080/15210960.2016.1228344

Hamblet, E. C. (2014). Nine strategies to improve college transition planning for students with disabilities. *TEACHING Exceptional Children, 46*(3), 53–59. https://doi.org/10.1177/004005991404600306

Illinois State Board of Education (ISBE). (n.d.). *College and career CTE curriculum.* https://www.isbe.net/Pages/cte-curriculum.aspx

Individuals with Disabilities Education Improvement Act (IDEA), Pub. L. No. 108-446, 20 U.S.C. § 1400 (2004).

Innovation Center for Design Excellence. (2022). *Design garage.* https://icde.co/pages/design-garage

International Society for Technology in Education (ISTE). (2022). *ISTE standards: Students.* https://www.iste.org/standards/iste-standards-for-students

MacArthur Research Network on Youth and Participatory Politics. (2018a). *Digital civics toolkit.* https://www.digitalcivicstoolkit.org/

MacArthur Research Network on Youth and Participatory Politics. (2018b). *The youth and participatory politics panel survey.* https://static1.squarespace.com/static/5e20c70a7802d9509b9aeff2/t/5f459161fbbbb05848efc9a2/1598394722560/YPP_Panel+Survey.pdf

McClain, C., Vogels, E. A., Perrin, A., Sechopolous, S., Rainie, L. (2021, September 1). *The internet and the pandemic.* Pew Research Center. https://www.pewresearch.org/internet/2021/09/01/the-internet-and-the-pandemic/

National Center for Education Statistics (NCES). (n.d.). *National Center for Education Statistics (NCES) locale classifications and criteria.* https://nces.ed.gov/surveys/annualreports/topical-studies/locale/definitions

National Disability Institute. (2021). *Financial wellness tools.* https://www.nationaldisability-institute.org/downloads/

Partnership on Employment and Accessible Technology (PEAT). (2021). *The Why of Teaching Accessibility.* https://www.peatworks.org/futureofwork/teach-access-a-case-study/the-why-of-teaching-accessibility/

Public Library Association. (n.d.). *DigitalLearn.* https://www.digitallearn.org/

Rehabilitation Act of 1973, Pub. L. No. 93-112, 29 U.S.C. §§ 701 *et seq.* (1973).

Rehabilitation Act Amendments of 1998, Pub. L. No. 105-220, 29 U.S.C. §§ 701 *et seq.* (1998).

Rowe, D. A., Carter, E., Gajjar, S., Maves, E. A., & Wall, J. C. (2020). Supporting strong transitions remotely: Considerations and complexities for rural communities during COVID-19. *Rural Special Education Quarterly, 39*(4), 220–232. https://doi.org/10.1177/8756870520958199

Schaeffer, K. (2021, October 1). *What we know about online learning and the homework gap amid the pandemic.* The Pew Research Center. https://www.pewresearch.org/fact-tank/2021/10/01/what-we-know-about-online-learning-and-the-homework-gap-amid-the-pandemic/

Scott, L. A., & Bruno, L. (2018). Universal design for transition: A conceptual framework for blending academics and transition instruction. *The Journal of Special Education Apprenticeship, 7*(3), Article 1. https://scholarworks.lib.csusb.edu/josea/vol7/iss3/1/

Self-Advocates Becoming Empowered (SABE). (n.d.). *Voter education toolkit.* https://www.sabeusa.org/govoter/vote-toolkit/

Stanford History Education Group. (n.d.). *Civic Online Reasoning Resource.* https://cor.stanford.edu/

Swan, K. (n.d.). *College, career, and civic life (C3) framework for Social Studies State Standards.* National Council for the Social Studies. https://www.socialstudies.org/sites/default/files/c3/c3-framework-for-social-studies-rev0617.pdf

Teach Access. (n.d.). *Study away.* https://teachaccess.org/study-away/

Teach Access. (2022). *Using this tutorial.* https://teachaccess.github.io/tutorial/

Ujifusa, A. (2020, July 22). *1 in 3 American Indian, Black, and Latino children fall into digital divide, study says*. Education Week. https://www.edweek.org/education/1-in-3-american-indian-black-and-latino-children-fall-into-digital-divide-study-says/2020/07

University of Washington. (2023a). *AccessComputing*. https://www.washington.edu/access computing/

University of Washington. (2023b). *AccessCSforAll*. https://www.washington.edu/access computing/accesscsforall

U.S. Department of Education. (2015, March 24). *Integrating technology in WIOA*. Office of Career, Technical, and Adult Education. https://www2.ed.gov/about/offices/list/ovae/pi/AdultEd/integrating-technology.pdf

van Dijk, J. A. G. M. (2017). Digital divide: Impact of access. In P. Rössler, C. A. Hoffner, & L. Zoonen (Eds.), *The international encyclopedia of media effects* (pp. 1–11). https://doi.org/10.1002/9781118783764.wbieme0043

Vocational Rehabilitation Act (VRA) of 1973, Pub L. No. 93-112.

Vogels, E. A. (2021, August 19). *Some digital divides persist between rural, urban, and suburban America*. Pew Research Center. https://www.pewresearch.org/fact-tank/2021/08/19/some-digital-divides-persist-between-rural-urban-and-suburban-america/

Workforce Innovation and Opportunity Act of 2014, Pub. L. No. 113-128, Stat. 129 (2014). https://www.govinfo.gov/content/pkg/PLAW-113publ128/pdf/PLAW-113publ128.pdf

11

Tying It Together

Implementing a UDT Framework

Colleen A. Thoma, Jarrod Hobson, and Regina H. Frazier

DIGGING DEEPER: What Teachers Have to Say

It is the beginning of the school year and I am developing my system for the year ahead. In my previous years, I managed transition planning around the time at which my students' individualized education program (IEP) meetings were due. A couple of months before the IEP meeting, I would begin to generate data by pulling my students out of class to give assessments, sending home surveys to parents, and asking general education teachers for classroom updates. Although this worked for my system, I have felt like transition planning took a backseat to all of my other responsibilities as a case manager, and I could have learned about myself more and involved the student and family more while backing up my data with additional examples within the classroom.

This year, I am trying something new. In my initial planning for the year, I am trying to include transition as an equal component of the IEP process. That means I have to start early and collect data throughout the year in a number of ways, just as I do with other IEP goals and academic performance. The information I plan to collect and present to the team includes firsthand accounts of the students' and families' perspectives and cultural values, student work samples connected to transition, and the various networking opportunities I've taken on to understand the resources available in our community. By the end of this process, I want my students in control of their future with the support of the rest of the IEP team. I am a key facilitator in making sure this happens.

Essential Questions

▶ What factors should I consider when determining 1) which transition components to incorporate into a unit or lesson plan and 2) how to incorporate them?

▶ How do my cultural background and life experiences influence my teaching and my perceptions of, and goals for, the students with whom I work? What biases or assumptions do I carry?

▶ What knowledge and strengths do my students have that I can build on as I implement universal design for transition (UDT) in my lesson and unit planning?

As you have read through each of the previous chapters of this book, you were provided with examples of how each of the UDT components can be incorporated into your instructional practices in addition to the perspectives of professionals who have been innovators in the implementation of a UDT framework. Because each chapter focused on one of these components, you have learned several strategies that you can incorporate into your own work. This chapter will help you make decisions about *how* to do that and *which* of the components make the most sense based on the overarching goal of the unit and/or individual lesson plans. Although incorporating a universal design for learning approach requires addressing all three of its component principles, you have more flexibility in implementing transition components. It is rare that you would create a unit plan that incorporates all four of the transition components, and it is probably counter-productive to do so in one lesson plan. Therefore, there are considerations when planning your lessons that we recommend, particularly as you map out lessons/goals that consider culturally sustaining practices.

LESSON PLANNING

The sections that follow elaborate on our recommended steps for planning lessons that incorporate UDT components and that are based in culturally sustaining practices.

Step 1. Become critical, self-reflective professionals. Educators must be critically conscious of themselves before building awareness and providing support for students from culturally and linguistically diverse backgrounds. In doing so, educators must unmask biases and prepare ways to share motivations for supporting students in their communities. This includes motivations for building relationships with students, families, and other stakeholders engaged in culturally sustaining practices.

Step 2. Think about the transition components that make the most sense, given the focus of the academic lesson. It's not difficult to find examples of transition goals when you look at the components of an academic standard. For example, mathematics and science objectives often require problem-solving skills (a core self-determination skill), and English objectives can include skills used in employment, such as public speaking, effective writing, and reading instructions for content. You can ask yourself to highlight components of academic standards that are closely linked to tasks one needs to be successful at work, in postsecondary education (PSE) courses, and/or in independent living.

Step 3. Think about the students in your classroom. What are their current interests outside of school? What do they know about possible employment, PSE, and/or independent living options, and what additional options could you help them explore? Which of these could be used to focus an assignment in history, English, technology, science, or math? What can you learn about their strengths, needs, preferences, and/or interests that can help guide transition planning and services?

Step 4. Think about the assets that students bring into your classroom. What are their ages, cultural/racial/gender/religious backgrounds? In what communities do they live? Who are some of the people beyond the typical transition stakeholders who can provide additional information about community assets? How could they possibly be involved in the classroom and/or in out-of-class experiences?

Step 5. Ask yourself: What are some ways you can involve parents in UDT-based unit/lesson plans? How can you involve them more in the transition IEP process and, prior to that meeting, in the gathering of critical transition assessment information to inform the transition planning process? How can you gain a better understanding of their cultures, values, and expectations for adult roles and responsibilities for their young adult with a disability?

Step 6. Think about what UDT transition components you are able to address through incorporating a UDT framework to your academic instruction and assessment processes. Based on this, determine what transition components/ information you still need to collect to develop effective, individualized transition goals for the students in your classroom. You should expect that you will still need to do some individually focused transition instruction, assessment, and planning because it does not easily fit within the academic instruction you need to address. The UDT framework should have you minimize this work so that it is more manageable, but it may not be possible to do it all in a blended manner, especially when you are first attempting to implement this approach. But, as the special educator/transition coordinator, you do not need to do it alone. These are opportune times to involve the vocational rehabilitation counselor through the Pre-Employment Transition Services process; the school counselor, who can provide information about PSE options (including the admissions process and financial assistance), community members who can help identify resources, job opportunities, and other needed services; as well as the family, who can help with many transition assessments as well as other resources.

Step 7. Gather resources that can be used to aid your efforts. If you develop a range of resources, it can help you make the connections between academics and transition and decide which transition components make the most sense to include in unit/ lesson planning. It can also help you explain the UDT approach to others whom you are involving in the process. These resources can also help you choose additional, individual transition assessment and services that can help students in your classroom meet their goals for adult life. Table 11.1 provides a listing of resources that can be used to implement a UDT framework (both universal design for learning and transition components). Additional resources are also included in the individual chapters in this book.

To help you think about how to incorporate a UDT framework, the following case study describes how one high school teacher, Mr. Boyd, made some of these decisions in his dynamic role of collaborating with multiple general education teachers. Mr. Boyd ensures that the focus continues to be on the students mastering the academic curriculum while bridging skills and knowledge related to postsecondary transition. Many of the decisions made by Mr. Boyd happens in advance, as he has set up a system to support his students' present needs while not losing sight of their future.

Table 11.1.   Resources for implementing a universal design for transition framework

Background of equity and postsecondary outcomes	The Post-High School Outcomes of Young Adults With Disabilities Up to 8 Years After High School (Newman et al., 2011; https://nlts2.sri.com/reports/2011_09_02/nlts2_report_2011_09_02_complete.pdf)
General transition resources	• National Technical Assistance Center on Transition: The Collaborative (NTACT:C) (Crane et al., 2018; https://transitionta.org/) • Transition Coalition (https://transitioncoalition.org/) • IRIS Center, Vanderbilt University (https://iris.peabody.vanderbilt.edu/) • CEC Division on Career Development and Transition (https://dcdt.org/) • Virginia Commonwealth University Center on Transition Innovations (https://centerontransition.org/) • Association of University Centers on Disabilities (www.aucd.org) • Office of Special Education and Rehabilitative Services: A Transition Guide to Postsecondary Education and Employment for Students and Youth with Disabilities (https://sites.ed.gov/idea/files/postsecondary-transition-guide-may-2017.pdf)
UDT framework	• The UDL Guidelines (https://udlguidelines.cast.org/) • The UDL Project: UDL Tools for All Grades and Subject Area (Nicol et al., n.d.; https://www.theudlproject.com/udl-tools–all-grades.html) • National Center on Accessible Education Materials (CAST, 2022; https://aem.cast.org/)
Stakeholder collaboration	NTACT Resource Mapping Toolkit (https://transitionta.org/resource-mapping-toolkit/)
Assessment	Transition Improvement Grant (2021), Age-Appropriate Transition Assessment and Resources) (https://witig.org/wp-content/uploads/2017/10/Age-Appropriate-Assessment-Guide.pdf)
IEP development	• IRIS Center (2022), IEP development module (https://iris.peabody.vanderbilt.edu/module/tran-scp/cresource/q1/p02/) • Next Steps New Hampshire (2022), Exemplar IEP transition plans (https://nextsteps-nh.org/transition-iep-tool/exemplar-iep-transition-plans/)
Postsecondary education	• Federal Student Aid (U.S Department of Education, 2022a; https://fafsa.ed.gov) • Information on College Preparation and the Federal Student Aid Programs (U.S Department of Education, 2022b; https://studentaid.gov/resources) • College Board (2022), College Search (https://bigfuture.collegeboard.org/college-search) • National Center for College Students with Disabilities (https://www.nccsdonline.org/) • Campus Disability Resource Database (National Center for College Students with Disabilities, n.d.; https://www.cedardatabase.org/) • Mapping Your Future (http://mappingyourfuture.org/)
Employment	• Job Accommodation Network (U.S. Department of Labor, n.d.; https://askjan.org/) • Explore Work (WINTAC, 2022) • T-Folio (CCTS, 2020; https://www.cctstfolio.com/#/) • O*Net Resource Center (U.S. Department of Labor, 2022) • I Want to Work Workbook (https://www.personcenteredpractices.org/pdfs/want_to_work_workbook.pdf) • Virtual Job Shadow (Pathful, n.d.; https://www.virtualjobshadow.com/) • Workforce Innovation Technical Assistance Center (http://www.wintac.org/) • Junior Achievement Work and Career Readiness Trainings (Junior Achievement USA, n.d.; https://sites.google.com/ja.org/ja-ed-resources/home)
Community involvement	• Administration for Community Living (U.S. DHHS, n.d.; https://acl.gov/) • Institute for Community Inclusion, ThinkCollege, UMASS Boston (https://thinkcollege.net/) • Engage All Abilities (University of Washington, n.d.; https://depts.washington.edu/particip/)
Recreation and leisure	Find Your Next Adventure (U.S. Government Recreation, 2022; https://www.recreation.gov/)

Self-determination	• Self-determination (Kansas University Center on Self-Determination, n.d.; https://selfdetermination.ku.edu/) • I'm Determined (Virginia Department of Education, 2021; https://www.imdetermined.org/)
Technology	• OCALI Assistive Technology Internet Modules (OCALI, 2021; https://atinternetmodules.org/) • Quality Indicators of Assistive Technology (QIAT) Assistive Technology Consideration Guide: (QIAT, 2013; https://www.qiat.org/docs/resources/AT_Consideration_Guide.pdf) • Assistive Technology for Transition Success (PACER's National Parent Center on Transition and Employment, 2022; https://www.pacer.org/transition/learning-center/assistive-technology/)

Key: CCTS, Center for Change in Transition Services; CEC, Council for Exceptional Children; DHHS, U.S. Department of Health and Human Services; IEP, individualized education program; UDL, universal design for learning; UDT, universal design for transition; WINTAC, Workforce Innovation Technical Assistance Center.

CASE STUDY: Mr. Boyd

Linking Academic and Transition Skills in Math

Mr. Boyd learned about the UDT framework through his transition coursework at his teacher preparation program. He is now a special education teacher with a wide variety of responsibilities, including case management for 17 students while collaborating with three general education teachers across multiple disciplines (science, math, and reading). Mr. Boyd's involvement in the collaborative lesson planning process includes a scan for opportunities to apply the UDT framework in order to bridge students' functional and academic skills simultaneously through daily lesson plans. He has found that this process reduces his overall workload through the infusion of multiple responsibilities within one academic task. Mr. Boyd has developed some key considerations to guide his part of the collaborative lesson planning process. These are listed in Figure 11.1.

In Mr. Boyd's first class of the day, his collaborative team is developing a unit plan on solving algebraic equations (e.g., $3x + 7 = 21$, $4a - 7 = 2a + 9$). A couple of

What to plan	What to do	Possible supports and strategies to support transition
• What is the lesson objective? • What are the academic standards? • How will the lesson be delivered? • How will the students participate and demonstrate competency? • What is the link to transition competencies?	• Identify the lesson. • Identify academic standards and UDT characteristics. • Locate resources and perspectives. • Use a variety of teaching methods and authentic learning objectives. • Give choices for participation.	• Make connections to meaningful transition outcomes and contexts (e.g., How does this translate into the postsecondary world for my students?). • Engage youth and families in identifying meaningful connections (e.g., How does this align with the goals and values identified by my students' family?).

Figure 11.1. Mr. Boyd's considerations for applying the universal design for transition framework in order to bridge functional and academic skills of the students.

Problem (academic)	Problem (transition)
• Charlie has $14. He has just enough money to buy 3 bottles of soda for his friends and have $2 left over for the bus ride home. How much does each bottle of soda cost? $3x + 2 = 14$	• Opportunity cost • Budgeting • What resources would I have in this real-world scenario that I would use (e.g., calculator)? • Do I have other options here (e.g., transportation)? • Can I manage a task that involves multiple components? • Opportunity to simulate the transaction (e.g., social interaction that occurs)
Lesson outcome (academic)	**Lesson outcome (transition)**
• Solving one- and two-step algebraic expressions	• Self-determination (financial decision making) • Problem solving • Self-advocacy (using supports in an out-of-school context) • Factoring in public transportation costs • Student may be able to solve this problem without using the academic method that is being assessed.

Figure 11.2. Connections between academics and transition in Algebra class.

his students have direct IEP goals linked to solving one- and two-step algebraic equations. Also, he knows the importance of this foundational algebraic skill. While they plan out their instructional delivery, Mr. Boyd advocates that the team consider a portion of instruction and final assessment to include real-life scenarios that are based on the current interests and projections of the class. Story problems, although difficult at times, provide an opportunity to infuse real-world scenarios that students may encounter while applying their understanding of math concepts. This includes opportunities to make decisions about the components of the story problems with dynamic solutions. In addition, this simulation provokes consideration of how essential supports may be advocated for in environments outside of the school setting (e.g., use of assistive technology [AT], communication of an answer in the context of the outside world). See Figure 11.2 for examples of the connections between academics and transition.

The data collected by Mr. Boyd can be used in a variety of ways to support his students, including the transition planning process. Data collected from the previous examples can be used to determine goals and inform instruction while also providing necessary information to guide transition decisions. For example, the methods used to complete story problems involving an algebraic expression using an equation and the student's ability to problem-solve this same scenario in a real-world environment may look very different. However, each provides key data that can be used to provide supporting evidence for academic and transition decision making.

CASE STUDY: Mr. Boyd, *continued*

Linking Academic and Transition Skills in English

After math class, Mr. Boyd enters his ninth-grade classroom where the students have just completed a popular novel and are now writing about their own interpretations and connections to the novel. One of Mr. Boyd's students has previously struggled with tasks that include lengthy written responses as the outcome assessment. However, Mr. Boyd anticipated this ahead of time and provided some choice options for the student to complete this assignment. Mr. Boyd has actively collected data throughout the semester to show that the student often becomes disruptive or tries to leave the classroom when asked to write independently. At this time, they are trialing some speech-to-text software for lengthy writing assignments and additional options to present his thoughts orally through one-to-one discussions, classroom presentations, and visual representations of his work (e.g., drawings, slide presentations, animations, video recordings). At the previous IEP meeting, the student's parents did not want the team to fully avoid writing because it may negatively affect his ability to go to college. However, they were open to trying the new ways presented. Mr. Boyd's ongoing communication with the family and use of data to back up his reasoning for presenting these options played a vital role in the team agreeing to address this through adjusting the parameters of the student's writing format expectations. See Figure 11.3 for connections between academics and transition for this student.

Problem (academic)	Problem (transition)
• How do the events in this novel connect to the current events happening in the world?	• Writing is commonly found among all of the transition domains. • Making decisions (presentation) • Making connections (in real-world context) • Learning to use assistive technology supports
Lesson outcome (academic)	**Lesson outcome (transition)**
• The student provides a written sample (using speech-to-text software).	• Student perspective of the world • Preferred method of presenting material • Opportunity to begin working toward using this method in other contexts • Considerations for identified transition pathways and how this support may need additional instruction • Use of data to show that production occurs (academic) while meeting the (transition) concerns of the family

Figure 11.3. Connections between academics and transition in English class.

This academic task, which previously resulted in the student exhibiting negative behaviors, was supported using a person-centered approach involving multiple perspectives. As a result of these adjustments, Mr. Boyd was able to do the following:

1. Provide a variety of choices to the student that more appropriately suited their individual needs

2. Assess the original academic question

3. Implement a meaningful piece of AT that opened instructional and transition avenues for the student

4. Utilize information acquired from the family that reflected their input

Mr. Boyd's students all possess specific skills that are transferable to cross-curricular and nonacademic environments. By considering options such as drawings, slide presentations, animations, and video recordings to fulfill submission assignments, students can decide to use any of these deliverables. Variations in deliverables may provide insight into preferred ways for expression or paths of student interest. After using this method a number of times, Mr. Boyd will have acquired data to share with the student's parents on progress related to behavior, academics, and student preferences. This information could be a driving factor for long-term adjustments in the student's plan.

CASE STUDY: Mr. Boyd, *continued*

Linking Academic and Transition Skills in Science

In the final class of Mr. Boyd's daily rotation, Earth Science, the students are ending a unit on rock formations and planning to take the unit assessment over the next couple of days. The general education teacher has provided slot notes to some of the students (as an accommodation), while others are taking open-ended notes in this last review of the material before the test. One of Mr. Boyd's students follows along with the slot notes; however, he has been adamant that he will likely not use these notes as the primary method for studying. The student and Mr. Boyd have developed a system where this student completes the slot notes, then transfers them into an electronic flashcard-style format for study purposes. The system has been successful for the duration of the semester and the student has gradually taken the lead. Mr. Boyd used to prepare flash cards for the students at the beginning of the school year. However, over time the student has taken responsibility as part of his transition plan. Mr. Boyd plans to use this as an example with the student during informal conversations and targeted transition making as a pathway to unlocking additional supports that may uniquely work for this student. See Figure 11.4 for connections between academics and transition for this student.

Problem (academic)	Problem (transition)
• Can I identify major rock-forming and ore minerals based on physical and chemical properties including 1) hardness, color and streak, luster, cleavage, fracture, and unique properties and 2) uses of minerals?	• Can I obtain and use the available supports that help me to be successful? • How would I access these supports outside of school? • What are my preferred ways of studying? • Can I self-manage the studying process on my own?
Lesson outcome (academic)	**Lesson outcome (transition)**
• The student completes an assessment showing knowledge of major rock-forming and ore minerals based on physical and chemical properties.	• The student utilizes available supports that will translate into postsecondary settings. • The student is making their own decisions about their learning. • The student has established a method for studying that works for them.

Figure 11.4. Connections between academics and transition in Earth Science class.

Not only has the student built a support that works in the Earth Science classroom, but it is also a support that can be generalized across settings with targeted planning and instruction. Recognizing things that do not work is also key information to include in discussion with the IEP team. This student has learned that the classwide strategy for notetaking and test preparation is not the most effective. For future considerations of transition planning, Mr. Boyd and his student could further investigate this individualized strategy to show how this student might use it to prepare for other classrooms during high school, upcoming college admissions testing, or actual strategies that the student may use in their PSE. By starting on this early, the student can become fluent in this process and reach independence.

These three scenarios are just a glimpse of the happenings within a school building. Activities like the ones described happen every single day. Through the UDT framework, we can make connections between the academic curriculum, the needs of the student, and the future implications of our decision making. Each of the scenarios occurred at different stages of the process of providing appropriate individualized instruction and support to the students. However, transition assessment data and connections to postsecondary skills were readily available within the context of the academic lesson. There were additional opportunities to deduce transition information from the context of the lesson without additional preplanning, while at other times Mr. Boyd intentionally targeted transition components within the daily lesson plan.

Reflection

Think about the actions Mr. Boyd took to use students' academic learning as a jumping-off point for developing skills that would be valuable for them in transition. Consider the students you work with who are preparing to transition into adulthood. In what ways could you make similar connections for your students—for example, by applying learning to real-world scenarios, building specific skills they will need after high school, or helping them carry strategies they currently use in school into other learning contexts?

WRAP UP: IMPLEMENTING CULTURALLY SUSTAINING UDT

As you have read throughout this book, there are many considerations for teachers who are supporting transition-age youth. The implications of these considerations can be life altering. As we come to a close, here are some simplified guidelines to begin the process of shifting your practice to be universally designed beyond your instruction and into transition planning.

▶ **Tips for Implementing Culturally Sustaining UDT**

1. **Be proactive.** Transition planning is an ongoing process. Throughout the school year, educators have many opportunities to be proactive and set the foundation to develop a comprehensive, person-centered transition plan. At a classroom level, this can be woven into various components of the day-to-day academic curriculum. Information from these lessons can provide essential data on prerequisite skills necessary for identified transition pathways, identify new opportunities to further explore within the transition domains, and help to connect the academic classroom to the outside world.

2. **Take a person-centered approach.** Person-centered planning is a creative process that focuses on a student's needs, strengths, and abilities to determine the services the student receives (Keyes & Owens-Johnson, 2003). The student is an active participant in this process. An understanding of one's disability and any accommodations that one finds useful and how to use them are examples that may come out of this process. As a result, the student gains control of their own life. This process empowers the student to be the primary driver of decision making with the support of their team.

3. **Connect and involve key stakeholders.** In order to be person centered, we must develop relationships with key stakeholders (e.g., parents, educators, service providers, community agencies, postsecondary institutions, employers) to be able to identify available supports, potential pathways, and reflect multiple perspectives. Progress reporting and report cards are opportunities for transition communication and should occur at minimum during these suggested intervals. However, frequent and ongoing communication with parents, in advance of the transition IEP meeting, may increase their comfort with sharing family and cultural values that are essential considerations in the transition planning process. Informal communication opportunities outside of typical transition assessments (e.g., rating scales, structured interviews, questionnaires, surveys) may provide necessary information or further context to understand the goals of the family. Similarly, key partnerships within communities may provide essential opportunities for students in their postsecondary life (Scott & Bruno, 2018).

4. **Utilize technology and other available supports.** AT is designed to meet individual student needs, support independence, and generate access to the curriculum. In addition, AT can provide access across the environment and within the community. For example, students' use of communication devices reflects the expected interactions within the academic school day. However, educators should also make additional considerations about the

devices, interactions outside of the school building, and lifelong use of these devices (if deemed appropriate). Doing so ensures that the device is set up properly for the student to be successful in each environment.

5. **Generate supporting evidence across multiple life domains.** Educators have many opportunities to intertwine various forms of assessment that cover the multiple life domains of postsecondary transition (Thoma et al., 2009). On a day-to-day basis, they have opportunities to extract data through intentional lesson planning to include transition, as well as opportunities to be more deductive with this information as it naturally comes out. This information can guide the transition process early on, provide a basis for additional assessment decisions, and open up opportunities to explore that would not have surfaced without a transition lens.

6. **Drive the IEP decision-making process with data.** A comprehensive person-centered approach that begins early, includes key stakeholder perspectives, considers the continuum of available supports, and consists of comprehensive information over multiple life domains can enhance the IEP development and decision-making process (Keyes & Owens-Johnson, 2003). This includes providing a detailed report of current student needs, strengths, preferences, and interests that is rooted in evidence that is observed by members of the team or supplied firsthand by the student.

7. **Empower the student.** Self-determination plays a critical role in the postsecondary success of the student (Mazzotti et al., 2021). Through self-determination, students develop an understanding of their individual uniqueness and how that impacts various sectors of their life, including areas outside of the academic setting. An understanding of their own values, goals, and needs can result in the student feeling empowered and following their true identity.

8. **Reflect on the potential impact.** Historically, students with disabilities have had poorer postsecondary outcomes than their typically developing peers (Newman et al., 2011; Sanford et al., 2011). Prioritizing transition planning as a primary focus, and weaving it into the academic curriculum through authentic connections, is one way to take control of this narrative for future students. The impact of this approach connects our students with their future world while handing over control as they navigate to the next stage of their life. Our work must be comprehensive, student centered, community connected, meaningful, and data driven to facilitate opportunities for our students to grow into their full postsecondary potential.

REFERENCES

CAST. (2022). *The UDL Guidelines.* https://udlguidelines.cast.org/

CAST. (2022). *National Center on Accessible Education Materials.* https://aem.cast.org/

Center for Change in Transition Services (CCTS). (2020). *T-Folio.* https://www.cctstfolio.com/#/

College Board. (2022). *College search.* https://bigfuture.collegeboard.org/college-search

Crane, K., Allison, R., MaGee, C., & National Technical Assistance Center on Transition: The Collaborative (NTACT:C). (2018). *Resource mapping and flow of services guide.* https://transitionta.org/

IRIS Center, Vanderbilt University. (2022). *Secondary transition: Student-centered transition planning, perspectives and resources.* https://iris.peabody.vanderbilt.edu/module/tran-scp/cresource/q1/p02/

Junior Achievement USA. (n.d.). *JA education resource links.* https://sites.google.com/ja.org/ja-ed-resources/home

Kansas University Center on Developmental Disabilities. (n.d.). *Self-determination.* https://selfdetermination.ku.edu/

Keyes, M. W., & Owens-Johnson, L. (2003). Developing person-centered IEPs. *Intervention in School and Clinic, 38*(3), 145–152. https://doi.org/10.1177/10534512030380030301

Mazzotti, V. L., Rowe, D. A., Kwiatek, S., Voggt, A., Chang, W.-H., Fowler, C. H., Poppen, M., Sinclair, J., & Test, D. W. (2021). Secondary transition predictors of postschool success: An update to the research base. *Career Development and Transition for Exceptional Individuals, 44*(1), 47–64. https://doi.org/https://doi.org/10.1177/2165143420959793

National Center on College Students with Disabilities. (n.d.). *Campus disability resource database.* https://www.cedardatabase.org/

Newman, L., Wagner, M., Knokey, A. M., Marder, C., Nagle, K., Shaver, D., & Wei, X. (2011). *The post-high school outcomes of young adults with disabilities up to 8 years after high school: A report from the National Longitudinal Transition Study-2 (NLTS2)* (NCSER 2011-3005). National Center for Special Education Research. https://nlts2.sri.com/reports/2011_09_02/nlts2_report_2011_09_02_complete.pdf

Next Steps New Hampshire. (2022). *Exemplar IEP transition plans.* https://nextsteps-nh.org/transition-iep-tool/exemplar-iep-transition-plans/

Nicol, J., Carr, J., Pettigrew, K., Goguen, T. (n.d.). *The UDL Project: UDL Tools for All Grades and Subject Areas.* https://www.theudlproject.com/udl-tools–all-grades.html

OCALI. (2020). *Assistive technology internet modules.* https://atinternetmodules.org/

PACER's National Parent Center on Transition and Employment. (2022). *Assistive Technology for Transition Success.* https://www.pacer.org/transition/learning-center/assistive-technology/

Pathful. (n.d.). *Virtual job shadow.* https://www.virtualjobshadow.com/

Quality Indicators of Assistive Technology (QIAT). (2013). *Assistive technology consideration guide.* https://www.qiat.org/docs/resources/AT_Consideration_Guide.pdf

Sanford, C., Newman, L., Wagner, M., Cameto, R., Knokey, A. M., & Shaver, D. (2011). *The post-high school outcomes of young adults with disabilities up to 6 years after high school: Key findings from the National Longitudinal Transition Study-2 (NLTS2).* (NCSER 2011-3004). National Center for Special Education Research.

Scott, L. A., & Bruno, L. (2018). Universal design for transition: A conceptual framework for blending academics and transition instruction. Journal of Special Education Apprenticeship, 7(3), 16.

Thoma, C. A., Bartholomew, C. C., Scott, L. A. (2009). *Universal design for transition: A roadmap for planning and instruction.* Paul H. Brookes Publishing Co.

Transition Improvement Grant. (2021). *Age-appropriate transition assessment and resources.* https://witig.org/wp-content/uploads/2017/10/Age-Appropriate-Assessment-Guide.pdf

U.S. Department of Education. (2022a). *Federal student aid resources.* https://fafsa.ed.gov

U.S. Department of Education. (2022b). *Federal student aid resources. Information on college preparation and the federal student aid programs.* https://studentaid.gov/resources

U.S. Department of Education, Office of Special Education and Rehabilitative Services. (2017). *A transition guide to postsecondary education and employment for students and youth with disabilities.* https://sites.ed.gov/idea/files/postsecondary-transition-guide-may-2017.pdf

U.S. Department of Health and Human Services (DHHS). (n.d.). *Administration for Community Living.* https://acl.gov/

U.S. Department of Labor. Employment and Training Administration. (2022, November). *O*Net Resource Center.* https://www.onetonline.org/

U.S. Department of Labor, Office of Disability Employment Policy. (n.d.). *Job Accommodation Network.* https://askjan.org/

U.S. Government Recreation. (2022). *Find your next adventure.* https://www.recreation.gov/

University of Washington. (n.d.). *Engage all abilities.* https://depts.washington.edu/particip/

Virginia Department of Education. (2021). *I'm Determined.* https://www.imdetermined.org/

Workforce Innovation Technical Assistance Center (WINTAC). (2022). *Explore work.* Employment Resources, Inc. https://explore-work.com/

Index

Note: Page numbers followed by *f* or *t* indicate figures or tables, respectively.